The New Deal in the Suburbs

THE NEW DEAL
IN THE SUBURBS

A History of

the Greenbelt Town Program

1935–1954

JOSEPH L. ARNOLD

OHIO STATE UNIVERSITY PRESS

Standard Book Number: 8142–0153–9
Library of Congress Catalogue Card Number: 74–141494
Printed in the United States of America

TO MY MOTHER
AND TO THE MEMORY OF MY FATHER

CONTENTS

vii

ACKNOWLEDGMENTS

This study could not have been completed without the help of dozens of individuals. The greatest debt I owe is to Professor Robert H. Bremner, who directed the original project at the Ohio State University. His helpful suggestions, kind encouragement, and deep scholarly interest in my work made the entire task as pleasurable as it was instructive.

The librarians and archivists with whom I worked were without exception helpful and cheerful in response to my many demands. Particularly helpful were Miss Ruth Erlandson and Mr. Roger Horn, of the Ohio State University Library, who obtained many scattered materials for me. Miss Helen Finneran of the National Archives, Dr. Jacquelen Bull and Miss Clair McCann of the University of Kentucky Library, Miss Elizabeth B. Drewery of the Franklin D. Roosevelt Library, and Mr. Ralph J. White of Records Division of the Public Housing Administration gave me substantial aid in locating materials in their respective libraries and repositories.

I was fortunate in receiving essential information from former administrators of the Resettlement Administration. John S. Lansill of Lexington, Kentucky, gave me complete access to the papers of the Suburban Division, which he fortunately took with him from Washington and placed in the University of Kentucky Library, and also to those papers he retained in his personal possession. Without his papers the history of the greenbelt town program could not have been written. Other former officials who gave me their smaller collections of papers and patiently answered all my questions were Tracy Augur, Tilford Dudley, Warren Vinton, C. B. Baldwin, and Albert Mayer. Finally, I am indebted to a number of citizens in each of the three greenbelt towns who shared with me their remembrances of local events.

In preparing this study for publication, I have been aided by a research grant from the University of Maryland Baltimore County, and by the excellent typing services of Mrs. Laura J. Justice of the Secretarial Center. Evelyn Smith, my student assistant at U.M.B.C., helped to prepare the index. Mr. Weldon A. Kefauver, director of the Ohio State University Press, has been most helpful and considerate. Mrs. Susan B. Collins of the editorial staff made many excellent suggestions and saved me from a number of difficult tasks during the various stages of preparation.

The entire process has left me with the deep desire to produce a finished work worthy of the labors of so many kind and dedicated people. Any errors of insight or accuracy are, of course, my own responsibility.

J.L.A.

October, 1970

INTRODUCTION

As long as mankind has been building cities, wealthy families have been escaping the resultant dangers and discomforts by removing themselves to suburbs. Suburban estates surrounded the Summerian city of Ur, Imperial Rome, Renaissance Florence, and Elizabethan London. By the 1820s, American real estate firms were advertising suburban houses for commuters who wished to combine the advantages of the countryside with the conveniences of the city. Extensive suburban settlements developed during the nineteenth century—infiltrating nearby villages, creeping out along highways and rail lines, and gradually filling in the open fields. By the end of the century many of these settlements on the urban fringe had been passed over by new waves of suburbanites seeking newer and larger homes now available through the extension of railroads and trolley lines. Increasing numbers of old suburban settlements had degenerated into slums—the trees replaced by telephone poles, the remaining open spaces filled with factories and stores, the old spacious houses subdivided for new, less affluent residents. A few settlements, like Greenwich Village or Georgetown, survive as quaint (and now very popular) islands in the concrete vastitude; but most were completely submerged. The gasoline engine and superhighway, the enormous growth of urban population, and the desire for more and yet more space has greatly accelerated the rate of urban expansion. The cycle of expansion and decay spiraled rapidly and covered much larger areas. The affluent now remove themselves deeper into the countryside, remote from the city and from each other. Central cities and old suburbs are converted into super-slums and ghettos on a scale undreamed of at the turn of the century. In spatial terms alone, the rich and poor have never been so far apart.

This study describes one major city planning project undertaken by the federal government in the 1930s in the hope that it would force a fundamental shift in the wasteful and unhealthy pattern of urban growth. The greenbelt towns were built to demonstrate that urban expansion by the construction of complete new towns would provide superior safety, convenience, beauty, and a deep sense of community spirit—all at a new low cost. These new suburban towns would therefore provide a superior environment for families heretofore condemned to live in urban slums. New towns would stop urban decay and end the economic segregation of the suburbs. They would, above all, restore to all classes the warm community life of the rural village without sacrificing the economic advantages of a metropolitan location.

This new deal in the suburbs failed. The Roosevelt administration never completed the project, and the three half-finished towns were thereby robbed of their full impact. The real estate and construction industry remained unmoved by the greenbelt town demonstration. The federal government washed its hands of new towns until 1968 when it authorized a few very modest aids to new town developers. Why did the New Deal abandon

the greenbelt town program? Why did the towns elicit so little
response from the public and such a negative one from the real
estate and construction interests? Was it the nature of the particular program under which the towns were built or was it
something about the towns themselves? Was the central problem perhaps the habits of mind of those who saw the towns?
To answer these questions requires an analysis of the interac-
tion between the New Deal, city planners, and the welter of
interest groups and individuals comprising the American people. The specific issue appeared to involve only a few small suburban communities; but the larger implications of the program
escaped few of the interested parties. An established pattern of
urban life was being challenged. Understanding the history of
the greenbelt town program provides a broad hint as to why the
suburban developers of the 1970s offer us little more than was
offered suburbanites fifty or one hundred years ago.

The New Deal in the Suburbs

1

🍁 SUBURBS AND NEW TOWNS

BEFORE THE NEW DEAL

The men who laid out the greenbelt towns in the 1930s drew on a rich international heritage of town planning theory and experimentation. In the second half of the nineteenth century increasing numbers of thoughtful people focused their attention on the problems and possibilities of suburban growth. The streetcar and commuter railroad allowed many affluent families to move beyond the edge of the city. The problem was to maintain the rural nature of an area once it came within reach of commuters. One readily apparent answer was to build whole new suburban towns or villages of sufficient size and cohesion to resist encroachments. For those who could afford it, nineteenth-century architects and planners devised a striking series of residential suburbs. Llewellyn Park, New Jersey (1859), and Riverside and Lake Forest, Illinois (1869 and 1873), were built under the influence of Andrew Jackson Downing's visions of suburban rusticity. It is to Downing and his brilliant associates, Calvert Vaux and Frederick Law Olmsted, Sr., that we owe the curvilinear street pattern and studied informality of the contemporary suburban development.[1]

Industrialists seeking larger tracts of land at lower cost vied with residential developers for choice pieces of suburban real estate. Some captains of industry followed in the footsteps of the New England textile manufacturers and built towns alongside of the factories. Pullman, Illinois, which was built in the 1880s to house over 8,000 people, was the largest and most famous industrial suburb of the era. George F. Pullman, the railroad car manufacturer, developed the town to give his employees a healthy environment while turning a profit for himself. The great Pullman strike of 1894–95 convinced other industrialists that company towns, regardless of the quality of construction, were troublesome and to be avoided whenever possible.[2] When Gary, Indiana, was built by the United States Steel Corporation a decade after the Pullman strike, company officials turned the entire town building task over to independent construction and real estate operators who laid out a prosaic gridiron city which soon became an ugly and unhealthy industrial community.[3] Slum reformers were divided in their opinions concerning company towns, particularly in areas adjacent to large cities where alternative employment was possible. The sociologists Adna F. Weber and Graham Taylor agreed that the movement of factories to the urban fringe offered the best means of ending overcrowding and the resultant economic and social evils. Taylor was convinced, however, that company towns were less satisfactory than communities owned by working men themselves—individually or cooperatively. Edith Elmer Wood, a housing reformer writing a few years later, said simply that company towns were "medieval, undemocratic and un-American."[4]

British manufacturers also experimented with the construction of industrial suburbs, but while the results were satisfactory for all concerned, they were not generally imitated by the business leadership. Saltaire, in the English Midlands, was completed in 1871 and with over 4,000 residents became England's largest new town. It was universally praised for its careful planning and hailed as an important factor in breaking down class antagonism. At the end of the century two other major British new towns, Bournville and Port Sunlight, were developed with equally happy results, but with few imitators. Efforts to encourage industrial decentralization were made by a Society for Promoting Industrial Villages (founded in 1888); but it was the publication of Ebenezer Howard's small book, *The Peaceful Path to Real Reform*, in 1898 that stimulated wide interest in Great Britain and throughout the industrialized world.[5]

Born in 1858, Howard lived all his life in the vicinity of London, except for a brief sojourn in the United States. A man of practical affairs (he was a skilled legal reporter), Howard was dismayed with the current structure of industrial cities but believed that socialization of factories offered no fundamental solution. The real path to reform lay in removal of factories and homes to inexpensive rural land in a manner which would preserve the best qualities of the urban and rural environments. Howard owed an intellectual debt to a wide variety of sources. He was deeply impressed by Henry George's *Progress and Poverty* and also by Alfred Marshall's economic studies of urban decentralization. His writings reveal a debt to Ruskin and Tolstoy's idealization of village life which was in itself part of a broad intellectual movement to get back to nature. This should not be overstated since Howard clearly emphasized the fundamental *urban* nature of his garden cities and never doubted the basic liberating effects of the industrial revolution.[6]

Howard's book, soon republished under the title *Garden Cities of Tomorrow*, laid out a concrete financial plan for the construction of a system of complete industrial cities on inexpensive land surrounding a central metropolis. Each community would be limited in area and population density. When a population of about 32,000 was reached, a new and separate city would be built. The land in these "garden cities"[7] would be mutually owned by the residents, who would thereby control its use by homeowners as well as factory and shop owners. Open spaces could be preserved and new houses or factories constructed only by majority consent of the residents exercising control through a land trust. Increasing real estate values would accrue for the whole community, thereby lowering costs and allowing families with small incomes to buy or rent garden city homes. To protect each city from undesirable encroachments, a wide belt of green fields and trees would surround the community. These greenbelts would serve as buffers between cities, establishing clear physical boundaries which would encourage community identity and local civic pride. Strong physical delineation and cooperative land tenure were the bases upon which Howard envisioned the rise of a deep spirit of communitarianism.[8]

Howard's proposal sparked almost immediate responses in Great Britain. Letchworth, the first garden city, was opened outside London in 1906. It stimulated the interest of many nations including the United States. The Garden City Association of America was founded the same year. Its president was a former New York state senator, Louis Childs, and its vice-president, Ralph Peters, was the head of the Long Island Railroad. Other officers and members included Josiah Strong, who had visited Letchworth during construction in 1904; Henry Potter, Episcopal bishop of New York; Felix Adler of Columbia University; and the banker, August Belmont. The association selected five locations for the construction of garden cities. Plans materialized most rapidly at an 800 acre tract near Farmingdale, Long Island. Thirty percent of a $500,000 limited dividend stock issue was sold in about six months, and the first factory had been promised. Unfortunately, the panic of 1907 disrupted these plans, and the garden cities were never built. The association became solely a disseminator of information through its publication *The Village*; both faded out in 1921. Its last and most noteworthy effort was a highly critical analysis of the new town of Gary, Indiana, showing how much unearned increment had accrued to private real estate interests between 1906 and 1921.[9]

During the early years of the twentieth century the garden city movement made no headway in the United States. Journals of the day often presented a distorted picture of Howard's concept. The magazine, *International Studio*, which advertised itself as "An Illustrated Monthly of Fine and Applied Arts," endorsed the garden city plan but urged that "the friends of any future Garden City or suburb should make up their minds to aschew the attempt to 'catch customers' by dangling the bait of cheapness before their eyes. It always means bad building and almost always bad design."[10] Other journals associated the garden city with an escape from the city into semirural suburban villages. Writing in *The Craftsman* in 1909, Gustav Stickley described the garden city as "a spontaneous movement of the people back to the land"; while Wilhelm Miller, a regular contributor to *Country Life*, emphasized the "garden" rather than urban aspects of the movement. While housing reformers such as Frederic C. Howe and Lawrence Veiller called public attention to the social reform goal of Howard's garden city, most American writers could visualize only middle-class residents being able to afford such attractive surroundings.[11]

Several "garden suburbs" (residential communites adjacent to industrial areas) constructed during the first decades of the twentieth century appeared to confirm the notion that spacious, well-planned communities were too expensive for the average worker. Goodyear Heights outside of Akron, Ohio, was designed for the company's employees by Warren H. Manning. The Norton Grinding Company employed John Nolan to build a garden suburb for its employees outside Worcester, Massachusetts. Aside from the fact that these garden suburbs were little more than attractive subdivisions instead of separate communities, they were so expensive that only foremen and skilled laborers could afford to live in them. Forest Hills, Long Island, built as a model garden suburb by the Russell Sage Foundation in 1912, was not for low-income residents. Its location on valuable urban property, its well-planned and carefully constructed homes, and its beautiful interior parks and playgrounds were delightful; but it offered no solution for the poor. The president of the Forest Hills Garden Housing Association, Robert W. DeForest, said the foundation might have something for the laboring man in the future, but not at Forest Hills Gardens. Even Letchworth was unable to house the unskilled laborer, in spite of Howard's desire to do so.[12]

By the time of the First World War, it was clear that few, if any, garden cities or suburbs would be built to siphon workers as well as the affluent out of congested areas. Garden city advocates began to recognize what Edward Bellamy's followers had learned somewhat earlier—that communal ownership of real estate cut against a very tough American grain.[13] In the case of the garden city, it was a seriously retarding factor. The physical planning alone was so revolutionary that it sounded somewhat impractical, and the public land ownership made the proposal sound socialistic or communistic. The notion that garden city publicists and planners were impractical visionaries or dangerous radicals was reinforced by testimony given before a Senate subcommittee in 1917. A subcommittee of the Senate Committee on Agriculture and Forestry held hearings on the progress of garden cities and suburbs in Europe and America and was given an excellent account of the movement by Richard Watrous, secretary of the American Civic Association. Watrous was followed, however, by a Mr. William T. Lone, who described his pet project at Lomax, Illinois—a vast garden city of 25,000 acres surrounded by 75,000 acres of farmland—all of it to be financed by what the senators correctly judged to be the most dubious stock arrangements. One senator told Mr. Lone that these sorts of projects were "drifting into socialism."[14] Planners and urban reformers noted that industrialists would not remove their factories to garden cities until they could be assured it would result in lower costs and higher profits. Until this could be proved to corporate executives, the reliance on philanthropy to draw factories out of central cities was regarded even by the reform-minded city planner Henry Wright as "somewhat visionary."[15] Those who did build factories in suburban areas maximized profits by ignoring any obligation to plan for the residential areas which grew around the factory gates. The result, wrote Carol Aronovici, was simply "the slumification of the countryside," with sanitary conditions as bad or worse than a city slum.[16]

America's entry into the First World War offered a unique opportunity to demonstrate the advantages of building entire communities for working-class families. The demands of the military for war matériel put a severe strain on American industry, particularly the shipbuilding trades. Thousands of laborers migrated to industrial centers but, upon finding no living accommodations, often left their jobs. Neither local private real estate people or the large corporations holding war contracts could house the laborers and their families. They turned to the federal government for aid. Faced with slowdowns in war production due to this housing situation, the government took the unprecedented step of building entire communities for war workers.

The two agencies created for this task were the United States Housing Authority and the Emergency Fleet Corporation. The U.S.H.A. obtained the services of Frederick Law Olmsted, Jr.; and the E.F.C. employed Frederic L. Ackerman, recently returned from Britain with plans of British war housing projects. The government allotted $175,000,000 in 1917 and 1918, and together the two agencies built seventy-nine projects in fifty-two localities constructing over fifteen thousand units of low-rent housing. The projects varied in size and quality; but the two best—the Bridgeport, Connecticut, projects designed by Jacob Crane, and Yorkship Village in Camden, New Jersey—provided war laborers with housing and town planning available in the past only to the middle class. While they were not garden cities, the two towns brought together all the latest principles of design being experimented with in England and America—curvilinear streets, cul-de-sacs, interior parks, row houses, and many other features. The program provided a whole generation of architects and planners with extremely valuable information and experience.[17]

The war housing program proved that the federal government could, if it wished, build excellent housing or even whole communities for moderate income families. There was hope on the part of housing reformers and planners that in view of the start already made, a permanent federal bureau of housing would be established to continue research and experimentation. Congress, on the other hand, was vociferously opposed. The House Committee on Buildings and Grounds was convinced that the U.S. Housing Authority had exceeded its mandate and hired droves of crackpots and utopians. "College professors and alleged experts in various lines were called in," declared the Committee *Report*, "and designated as 'town planners, town managers,' etc., ad nauseum and ad absurdum."[18] The Senate committee was likewise furious that the war agencies had engaged in demonstrations of model housing, presumably feeling that military-type barracks would have been more suitable. The war housing projects were quickly disposed of and requests for a permanent agency rejected. Aside from the planners and a few other individuals, there was no pressure to reverse the view of Congress. Not even the American Federation of Labor spoke out in favor of the housing-planning bureau. The New York Federation merely asked that the war projects be retained for the laboring men who lived in them.[19]

The suburban trend became dominant in the years following the First World War. The growth rate of the suburbs finally surpassed that of the central cities in the 1920s. Suburban communities burgeoned from New York to Los Angeles; growth rates of four or five hundred percent were not uncommon, while during the same period the number of wage earners in some central core areas began to decline. By the end of the decade, 5,176,000 persons had moved to suburban homes. The automobile and concrete highway opened thousands of heretofore inaccessible acres of land around the cities, and the increase of motor vehicle registrations from 9.2 million in 1920 to 26.5 million in 1930 gives a rough picture of the number of Americans who were able to live beyond the end of the streetcar line.[20]

The suburban movement remained, however, a fundamentally upper-middle-class trend. The cost of an automobile was still too high for most families. Beyond that, suburban houses required a large down payment and monthly charges which put them even farther out of reach. The average laborer could not buy a suburban home. One careful estimator contended that close to three-quarters of the suburban houses built in 1924 were within reach of only one-tenth of the nation's families.[21]

Well-planned suburbs of the 1920s catered exclusively to the small class of upper-income families. Mariemount, Ohio, outside Cincinnati was launched by the philanthropic widow of a Cincinnati industrialist, who wished to bring a wholesome community life to "all classes of people." The famed planner, John Nolan, was called in to lay out the community. As the project developed, particularly after its sponsor's death, the cost of its houses rose until it was open only to upper-income buyers.[22]

The most famous of all planned suburbs (from the point of view of real estate developers) was the Country Club District of Kansas City whose developer, Jesse Nicholes, was a charter member of the American Institute of Planners and a national leader among real estate developers. His 6,000 acre community on the edge of Kansas City pioneered the construction of suburban shopping centers, control of land use through deed restrictions, and comprehensive delivery of community services—everything from garbage removal to recreational services. Obviously, the working classes did not seek homes in the Country Club District, and blacks were carefully prohibited by perpetual deed covenants.[23]

Some lower-income families did manage to buy suburban homes. Outside of Detroit, auto workers secured building permits for "garage dwellings" and lived the suburban life in one or two room shacks on land purchased at inflated prices. Those who did manage to buy a house often purchased a flimsy structure squeezed onto a tiny lot in a gridiron pattern that raised the cost of both streets and utilities. Ugly, expensive, and poorly constructed, most suburbs of the 1920s were an easy mark for critics.[24]

At the opening of the decade, an article in *The Atlantic Monthly* attacked upper-class suburbs for their garishness and banality as well as for their snobbery and introversion. Behind their facade of relaxed friendliness was "a hardness and selfishness beyond belief."[25] The young critic Lewis Mumford wrote in *The New Republic* of "The Wilderness of Suburbia," which he claimed was only part of a deeper urban malaise. The modern industrial agglomeration, with none of the cultural resources of the great cities of the past, was "the negation of a city," and the new suburbs were "a negation of that negation." Suburbia was not a new and better type of city; it was "the city become a traffic thoroughfare; the home, a dormitory; and the neighborhood, a stony wilderness . . . a vast aimless drift of human beings." Having failed to create a decent life in the cities, Americans built suburbia, which, instead of offering a remedy, was "an aggravation of the disease."[26]

Popular magazines and writers attacked the exclusiveness of wealthy suburbs and shoddiness of less affluent ones. Sociologists, architects, planners, and other urban reformers examined concrete alternatives to the slipshod methods of the suburban developers. Two of the decade's most deft satirists trained their sights on the new suburbs. Ring Lardner's *Own Your Own Home* (1917) exposed the stupidity and criminality of "easy finance" home ownership, while Sinclair Lewis created one of the enduring stereotypes of the age with his creation of George Babbitt, dealer in suburban real estate.[27]

Literary attacks on the shortcomings of suburbs were supported by evidence from the social sciences. In 1925 Harlan Paul Douglas published *The Suburban Trend*, a pioneering study of suburban society. While deploring the physical and financial sins of suburbs resulting from "almost criminal misdirection of effort and investment," Douglas found their most serious problem to be a lack of community identity. He noted the divided loyalties of the suburbanite between the community where he lives and the city where he works and spends most of his waking hours. Unlike rural towns which were centers for an agricultural hinterland, the modern suburb had no comparable town center in which its residents could meet. He found suburbs that were built around former small agricultural towns with their old traditions, institutions, and machinery for social life appeared to be significantly different from suburbs built on raw land. Finally, he found that the high cost of suburban homes not only excluded the poor but also young married families and retired couples, which, aside from its effects on the excluded groups, rendered suburbia socially unbalanced.[28]

The gasoline-fueled suburban boom impelled metropolitan areas to establish regional planning agencies to at least tie the growing suburbs into some system of highways and utility lines. Between 1923 and 1929 almost every large metropolitan area of the nation created such an agency under private auspices, such as the Chicago Regional Planning Association, or as a public bureau such as the Los Angeles County Regional Planning Commission.[29] The first, and most famous of these commissions was the New York Regional Plan Commission, which was established in 1921 by Charles D. Norton and financed by the Russell Sage Foundation. Norton died in 1923 (being replaced by Frederic A. Delano, an uncle of Franklin Roosevelt); but he had already set the project in motion by selecting as its research director the former secretary of the British Garden City Association, Thomas Adams. The multivolume *Regional Plan of New York and its Environs* was the most comprehensive regional investigation ever undertaken. The *Regional Plan* steered a middle course between timid acquiescence to prevailing methods and patterns of metropolitan growth and a plan which would so fundamentally alter existing trends that it would not be taken seriously. Encompassing an area of 5,528 square miles, the plan yielded to already established directions of metropolitan growth but suggested controlling these movements through comprehensive zoning, anticipatory purchases of park land, and prior construction of highways, streets, and utility lines. As might be expected, Adams suggested the construction of entire satellite cities, but this was not a paramount part of the plan.[30] There were no suggestions for new ways to finance suburban homes for working-class families beyond the well-worn call for limited-dividend housing corporations.[31]

None of the regional planning commissions of the 1920s was (or could have been) as boldly comprehensive as most planners wished, for they lived at the behest of local business and political leaders. No commission presented plans which aimed at diverting the growth of metropolitan cities because their sponsors never questioned the assumption that bigger was better. The regional commissions were supposed to facilitate growth by making certain that when real estate developers and industrialists moved into new areas, they would soon have the necessary streets and utilities.

It was therefore logical that the most radically comprehensive regional planning would, in the 1920s, be carried out by a private organization—the Regional Planning Association of America. Founded in 1923 by a group of architects and planners living in the New York area, the RPAA drew to its informal gatherings architects Henry Wright, Clarence Stein, Frederick L. Ackerman, Robert D. Kohn, and Frederick Bigger; the economist Stuart Chase; the reform-minded real estate developer Alexander Bing; the naturalist Benton McKaye; and the man of many talents, Lewis Mumford. They were later joined by Tracy Augur, fresh from the Harvard School of Landscape Architecture, and Edith Elmer Wood and Catherine Bauer, both of whom were drawn to the group by an interest in low-income housing. Stein, Wright, Kohn, Bigger, Augur, and Bauer later served as planners or consultants to the greenbelt town program. Lewis Mumford perhaps overstated the case years later in claiming that without the RPAA, the greenbelt town program of the 1930s "would have been inconceivable"; but the intellec-

tual debt was very great.[32] The RPAA resembled the old Garden
City Association of America in its advocacy of new towns,[33]
but did so in the framework of regional-ecological theories undreamed of by the earlier group. Likewise, the RPAA conceived
far more detailed and sophisticated plans of the new towns
themselves.[34] On the regional scale it was argued that the motor
vehicle and electric power transmission lines now permitted
industrial and commercial enterprises to move far into the country. New towns (or carefully expanded villages) could now have
all the modern necessities but planned to preserve their rural
character. In this manner the large cities would cease their unhealthy growth rates and millions of Americans would not have
to forgo modern conveniences or economic necessities to remain in the countryside. Within metropolitan areas such
growth as did occur should be channelled into satellite towns
close enough for commutation, but built on tracts which would
interlace the residential areas with parks and open spaces to
provide a rural atmosphere and delimitate clear neighborhoods,
villages, and towns. This would prevent compact urban centers
from dissolving into the formless anticities Mumford decried
in 1920.[35]

The RPAA apparently never formulated a concrete plan for
a rural new town; but Stein and Wright, in conjunction with
Alexander Bing's City Housing Corporation, determined to
build a demonstration satellite town outside New York City. A
1,258 acre tract was assembled near Fairlawn, New Jersey, near
a major approach to the George Washington Bridge (then under construction). Construction of the new town of Radburn began in 1928, and the first of a projected 25,000 residents moved
in during the summer of the fateful year 1929.

The Radburn plan embodied many elements built into the
greenbelt towns.[36] The entire town was divided into three major villages, each having its own elementary school. Each village was divided into more basic neighborhood units by creating superblocks of thirty-five and forty acres with the houses
facing away from the street towards interior parks. Neighbors

would face each other across grassy parkways rather than traffic thoroughfares. Streets varied according to use: narrow lanes for direct access to the buildings, secondary roads around the superblocks, main streets connecting the large neighborhoods, and express highways linking Radburn with the outside world. All pedestrian and vehicular traffic was separated—the walkways often running through the interior parks and crossing roads through underpasses.

Radburn differed from the classic garden city in several ways. Common public landholding was rejected in favor of individual ownership. The City Housing Corporation held title only until the area was subdivided, but in so doing it continued to control overall town planning. The limited financial resources of the corporation forced abandonment of both the encircling greenbelt and an industrial area. These were partially compensated by the extensive interior park system and the availability of factory sites adjacent to the town. Finally, the town lacked a separate government, but developed an active homeowners association.

Not wishing to build another attractive suburb open only to the affluent, Radburn's planners designed both the superblocks and houses to take advantage of every possible economy. Nevertheless, each acre of park or open space increased land prices for the residential lots, and homes at Radburn were still beyond the reach of the average family.[37] Such financial exclusiveness was unavoidable. The corporation had to show a decent profit if the project was to be taken seriously by the real estate industry. The RPAA was no more successful than any other groups in devising ways that moderate-income families (not to speak of the poor) could be adequately housed at a profit. The RPAA joined slum housing reformers in advocating some form of public subsidy for the construction of new towns.[38]

The Great Depression destroyed Radburn long before it was even half finished. Only two superblocks were completed. Like thousands of other real estate developers, the City Housing Corporation went into receivership in 1933 and was forced to dispose of almost all of its undeveloped land. A number of Radburn's middle-class wage earners lost their jobs and consequently lost their new homes. The town thus suffered blows at every level. The only rapidly growing new towns in America in 1933 were the tarpaper "Hoovervilles."

Herbert Hoover's administration showed no interest in giving direct aid to new town developers or to builders. During his years as secretary of commerce, the president took an active interest in preparing and distributing information on housing and city planning. The publication of a Standard City Planning enabling act was a significant achievement.[39] These aids, he thought, were the proper limit of federal encouragement to the real estate and construction industries. After the collapse of 1929, all the technical information seemed superfluous. To meet the crises Hoover suggested the creation of a Home Loan Bank System which, in normal times, might have been helpful, but was woefully inadequate in 1931. Curiously, in the midst of the depression when residential construction had virtually ceased, Hoover launched his most ambitious research project, the President's Conference on Home Building and Home Ownership. On December 2, 1931, Hoover opened the conference by addressing over a thousand delegates representing governmental, housing, labor, and city planning groups. He lauded the character-building role of home ownership, saying, "To own one's own home is a physical expression of individualism, of enterprise, of independence, and of freedom of spirit."[40] Turning finally to the problem of home financing, the president took almost no note of the depression, alleging instead that the "chief problem" related to people who could only afford a ten to twenty percent down payment. His proposed creation of the Home Loan Bank System would solve this problem and thus destroy the last hurdle to universal home ownership. He saw no necessity for further aid. The purpose of the conference, he warned the delegates, was "to stimulate individual endeavor" and not "to set up government in the building of homes."[41] Hoover remained a life-long opponent of public housing.

Albert Shaw, editor of the *Review of Reviews* and chairman

of the Conference Committee on Education and Service (the committee charged with publicizing the conference's findings), wrote that he was confident the conference would show how "millions of workers may own homes with gardens." He too warned that "this cannot be done by building barracks as in Russia" or "by such re-housing schemes at municipal and national expense [as] adopted in Great Britain." Shaw concluded, "The American plan is to train and develop the individual in the capacity and ambition to own his own decent home."[42] Obviously, the conference did not begin on a very hopeful note.

Many conference delegates disagreed with Hoover and Shaw. Two major conference committees reported for sweeping changes. The Committee on City Planning and Zoning, which included John Nolan, Jacob Crane, and Henry Wright, pictured Radburn on the frontispiece of its report and called for the construction of new towns as the best way to build a decent environment at reasonable cost.[43] The Committee on Slums, Blighted Areas, and Decentralization recommended the construction of subsidized low income housing on the urban fringe.[44]

In the opinion of one delegate, Hoover's plea for rugged individualism fell on deaf ears, for "the spirit of the conference was for a right-about-face on this principle."[45] A large number of delegates spoke in favor of direct government action to build homes. Hoover's own secretary of the interior, Ray L. Wilbur, concluded at the conference that publically financed housing was "inevitable" unless private builders could somehow meet the demand for low-cost housing.[46] Other committees, such as the important Committee on Home Finance, were presided over by conservatives who did not share this view. The conference, like the nation itself, hovered indecisively between old methods and new experiments. The President's Conference did bring together the widely scattered professionals interested in housing and city planning, and a wealth of material was gathered and published. The conference reports distilled over thirty years of housing and city planning experiments, and synthesized the research of hundreds of urban investigators. President

Hoover, locked into an outmoded conception of limited government, was unwilling to use this data to launch his own housing and urban planning programs. The conference material, and many of the architects and planners who wrote it, remained unemployed until the coming of the New Deal.

1. Alan Gowans, *Images of American Living: Four Centuries of Architecture and Furniture as Cultural Expression*, p. 314; Christopher Tunnard, "The Romantic Suburb in America," *Magazine of Art* 40 (May, 1947): 184–87; John W. Reps, *The Making of Urban America* (Princeton, N.J.: Princeton University Press, 1965), p. 342.

2. Stanley Buder, *Pullman: An Experiment in Industrial Order and Community Planning, 1880–1930* (New York: Oxford University Press, 1967), pp. 43–45, 89, 147 ff.

3. Graham Taylor, *Satellite Cities: A Study of Industrial Suburbs* (New York: A. A. Appleton & Company, 1915), pp. 165–230; Harold M. Mayer and Richard C. Wade, *Chicago: Growth of a Metropolis* (Chicago: University of Chicago Press, 1969), pp. 242–46.

4. Edith Elmer Wood, *The Housing of the Unskilled Wage Earner: America's Next Problem* (New York: The Macmillan Company, 1919), p. 131. The views of Weber and Taylor are found in Adna F. Weber, *The Growth of Cities in the Nineteenth Century* (New York: The Macmillan Company, 1899), p. 475; and Taylor, *Satellite Cities*, pp. 285–90.

5. William Ashworth, *The Genesis of Modern British Town Planning* (London: Routledge & Kegan Paul Ltd., 1954), pp. 126–38. For an American view of Bournville and Port Sunlight, see Wilhelm Miller, "What England Can Teach Us about Garden Cities," *Country Life* 17 (March, 1910): 531–32.

6. The two best sketches of Howard's life are J. F. Osborn, "Introduction" in *Garden Cities of Tomorrow*, ed. Ebenezer Howard; and Dugold Macfayen, *Sir Ebenezer Howard and the Town Planning Movement* (Manchester: Manchester University Press, 1933).

7. The term "garden city" was first used by Alexander T. Stewart to describe his model town on Long Island, New York, in 1869; but Howard may have first heard the term in Chicago, during his residence there from 1871 to 1876. Proud of its new parks and gardens purchased in 1870, the city of Chicago adopted the name Garden City and placed it on the coat of arms. See Thomas Adams, *Outline of Town and City Plan-*

ning, p. 168. There is even the possibility that Howard drew from Chicago his inspiration for the system of satellite cities separated by green belts. The Chicago architect, Henry Lewis Sullivan, recalled that Chicago in the 1870s was surrounded by an arc of smaller towns each "nestled in the spacious prairie . . . within its own companionable tree growth." See Henry Louis Sullivan, *Autobiography of An Idea* (New York: Dover Publications, 1956), p. 241. For British use of the term before 1898, see Ashworth, *Genesis of Modern British Town Planning,* p. 141 n.

8.   Howard, *Garden Cities of Tomorrow,* pp. 46–48, 113–14, 126–27.

9.   There is no history of the Garden City Association of America. Its genesis and early development can be traced in Josiah Strong, "The Industrial Revolution: Its Influence on Urban Development," *The Garden City* 1 (October, 1904): 2–4; "Garden City Association in America," *The Garden City* 1 (December, 1906): 252; W. D. P. Bliss, "The Garden City Association of America," *The Garden City* 2 (February, 1907): 268–69; "Garden Cities in America," *Charities and the Commons* 17 (April 27, 1907): 114; "Notes from Abroad," *The Garden City* 2 (September, 1907): 411–14. The association also is discussed briefly in Tracy B. Augur, "Industrial Growth in America and the Garden City" (Master's thesis, Harvard University, 1921), pp. 50–55. Augur later served as an advisor to the greenbelt town planners.

10.   "Garden Cities and Suburbs" *International Studio* 28 (June, 1906): 376.

11.   Gustav Stickley, "Rapid Growth of the Garden City Movement," *The Craftsman* 27 (December, 1909): 296–310; Miller, "What England Can Teach Us about Garden Cities," pp. 531–32; Frederic C. Howe, *European Cities at Work* (New York: Charles Scribner's Sons, 1914), pp. 17, 37, 172–74; Roy Lubov, *The Progressives and the Slums: Tenement House Reform in New York City, 1890–1917* (Pittsburgh: University of Pittsburgh Press, 1962), pp. 221–29.

12.   Wood, *Housing of the Unskilled Wage Earner,* pp. 105–23, 131–32; Nelson P. Lewis, *The Planning of the Modern City* (New York: John Wiley & Sons, Inc., 1916), p. 311; Ebenezer Howard, "Cottages for Labourers," *The Garden City* 2 (February, 1907): 265.

13.   Arthur C. Comey, "Copartnership for Housing in America" *The Annals of the American Academy of Political and Social Science* 51 (January, 1914): 140–47.

14.   U.S., Congress, Senate, Subcommittee of the Committee on Agriculture and Forestry, *Hearings on Senate Resolution No. 305,* 64th Cong., 2d sess., 1917, p. 24.

15.   Henry Wright, *The American City: An Outline of Its Development and Functions* (Chicago: A. C. McClurg & Co., 1916), p. 171.

16. Carol Aronovici, "Suburban Development," *The Annals of the American Academy of Political and Social Science* 51 (January, 1914): 236.

17. The war housing program is described in Roy Lubov, "Homes and A Few Well Placed Fruit Trees: An Object Lesson in Federal Housing," *Social Research* 27 (January, 1961): 469–86; and Charles H. Whitaker et al., *The Housing Problem in War and Peace.* Its effect on planning is assessed in Thomas Adams, *The Design of Residential Areas,* p. 241; and in Mel Scott, *American City Planning Since 1890* (Berkeley: University of California Press, 1969), p. 174.

18. U.S., Congress, House, Committee on Buildings and Grounds, *House Reports, Miscellaneous,* 66th Cong., 1st sess., 1919, no. 181, pp. 2–3.

19. Ray W. Bronez, "Interest Groups and Public Housing Policy," pp. 36–37.

20. Charles N. Glaab, "Metropolis and Suburb: The Changing American City," in *Change and Continuity in Twentieth Century America: The 1920's,* eds. John Braeman, Robert Bremner, and David Brody, (Columbus, Ohio State University Press, 1968), pp. 404–5, 407. Warren S. Thompson, "Population Growth and Housing Demand," *The Annals of the American Academy of Political and Social Science* 190 (March, 1937): 135.

21. Harlan Paul Douglas, *The Suburban Trend* (New York: The Century Company, 1925), p. 146.

22. Scott, *American City Planning,* pp. 232–33.

23. Glaab, "Metropolis and Suburb," 426–30.

24. Catherine Bauer, *Modern Housing,* pp. 54–55.

25. Edward Yeomans, "The Suburban Delux," *Atlantic Monthly* 125 (January, 1920): 107.

26. Lewis Mumford, "The Wilderness of Suburbia," *The New Republic* 28 (September, 1921): 44–45.

27. Ring Lardner, *Own Your Own Home* (New York: Charles Scribner's Sons, 1917); Sinclair Lewis, *Babbit* (New York: Harcourt, Brace & World Inc., 1922). See also Frederick Lewis Allan, "Suburban Nightmare," *Independent* 114 (June, 1925): 670–71.

28. Douglas, *Suburban Trend,* pp. 103–4, 112–13, 145–46, 180–83, 226–34.

29. Scott, *American City Planning,* pp. 204–13.

30. Ibid., pp. 223–25. On the building of satellite cities, see New York Regional Plan Committee, *The Regional Plan of New York and Its Environs* (New York: The Regional Plan Committee, 1929), 1: 383–84.

31. A heated controversy developed between Thomas Adams and Lewis Mumford over the latter's attacks on the Regional Plan. For a description of both the Regional Plan and the Adams-Mumford exchange, see Roy Lubov, *Community Planning in the 1920's: The Contribution of the Regional Planning Association of America* (Pittsburgh: University of Pittsburgh Press, 1963), pp. 114–22; and Scott, *American City Planning*, pp. 290–93.

32. Lewis Mumford "Introduction," in *Towards New Towns for America*, ed. Clarence S. Stein, p. 14.

33. The term "new town" gradually replaced "garden city" in the 1920s, due to increasing use of the old term for exclusively residential suburbs or any type of suburban development that included a few trees and flowers. See "What Is and What Is Not a Garden City?" *The Survey* 41 (January, 1919): 539, and Alexander M. Bing, "Can We Have Garden Cities in America?" *The Survey* 54 (May, 1925): 172.

34. These differences arose because the old GCAA was composed of technically untrained reformers, philanthropists, and civic-minded businessmen while the RPAA was predominantly professional architects and planners with wide technical and intellectual experience. The RPAA's membership was weak in view of the fact that it had only one real estate developer (Alexander Bing) and no one from the financial or political worlds. These omissions are no doubt a comment on the pedestrian views of bankers and politicians in the 1920s, rather than an oversight by the RPAA.

35. Lubov, *Community Planning in the 1920's*, pp. 35, 47–50, 83–105.

36. Descriptions of the planning of Radburn and brief descriptions of its development as a community are found in Stein, *Towards New Towns in America*, pp. 37–73; and Henry Wright, *Rehousing Urban America*, pp. 36–46.

37. The annual income of Radburn residents was $2,000–$5,000. The average annual income of employed wage earners in the United States in 1928 was $1,405. See Stein, *Towards New Towns*, pp. 59–60; and George Soule, *Prosperity Decade: From War to Depression, 1917–1929*, The Economic History of the United States, Vol. 8 (New York: Harper & Row Publishers, 1968), p. 221.

38. Lubov, *Community Planning in the 1920's*, p. 47.

39. Herbert Hoover, *The Memoirs of Herbert Hoover*, 2: 92–94. See also U.S., Department of Commerce, *A Standard City Planning Enabling Act* (Washington: U.S. Government Printing Office, 1928).

40. Hoover, *Memoirs*, 2: 257.

41. Ibid., pp. 257–58.

42. Albert Shaw, "The Conference for Better Homes," *Review of Reviews* 84 (December, 1931): 41–43.

43. U.S., President's Conference on Home Building and Home Ownership, *Planning for Residential Districts,* Vol. 6 of *President's Conference on Home Building and Home Ownership* (Washington: U.S. Government Printing Office, 1932), frontispiece.

44. President's Conference on Home Building and Home Ownership, *Slums, Large-Scale Housing and Decentralization,* Vol. 3 of *President's Conference on Home Building and Home Ownership,* pp. 12–17.

45. Arthur E. Wood, "Home and the Housing Experts," *The Nation* 133 (December, 1931): 692–93.

46. U.S., Presidents Conference on Home Building and Home Ownership, *Slums, Large-Scale Housing and Decentralization,* Vol. 3 of *President's Conference,* p. xii.

2

🍁 ORIGINS OF THE SUBURBAN
RESETTLEMENT PROGRAM

The greenbelt towns owe their existence to Rexford Tugwell. In the spring of 1935 he convinced President Roosevelt to pay for their construction out of the unemployment appropriation currently being considered by the Congress. The greenbelt idea germinated at a time when a number of rural land-use and community construction agencies were consolodated by Tugwell, Secretary of Agriculture Wallace, and Roosevelt into a single organization—the Resettlement Administration. The agencies absorbed by the R.A. were the Subsistance Homesteads Division of the Department of Interior, the Rural Rehabilitation Division of the Federal Emergency Relief Administration, the Land Utilization Division, also under the F.E.R.A., and the Land Policy Section of the Agricultural Adjustment Administration. The greenbelt town program was the only fundamentally new activity to be undertaken by the Resettlement Administration.[1]

The purpose of the Resettlement Administration as seen by Tugwell and its other officials was threefold. First, it was to provide aid for marginal but economically "savable" farms through small loans, educational programs, and technical aid. The Rural Rehabilitation Division had already made a start in these activities, and those programs were expanded. Second, the Resettlement Administration was to execute a land reform program allowing rural families to move from unproductive land and resettle in more fertile areas—on individual farms or in cooperative farm communities. The unproductive lands which they left were to be used for some nonfarming purpose. The Land Utilization Division had been purchasing unproductive land before it came under the Resettlement Administration, but had not developed a program for resettling those families whose land had been purchased. The Rural Rehabilitation Division had constructed a few small farm communities; but the Subsistence Homesteads Division, engaged exclusively in rural community building, had been far more active. Both programs were eventually completed after being coordinated under the Resettlement Administration.[2] Third, it was obvious to Tugwell that the basic rural problem was the increasing technological efficiency of farming which, each year, drove thousands of families out of agriculture. These unfortunate families could not be resettled in any substantial numbers on more productive land because they would simply increase total farm output and further depress the market. Therefore, in spite of a temporary halt in the migration to urban areas, business would again pick up and the inevitable cityward trend would reappear.[3] The rural family, forced by economic circumstances to seek a living in the city, had usually joined other low-income families in the urban slums. Slums, like the submarginal farms, persisted because no institution offered slum dwellers an alternative which they could afford. They paid a high proportion of their income for very low quality housing—tiny apartments unsafely crowded together because the land on which they stood was valuable and highly taxed. But in the countryside land was inexpensive and unencumbered by outmoded street patterns and buildings. A builder could construct a large number of homes plus all the facilities of urban neighborhoods on inexpensive suburban land. There would be room for trees, grass, and sunlight—all available for the same rent paid in the city slums.

Tugwell, like Roosevelt, believed that resettling thousands of slum dwellers in semiagricultural communities was economically unfeasible. Employment would continue to concentrate in the urban areas because industries would not move out to aggregations of willing workers in rural areas.[4] The suburban fringe was the only location where the advantages of the countryside could be combined with the employment opportunities of the city.[5] Ebenezer Howard had seen this years before when he located his garden cities within commuting distance of a large central metropolis. However, when Howard's ideas for metropolitan planning were combined with the rural resettlement plans of the R.A., a broad program emerged that would "make America over."[6]

It is not surprising that Roosevelt approved both the coordination of the existing programs and the inauguration of a new program to build suburban towns. He had long been interested in city and regional planning. Alfred Bettman, in his Presidential Address to the 1933 National Conference on City Planning, said that "the outstanding item" in America's city and regional planning was "a President who knows and cares about planning."[7] Roosevelt said in 1932 that as a young man he had listened to his uncle Frederic Delano discuss city planning with the giants of the field and had thereafter kept a vital interest not only in the "mere planning of a single city, but in the larger aspects of planning."[8] He was quite aware of past mistakes in the physical planning of our existing structures and the need for imaginative solutions.

> We go gaily into projects for putting up new buildings without realizing that there is a limit beyond which we are cutting off more than we are adding on. And this is true not only in the city, but in the suburbs and the country.

I am convinced that one of the greatest values of this total regional planning is the fact that it dares us to make experiments, for this country will remain progressive just so long as we are willing to make experiments.[9]

In his second Inaugural Address as governor of New York, Roosevelt called attention to the failure of local government to meet the needs of the modern metropolis. He saw "the unparalleled growth of city populations" and the "birth of a new type of community known as the suburban area" creating a host of new requirements for highways, sewers, water, and schools.[10]

In his Annual Message to the New York Legislature in January, 1931, he told them that the machinery of local government "is now obsolete" and recommended a constitutional amendment allowing local governments greater freedom in adopting "modern forms of government."[11]

As governor of New York, Roosevelt was an outspoken critic of the slums and conceded that private philanthropy in the housing of the poor was a failure, but he did not suggest a specific solution.[12] During the 1932 presidential campaign he followed a cautious policy in discussing public housing. He endorsed the construction of slum clearance projects for the poor but mainly as a means to alleviate unemployment.[13] The Democratic Platform of 1932 approved a federal public works program for flood control and waterways, but made no mention of housing for the poor, urban decentralization, or new towns.[14]

Roosevelt did show concern for what he told the 1931 Governor's Conference was "the dislocation of a proper balance between urban and rural life."[15] In his Inaugural Address to the nation on March 4, 1933, he said "We must frankly recognize the overbalance of population in our industrial centers."[16] The word "balance" may be the most descriptive term not only for Roosevelt's idea of urban-rural relationships but also for the entire philosophy underlying the New Deal. Several historians have remarked on the desire of the New Dealers to strike a balance of power between the traditionally antithetical factions of the nation—urban and rural, management and labor, as well as interindustrial competition.[17] Roosevelt was concerned not only with the economic imbalance of society but with the physical imbalance of people unnecessarily crowded into congested city slums and those in isolated or unproductive rural areas.

The president was not an advocate of the back-to-the-land movement. While he had a deep feeling for rural life and encouraged the "breaking down of artifical and unnecessary barriers between the rural and urban communities," he saw the futility of attempting to move large numbers of urbanites to farms.[18] He thought the back-to-the-land question was too narrowly debated between the advocates of either strictly urban or strictly rural communities. He saw "a definite place for an intermediate type between the urban and rural, namely a rural-industrial group."[19] Whether he was thinking specifically of a garden city or greenbelt type of community is not clear, but it is very likely that he was aware of them through his uncle or through Thomas Adams, the director of the Regional Plan of New York and former secretary of the British Garden City Association.[20] Mrs. Eleanor Roosevelt must certainly have had some knowledge of the garden city movement and the work of the Regional Planning Association of America through her position as a board member of Alexander Bing's City Housing Corporation, the limited dividend company which built Radburn, New Jersey.[21] Eleanor Roosevelt was later to become one of the most valuable defenders of the greenbelt town programs.

The Resettlement Administration itself was officially created by Executive Order 7027 on April 30, 1935. Subsequent executive orders transferred the land programs, rural rehabilitation programs, rural communities, and subsistence homesteads to the Resettlement Administration.[22] Tugwell retained his post as undersecretary of agriculture, but under E.O. 7027 he also became the administrator of the Resettlement Administration, responsible only to Roosevelt. Three of the R.A.'s four divisions were transfers from other agencies—Land Utilization, Rural Rehabilitation, and Rural Resettlement. The fourth division was named the Suburban Resettlement Division. It's task was the construction of the greenbelt towns under authority granted in section (a) of E.O. 7027 which empowered the R.A. to

administer approved projects involving resettlement of destitute or low-income families from rural and urban areas, including the establishment, maintenance, and operation, in such connection, of communities in rural and suburban areas.[23]

Tugwell was assisted in the overall Resettlement program and in the Suburban Division specifically by personnel transferred into the R.A. from the three existing agencies and by others brought in from outside the government. His deputy administrator, a southern liberal named Will W. Alexander, came to the R.A. from Dillard University in New Orleans where he had been president since 1931. There were a number of assistant administrators, but the most important was Calvin B. Baldwin, who had been an administrative aid to Henry Wallace. Baldwin handled most of the internal administration of the Resettlement Administration including personnel problems, a number of which arose in the Suburban Division in 1935.[24] First Alexander, and then Baldwin, was to succeed Tugwell as administrator of the Resettlement Administration.

The Suburban Division was headed by John S. Lansill, the former chief of the Land Utilization Division of the F.E.R.A. and an old friend of Tugwell. The two men met at the Wharton School of Finance, but while Tugwell remained in the academic profession, Lansill went to work on Wall Street. When they met again in 1933, Lansill was independently wealthy. Lansill had read about Tugwell's new role as an advisor to the New Deal administration and stopped to greet him in Washington before he and Mrs. Lansill sailed for Europe. Tugwell was delighted to see his old friend and immediately offered him the job of directing the F.E.R.A.'s land program. Lansill demurred, saying he did not want a job with the government. As a Republican he was not sure he agreed with the New Deal program, and he knew very little about land-use planning. Tugwell and Harry Hopkins (who was administrator of the F.E.R.A.) finally prevailed on him to take the job on a temporary basis. He remained in the government until the spring of 1938 and became an enthusiastic advocate of both the land utilization program and the suburban town program as well as an admirer of Roosevelt.[25]

Like Tugwell, John Lansill was strikingly handsome and well dressed; but his gentlemanly manner and warm Kentucky accent were in sharp contrast to Tugwell's brusque self-confidence—indeed, arrogance—which so often infuriated friend and foe alike. Lansill was well suited to handle the administration of a project in which so many formerly self-employed and individualistic architects were forced to work out daily compromises with each other and with the Resettlement Administration. Controversies would often become so heated that Lansill would adjourn them to his home where—over potently refreshing mint juleps—compromises emerged.[26]

When Lansill became chief of the Suburban Division, he took with him two former assistants from the Land Utilization Division. Wallace Richards, Lansill's administrative assistant in the land program, remained one of Lansill's closest advisors and became the coordinator of the first suburban project—Greenbelt, Maryland. The other assistant was Tilford E. Dudley, who became chief of the Land Acquisition Section of the Suburban Division. Dudley's experience in assembling large tracts of land for the government was to prove crucial to the entire suburban program.

In June, 1935, the Suburban Division established a Research Section to determine the location for the projects. Its director was Warren J. Vinton, a bright, young economist from Columbia University and a sharp leftwing critic of the New Deal. Vinton remained in the field of public housing and later became chief of research for the Public Housing Administration. His opinions carried great weight in the Surburban Division and with the directors of the Resettlement Administration.[27]

Placement of the greenbelt town program in Tugwell's agency was not entirely advantageous. The Suburban Division was given unusual freedom in the planning and construction of the towns—which it would not have had if placed (perhaps more logically) under the direction of Harold Ickes's P.W.A. Housing Division. The chief disadvantage of the Suburban Division was its association with the more controversial (and less successful) programs of the Resettlement Administration. From the inception of the R.A. its programs were controversial—as was everything which involved the name of Rexford Tugwell. He had a reputation as Roosevelt's most leftist advisor. During the 1936 campaign Tugwell was described as "a visible and personal link, as it were, between the Comintern in Moscow and the aspiring young reformers in Washington."[28] When the press dubbed the greenbelt towns "Tugwelltowns," it was enough to convince many Americans of their sinister portent.

As a product of the Emergency Relief Appropriation Act of 1935, the R.A. became a pawn in the larger controversy surrounding the New Deal relief programs. This relief act of 1935 was the largest single peacetime appropriation in the history of the nation. Its size, $4,880,000, and the wide discretionary powers given President Roosevelt in its use marked a turning point in the New Deal and in the long struggle between the two branches of government located at either end of Pennsylvania Avenue.[29] During the debate on the Appropriation Act, Democratic Congressman James P. Buchanan, a House conference manager of the bill, said that at his request the comptroller general had issued an opinion stating that the president was not bound to a strict interpretation of the types of projects he could authorize. The president could "adopt any otherwise lawful Federal projects he desired" with the work relief funds. Congressmen John W. Taber and Bertrand Snell, speaking for the Republican opposition, agreed with the comptroller and thought it all the more reason to scuttle the bill.[30]

In September, 1935, the Resettlement Administration itself provided opponents with more ammunition. The president was asked to further widen the R.A.'s authority under E.O. 7027, the order originally creating the R.A. to initiate and administer soil erosion, stream pollution, and several other types of projects; the words "and other useful projects" were added.[31] Stanley Reed, acting attorney general of the United States had himself questioned the "very broad" power granted by the additional phrase. He was told "informally" by the R.A. that the phrase was needed so that the agency could administer some projects for the white-collar class which were not directly authorized by the original Executive Order 7027. There is no direct mention of the greenbelt towns, but they were the only white-collar projects undertaken by the Resettlement Administration. It may have been thought that the authorization in paragraph (a) to build suburban projects for the "resettlement of destitute or low-income families" would prohibit the R.A. from placing any higher-income families in the greenbelt towns.[32]

The additional phrase did not pass unnoticed. Felix Bruner of the *Washington Post* pointed to it in the first of an extremely influential series of articles on the Resettlement Administration. He said that the unpublicized addition to E.O. 7027 gave Tugwell the power to "initiate and administer anything." Tugwell, he warned, possessed almost every power "except the power to declare war."[33]

Thus the New Deal's new town program was created in the midst of increasingly bitter political conflict, with its creator and chief administrator the object of some of the most heated attacks. The R.A. itself existed on a tenuous grant of presidential authority with no assurance of congressional support. Its funds, allocated from unemployment relief appropriations, placed the greenbelt program in the ambiguous position of both an efficient demonstration of planning and construction and a speedy make-work project for the unemployed.

1. Sidney Baldwin, *Poverty and Politics: The Rise and Decline of the Farm Security Administration* (Chapel Hill: University of North Carolina Press, 1968), pp. 85–93; Bernard Sternsher, *Rexford Tugwell and the New Deal*, pp. 263–64.

2. The best published discussion of the origins of the Resettlement Administration with particular attention to community programs is Paul K. Conkin, *Tomorrow a New World: The New Deal Community Program*, pp. 73–89, 93–145. The most concise statement of the R.A.'s goals is found in Rexford G. Tugwell, "Changing Acres," *Current History* 44 (September, 1936): 57–63. The entire problem of land use management in rural America was discussed by Tugwell in two public addresses given in 1933 and published as chapters 13 and 14 of Tugwell's *The Battle for Democracy.*

3. Rexford G. Tugwell, "Down to Earth," *Current History* 44 (July, 1936): 38. See also Tugwell, *Battle for Democracy*, pp. 109–11, 153–56.

4. In the early years of the New Deal, Roosevelt saw more hope in the back-to-the-land movement than did Tugwell, who later said that this "utopian notion out of the past . . . was an old weakness of both Eleanor and Franklin and was shared by Louis Howe." See Rexford G. Tugwell, *The Democratic Roosevelt*, p. 158. Tugwell's opinion on the future of industrial decentralization is presented in his article, "Cooperation and Resettlement," *Current History* 45 (February, 1937): 74.

5. Tugwell's ideas on the role of the suburban town program in the general plans of the Resettlement Administration and the specific planning concepts for the towns was first expressed in an N.B.C. Radio Address, December 2, 1935 (mimeographed copy in Franklin D. Roosevelt Papers, O.F.), Franklin D. Roosevelt Library, Hyde Park, New York. The most detailed discussion of the towns by Tugwell was given in his "Address to the Regional Planning Association of Hamilton County, Ohio, February 3, 1936" (bound copy in the Library of Congress, Washington, D.C.). The most widely published and cited of his statements on the towns is Rexford G. Tugwell, "The Meaning of the Greenbelt Towns," *The New Republic* 90 (February 17, 1937): 42–43.

6. The plan to "make America over" was recalled by Will Alexander, Tugwell's deputy administrator and successor in his *Oral History Memoir*, p. 386. The early visions of revolutionizing the land and community systems of America faded, but there is little doubt that Tugwell shared them with Alexander. Alexander may have taken the phrase "make America over" from Tugwell. It was the last line in a reformist poem Tugwell wrote in 1912 while an undergraduate at the University of Pennsylvania

and was widely reprinted in the 1930s. See Russell Lord, *The Wallaces of Iowa*, p. 349.

7. Alfred Bettman, "City and Regional Planning in Depression and Recovery," *Planning and National Recovery: Planning Problems Presented at the Twenty-fifth National Conference on City Planning*, p. 124.

8. Franklin D. Roosevelt, "Growing Up by Plan," *The Survey* 67 (February, 1932): 483–85, 509. The article was a slightly altered version of his "Address on Regional Planning in New York City, December 11, 1931. See Samuel I. Rosenman, ed., *The Public Papers and Addresses of Franklin D. Roosevelt*, 1: 496–98. During the 1920s Delano was director of the Regional Plan of New York.

9. Roosevelt, "Growing Up by Plan," pp. 483–85.

10. Rosenman, *Public Papers and Addresses*, 1: 96.

11. Ibid., 1: 108.

12. See Roosevelt's address on housing conditions made in New York City on February 28, 1930 (Rosenman, *Public Papers and Addresses*, 1: 310–12).

13. See Roosevelt's radio address on unemployment and social welfare of October 13, 1932 (ibid., 1: 790–91).

14. Kirk H. Porter and Donald B. Johnson, *National Party Platforms: 1840–1960*, p. 331.

15. Rosenman, *Public Papers and Addresses*, 1:493. Roosevelt's address to the Governor's Conference, "Land Utilization and State Planning" was reprinted as a chapter on "State Planning for Land Utilization" in his book *Looking Forward* (New York: John Day Co., 1933).

16. Rosenman, *Public Papers and Addresses*, 1:13.

17. William E. Leuchtenburg, *Franklin D. Roosevelt and the New Deal*, pp. 35–36; also Arthur M. Schlesinger, Jr., *The Coming of the New Deal*, pp. 179–94.

18. See Roosevelt's Annual Message to the New York Legislature, January 1, 1930 (Rosenman, *Public Papers and Addresses*, 1:93). For two other assessments of Roosevelt's thoughts on rural life, see Daniel R. Fusfield, *The Economic Thought of Franklin D. Roosevelt and the Origins of the New Deal*, pp. 124–30; and Thomas H. Greer, *What Roosevelt Thought: The Social and Political Ideas of Franklin D. Roosevelt*, p. 60.

19. Roosevelt, *Looking Forward*, pp. 56–57.

20. See the interesting "Foreword" Roosevelt wrote in December, 1932, for Thomas Adams's *Outline of Town and City Planning*.

21. See the advertisement for the City Housing Corporation's Radburn project in *The Survey* 54 (May 1, 1925): 54.

22. Executive Order 7027, April 30, 1935, and Executive Order 7041, May 15, 1935, cited in Rosenman, *Public Papers and Addresses*, 4:144–50.

23. Ibid., 4:143.

24. Interview with Calvin B. Baldwin, Greenwich, Connecticut, August 17, 1967.

25. Interview with John S. Lansill, Lexington, Kentucky, February 3, 1965.

26. Ibid.

27. Warren Vinton's critique of the New Deal, written before he entered the government, is found in Benjamin Stolberg and Warren J. Vinton, *The Economic Consequences of the New Deal*. Vinton's wide influence in the Resettlement Administration was recalled by C. B. Baldwin and Tilford E. Dudley.

28. Editorial in *New York Times*, November 19, 1936.

29. Leuchtenburg, *Roosevelt*, p. 125. See also *Emergency Relief Appropriation Act of 1935*, in U.S., Statutes at Large, 49: 115.

30. U.S., *Congressional Record*, 74th Cong., 1st sess., 1935, 79: 5144, 5147–48.

31. The phrase was added to paragraph (b) of E.O. 7027 by E.O. 7200, September 26, 1935 (Rosemann, *Public Papers and Addresses*, 4: 603).

32. Letter from Acting Attorney General Stanley Reed to Franklin D. Roosevelt, September 25, 1935, Roosevelt Papers, O.F. 1568.

33. Felix Bruner, "Utopia Unlimited," *Washington Post*, February 10, 1936.

3

CONFLICTS IN THE FORMATION OF THE GREENBELT TOWN PROGRAM

The R.A. administrators did not immediately turn to city planners for design staffs or advisors. Only after considerable planning had been done did members of the old Regional Planning Association of America and other planners even learn of the program. Their entrance resulted in a major reorganization of the Suburban Division and a very marked improvement in the quality of the towns.

The planning of the towns began on an unusually warm day in February, 1935, when Tugwell took John Lansill and Wallace Richards out to the Beltsville National Agricultural Research Center. It was located a few miles outside Washington in a rolling terrain that was still quite rural. As the three men walked across the windblown fields adjacent to the center, Tugwell explained for the first time his idea for the construction of a model community that could be built on this land.

The town could house not only the employees in the expanding research center, but low-income families from Washington's slums. He discussed the feasibility of Lansill's Land Utilization Division building such model towns outside a number of metropolitan areas. Tugwell concluded with a confidential offer to incorporate Lansill's division into a new agency which he would soon suggest to the president—the agency that emerged three months later as the Resettlement Administration. The initial funds would come from the Emergency Relief Appropriation Act then being debated in the Congress.[1]

Lansill and Richards knew little about model suburban towns but were enthusiastic. By March 12, the Land Utilization Division began taking options adjacent to the Agricultural Center for what they called Maryland Special Project No. 1. On April 2, Tugwell, Lansill, and Richards met again to discuss the Beltsville project. Tugwell told them in confidence that the president had approved his idea for a Resettlement Administration authorized to build several suburban community projects. Tugwell had second thoughts on the desirability of building a large project so close to Washington where it would be under the daily scrutiny of the Washington press, the Congress, and all the other government agencies. Lansill agreed with Tugwell, but Wallace Richards thought this a minor disadvantage compared to the unique opportunity of establishing a housing laboratory in conjunction with the Agricultural Research Center. On April 5, Tugwell discussed the project again with the two men and gave his general approval for a "housing development" adjacent to Beltsville Center.[2]

Preliminary reports were prepared on all major aspects of a proposed model town program which they called "rurban housing."[3] The projects would, according to Lansill and Richards, combine work relief for the unemployed, low-cost housing for the slum dweller, long-term community planning, and subsistence farming. Thus, even at this early date, most of the essential features of the greenbelt town program were laid out. There was no specific mention of garden cities; and while one of the purposes of long-term community planning was to "establish a more satisfactory relationship for the worker between home, community and work," there was no suggestion of including factories within the project.[4]

While Richards's reports were vague as to whether the towns were considered to be fullfledged communities along garden city lines, they were quite clear regarding housing. Richards quickly grasped the significance of low-income housing projects in the suburbs. The towns should demonstrate an attempt to make housing a "public utility" and remove necessary shelter from speculative fields.[5] More importantly, Richards saw *suburban* public housing as an alternative to the P.W.A. slum clearance program which was slow, worked too great a hardship on slum dwellers being cleared, and was expensive for tenants when completed. The chief problem for the P.W.A., as everyone from the president on down knew, was land. Assembling many small parcels of urban land into a large tract was so costly that no adequate low-rent housing could be built on it without a large subsidy. Richards concluded that "rurban" housing projects should be built on inexpensive suburban land before any slums were cleared and rent for prices with which slum housing "would not be able to compete," thus correcting "a fundamental error in federal slum clearance."[6]

While Lansill and Richards were deciding what kind of towns they wanted to build, Vinton's Research Section of the Suburban Division began to look for cities near which to build them. The most important criterion for selecting a city was its past and projected stability of employment. A study was made of over one hundred major cities to find those with the steadiest growth of population, employment, and payrolls from 1900 to 1933. Primary consideration was given to a city that maintained, in addition to steady growth, enlightened labor policies, above average wage levels, a diversity of industry, and, finally, a suitable site on its fringe for the construction of an entire new suburb.[7] The preliminary survey resulted the recommendation of nineteen metropolitan areas: New York, Boston, Pittsburgh,

Detroit, Philadelphia, Chicago, Providence-Fall River, Bridge-port-New Haven, Youngstown, Worcester, Wheeling, St. Louis, Cincinnati, Buffalo, and Los Angeles. On a secondary list were Baltimore, San Francisco, Milwaukee, and Minneapolis-St. Paul.[8]

Further consideration by Vinton led to a major revision in the original group of cities. Los Angeles and San Francisco were dropped because they were too far from the R.A.'s offices in Washington. The program was going to be closely supervised and coordinated—the planners doing most of their work in Washington. Detroit was eliminated because it was too depend-ent on a single industry and was far from qualifying as a center of enlightened labor policies. A revised list was prepared in August. It proposed the construction of nine suburban towns. The cities of St. Louis, Cincinnati, Milwaukee, and Chicago were retained. Three new cities were added—New Brunswick, New Jersey; Dayton, Ohio; and Chattanooga, Tennessee.[9]

The three new cities were selected for reasons not altogether dependent on the original criteria. New Brunswick, New Jersey, was selected at the suggestion of Russell Black, a city planner from New Hope, Pennsylvania, just across the Delaware River from New Jersey. Vinton visited the New Brunswick area and found an excellent site midway between that city and the smaller industrial town of Bound Brook, New Jersey. He be-lieved that the area would experience a rapid industrial expan-sion out from New York—an assumption which proved to be correct. Also, he convinced the R.A. administrators that it was important to demonstrate their suburban program in the New York metropolitan area since it was the center of the communi-cations media and had the largest concentration of architects and city planners. Chattanooga, Tennessee, was selected in part because the R.A. wanted to construct one of its towns in the area of the Tennessee Valley Authority. The selection of Dayton, Ohio, is less clear and Vinton does not recall why it was chosen.[10] The first subsistence homesteads project to receive federal funds was located outside Dayton, but there is no evidence that this influenced the selection of that city for a suburban town.[11] It is curious, however, that both Beltsville, Maryland, and Cincinnati, Ohio, were under consideration for subsistence homesteads when that program was shifted to the Resettlement Administration. They were two of sixty-four tentative subsistence homestead projects transferred to the Suburban Division of the Resettlement Administration for further study.[12] Greater Cincinnati Homesteads, as the one project was called, was never given serious consideration by the Suburban Division for subsistence homesteads. No site was ever selected nor any land optioned. Beltsville Homesteads, on the other hand, remained in the overall plans for Greenbelt until 1936, but it too was finally dropped.[13] The only subsistence homestead project in which the Suburban Division played a major developmental role was Jersey Homesteads outside of Hightstown, New Jersey. This highly publicized project for Jewish garment industry workers was initiated in 1934; but due to a disagreement between the R.A., the project sponsors, and the garment unions, construction was in abeyance when the Suburban Division took charge of the half-completed site. The community became one of the nine towns to be financed with the Suburban Division appropriation, but was later separated from the division's program and completed by the R.A.'s Construction Division.[14]

Guessing the cost of the towns was very difficult. The R.A.'s estimate was much too low. The nine sites selected by the research staff became the basis of Tugwell's first proposal for an allotment of funds from Roosevelt. The cost of each town was set at $7,550,000 which meant a total cost of $68,000,000 for the nine towns.[15] The funds were to be allotted by the president from the Emergency Relief Appropriation Act of 1935; and therefore Tugwell had to compete for it with Harry Hopkins and Harold Ickes.

The Relief Act of 1935 had been requested by Roosevelt in his Annual Message to Congress on January 4, 1935, and Congress followed his guidelines for the manner in which the money was to be spent. Unfortunately, a number of these guidelines were very unsuitable to the greenbelt towns. The act was intended to take all those still on relief rolls and put them to work on government projects. These projects would (1) be of permanent use to the nation, (2) provide an income to the worker greater than relief payments but below prevailing wages in private business, (3) use large numbers of laborers, (4) be self-liquidating or reasonably close to it, (5) be as noncompetitive with private industry as possible, (6) be planned so that relief laborers could be quickly put to work and speedily dismissed when private employment increased, and (7) be located in areas of the most severe unemployment.[16]

Guidelines four through seven were particularly difficult, if not impossible, to meet. The towns could be self-liquidating only if high rents were charged, but this would open them only to middle-class tenants and put the federal government into competition with private builders and landlords. If the towns were to demonstrate the best in American city planning and architecture, they could not be quickly thrown up to give people immediate employment, nor could they be built efficiently by relief laborers, few of whom had the necessary skills. Also, the cities selected by the R.A. for the suburban towns were chosen because of their economic health, whereas the relief projects were to be located in areas with the most serious unemployment problems.

The greenbelt towns shared much in common with Ickes's P.W.A. housing projects; but Ickes, suspicious of both Hopkins and Tugwell, was not initially pleased with R.A.'s suburban housing program. On August 27, 1935, Tugwell proposed that the president allocate the funds necessary for the suburban towns, but Ickes blocked it in the President's Advisory Committee on Allotments, noting in his diary, "It is extraordinary how duplicating agencies intending to do precisely the same thing keep bobbing up here like mushrooms after a rain."[17] Knowing Ickes's jealousy for rivals, the Suburban Division and the R.A. resolved to win him over. The opportunity presented itself most naturally in the Central Housing Committee rather than the Advisory Allocations Committee. The Central Housing Committee was composed of representatives from all the federal agencies engaged in housing activities—the Resettlement Administration being represented by Tugwell, Lansill, and Warren J. Vinton.[18] Ickes was told that the R.A.'s Suburban Division wished only to build a limited number of demonstration projects. The interior secretary was convinced that these projects were not intended to challenge his position as the chief federal home builder, and he lent staff members and records freely to the Suburban Division.[19]

Harry Hopkins, first with the Federal Emergency Relief Administration and then in 1935 with the Works Progress Administration, placed special emphasis on getting people to work quickly on small, very flexible projects. Hopkins was not concerned about the Resettlement Administration duplicating the housing function of Ickes's P.W.A., but he wanted as much of the E.R.A.A. money as possible to be quickly translated into jobs for the unemployed.[20] A powerful ally of Hopkins was the secretary of the treasury, Henry Morgenthau. Morgenthau was never interested in Tugwell's greenbelt towns or any other resettlement projects. When Tugwell, as assistant secretary of agriculture, obtained a $67,000,000 allotment from the president for rural rehabilitation, Morgenthau succeeded in taking it away from him by telling Roosevelt that Tugwell had not even spent all of his previous allocations.[21] Morgenthau believed that Hopkins's methods provided the best use for federal relief funds.

The crucial decision for the greenbelt town funds came on September 12, 1935. Roosevelt called together all the chief administrators of the relief and public works programs to meet with him at Hyde Park and decide on the allocations for the balance of the $4,880,000,000 relief appropriations. The conference was attended by Morgenthau, Hopkins, Ickes, Tugwell, Lee Pressman (Tugwell's general counsel in the R.A.), Daniel Bell (the president's budget director), and several others.[22] There is no record of the conference, but it is clear that with approximately 1,500,000 employable people still on relief rolls, Hopkins's quick-action projects were the obvious solution. Secretary Morgenthau urged that most of the funds go to Hopkins, which is the policy Roosevelt followed.[23] Tugwell received a total of $126,500,000 for the Resettlement Administration and $31,000,000 of this amount was allotted to the greenbelt towns, with the implication that another $37,500,000 might be forthcoming at a later date. The president, that is, approved a construction program totalling $68,500,000 but allocated only $31,000,000 in September:[24] it was a typical Rooseveltian compromise.

The failure of the Suburban Division to get the full $68,500,000 was a disappointment because there was no certainty that Congress would again appropriate relief money or allow the president to use it for model suburban towns—or, indeed, as turned out—that the president himself would be willing to sink any more into the program. Far more serious, however, were the stipulations which the president attached to the allocation. First, the Suburban Division had to obtain permission from the Works Progress Administration to begin each town. The W.P.A. would ascertain whether the supply of relief labor in the area of each proposed project warranted the expenditure of relief funds. Second, the W.P.A. had to certify that each worker hired by the Suburban Division was on relief, unemployed, or in need of a government job. Third, and most improbable, the land for the towns had to be purchased and construction begun by December 15, 1935; and the towns had to be completed by the end of fiscal 1935 (June 30, 1936).[25] These stipulations—made out of the justifiable desire to give immediate employment to people in desperate need of work—greatly complicated, confused, and ultimately crippled the suburban town program. Tugwell phoned Lansill's office from Hyde Park to tell him and his staff the good—and the bad—news concerning the allocation. Lansill explained the strings attached to the money and turned to Tilford Dudley saying, "Well Ted, it's all up to you now." Dudley remembers that nobody in the room was smiling. The task of assembling large tracts of land in ninety days seemed impossible. They didn't even begin to discuss how plans for the towns would be ready for construction crews by December 15.[26]

The number of towns was cut from nine to five even though there still appeared some possibility of obtaining the full $68,500,000. Only those projects could be started at which some progress had been made in land optioning. The Beltsville site was already in the hands of the Resettlement Administration —the land having been purchased with unexpended funds from the old subsistence homesteads program.[27] Likewise, the Hightstown site had been purchased by the Subsistence Homesteads Division prior to its transfer to the Resettlement Administration.[28] Tilford Dudley's Land Section—charged with the responsibility of obtaining the other suburban sites—had begun work at four other locations (Cincinnati, Milwaukee, Bound Brook, and St. Louis). It was clear that Dudley's task at these four sites was all he could handle; and therefore, the others were dropped. St. Louis was excluded at the end of October when the land could not be purchased by December 15.[29]

While the Land Section furiously set to work collecting options at the project sites, the R.A. jostled and cajolled its way through the certifications and approvals necessary to obtain the funds. Any delay in the program could have resulted in the Suburban Division funds being transferred to a program that would employ people more quickly. On September 23 the president officially requested the $31,000,000 by Allocation Memo No. 551. However, the allocation was appended by a memo from Budget Director Bell stating that he was advised by the W.P.A. that no supply of relief labor existed in the Beltsville, Maryland, area, the Bound Brook, New Jersey, area, or the Chattanooga area and that it was doubtful if a sufficient supply existed at any of the other sites.[30] Nevertheless, Corrington Gill, assistant administrator of the W.P.A., certified the Beltsville project on September 30 and the remaining projects on October 18.[31]

The first hurdle for the Suburban Division to surmount was a formidable one—Comptroller General McCarl. McCarl was the chief of the General Accounting Office which had been created by Congress in 1921 to oversee executive allocations. McCarl performed his duties diligently and was approached with great care by the R.A. for fear that he would not allow funds from the Emergency Relief Appropriation Act to be used for building greenbelt towns. Before any funds were transferred, the top R.A. and Suburban Division officials went personally to McCarl to explain the suburban projects to him, which flattered the comptroller considerably.[32] On October 9, Lee Pressman and Wallace Richards officially requested approval of the fund transfer from Comptroller McCarl for the purpose of executing suburban projects at nine locations. The comptroller general said he would approve the funds under the authority of section 1, paragraph (b) of the Emergency Relief Appropriation Act of 1935. However, he questioned the large number of projects and whether they could be defined as "rural rehabilitation." Tugwell answered that on the nine approved locations only three or four would be selected for actual use. Thus the R.A. could "prevent any group of speculators in any one place from attempting to hold up the Administration for exorbitant prices for the land." The projects would derive part of their income from "agricultural work performed within the community," thereby satisfying the rural rehabilitation requirement.[33] McCarl approved the fund transfer on October 10. The next day, October 11, the suburban town program was to be announced to the press, and a few men were to begin clearing the site at Greenbelt.

Late in the day on the 10th, Lansill received a call from District of Columbia Commissioner George Allen. Allen, as chief of the District W.P.A., was sending 800 transient laborers to Greenbelt the next day and another 700 the day after.[34] The president himself had thought this was a good way to rid the capital city of 1500 unemployed and somewhat undesirable men—leftovers from the bonus marchers, unemployed men who had drifted into the capital, and local unemployed, homeless men.[35] Roosevelt issued an Executive Order transferring all the transients in the District of Columbia to the Resettlement Administration by November 1. Allen was quoted as saying that this action solved "the greatest single relief problem which the District government faces."[36] The local press regarded it as a coup for the District government and an important step in the national administration's program to move unemployed persons from relief rolls to useful work projects.[37] One can only imagine the consternation of the Suburban Division officials.

The construction at Greenbelt was begun on October 12; but the Greenbelt planners were not ready with blueprints, so the entire labor force was put to work creating a lake.[38] The lake was of marginal utility to the plans for Greenbelt and began to devour large amounts of money before a single foundation was laid. The press release announcing the commencement of the Beltsville project and the suburban town program—issued on October 11—said that Beltsville would be built "with efficiency, economy and speed"; but the emphasis was obviously on speed at the cost of both efficiency and economy.[39] At Greenbelt the planners were at least well under way, but the other projects were still far from the drawing board stage as the Suburban Division had not even completed hiring of planning directors or draftsmen.[40] C. B. Baldwin later summarized his feelings at the time: "I was scared to death."[41]

The unexpected addition to the Beltsville labor force underscored the necessity for an acceleration of the program. A speedup in planning, however, appeared unlikely because a major conflict within the Suburban Division reached its climax at this same time. The planning staff, assembled in the summer of 1935, divided its attention between the Beltsville and Hightstown projects since the government already owned the land and could begin construction immediately.[42] The chief of the Planning Section was Thomas Hibben, an engineer. He turned the planning of Hightstown and Beltsville over to his Engineering Section which was under the direction of another engineer,

Frank Schmitt. The houses and other buildings were planned by architects in an Architectural Section.[43] Engineers were employed to plan the towns because Lansill, C. B. Baldwin, and even Tugwell did not have sufficient confidence in professional town planners, whom they regarded as impractical and utopian.[44] This was a serious error. The engineers produced an undistinguished plan for Hightstown and a plan for Beltsville that was expensive and clumsy. It called for sixty miles of streets laid out in a geometric pattern.[45]

Fortunately, Lansill asked Tracy Augur, the chief town planner for the T.V.A., to give his advice on the plans being prepared by the engineers. Augur, a member of the Regional Planning Association of America in the 1920s, was dismayed with the work of the Engineering Section. The engineers were reluctant to show anyone their drawings; but in late July or early August, Augur and Warren Vinton were able to spirit a copy of the Beltsville plan out of the engineers' office and show it to Lansill, Baldwin, and Tugwell. They urged the three administrators to turn the job over to professional planners. Augur brought Henry Wright, Clarence Stein, and Frederick Bigger to Washington to meet the R.A. officials and review the town plans.[46] The great English town planner and architect of Hempstead Garden Suburb, Sir Raymond Unwin, was also brought to the R.A. offices in August to discuss the program and added his approval of a change.[47] The result of all this advice was to convince Tugwell and the other R.A. officials that a basic reorganization should be made. All the engineers should be replaced with town planners—a separate team for each town. The suburban town planning should also be completely separated from the subsistence homestead program.

Thomas Hibben was transferred on August 16 to Tugwell's office as advisor on engineering problems for the entire Resettlement Administration—thus removing him from the Suburban Division. Frank Schmitt, and his staff in the Suburban Division Engineering Section, were reorganized as a separate Construction Division and took no further part in the planning of the

suburban towns.[48] The two architects who directed the Architectural Section were gradually eased out. During October and
November almost every one of the original planning officials
had either been transferred or fired.[49]

Hibben's replacement was Frederick Bigger, the associate
of Stein and Wright. He took over direction of the planning
on October 4—one week before construction began at Greenbelt.[50] In his capacity as chief of planning for the Suburban
Division, Bigger became the key figure in the new planning program. He wielded great authority because he was a senior administrator with technical training in architecture and town
planning. He was slight of build and quiet. Certainly he had
none of Tugwell's dashing brilliance or Lansill's savoir faire. He
did possess a detailed working knowledge of every aspect of
architectural planning combined with a shrewd administrative
ability and great patience. He and Lansill worked extremely
well together and are the two men most responsible for executing the greenbelt town program. While Tugwell deserves the
credit for originating the program, that remains his most significant contribution. Any discussion of the towns should mention
all three names equally. Frederick Bigger was the one responsible for all the key policy statements and basic decisions concerning the planning of the towns.

Bigger, along with John Nolan of the Harvard City Planning School, selected all the new planners and architects. During the 1920s, Nolan headed the nation's largest city planning
firm and had been in close contact with British planners such as
Ebenezer Howard and Raymond Unwin.[51] The R.A. had the
pick of the best planners and architects in America—this group
was one of the hardest hit of all professions during the depression. Architectural work declined eighty-six percent between
1928 and 1932, and construction had increased little by 1935.[52]
A staff of twenty-six planning directors was quickly assembled:
Greenbelt: Wallace Richards, project coordinator; Hale
Walker, town planner; Reginald J. Wadsworth, principal architect; Douglas D. Ellington, principal architect; Harold Bursley,

engineering designer; *Greenbrook*: Isaac McBride, project co-ordinator; Henry Wright, town planner; Allan F. Kamstra, town planner; Albert Mayer, principal architect; Henry S. Churchill, principal architect; Ralph Eberlin, engineering designer; *Greenhills*: Albert L. Miller, project coordinator; Justin A. Hartzog, town planner; William A. Strong, town planner; Roland A. Wank, principal architect; G. Frank Cordner, principal architect; William G. Powell, engineering designer; *Greendale*: Fred L. Naumer, project coordinator; Jacob Crane, town planner; Elbert Peets, town planner; Harry H. Bentley, principal architect; Walter G. Thomas, principal architect; Charlton D. Putnam, engineering designer; Tracy Augur, Catherine Bauer, Russell Black, Earle Draper, J. Andre Fouilhoux, and Clarence Stein, general advisors.[23] The directors were assisted by a staff of over four hundred people. The size of the staff was large because of the speed with which plans had to be prepared. This, of course, further increased the ultimate costs of the towns.[54]

The planning staffs and supporting personnel moved into their offices at the end of July. They were housed in the fifty-four-room Evelyn Walsh-McLean mansion at 2020 Massachusetts Avenue. Built by the copper king, Thomas Walsh, the house had been a center of Washington social life for over thirty years. The offices became a curiosity to visitors who joked about the clattering of typewriters in rococo bathrooms and architectural conferences in converted bedrooms. The main ballroom was crammed with drawing tables over which long-necked drawing lights bobbed like a fleet of sailboats on a sea of blueprints.[55] Contemporary photos of shirt-sleeved engineers working under high baroque ceilings looked very much of the "realist school" of Soviet painters depicting the engineers of the new society at work in the former palaces of the czars.

As a matter of fact, the planners of the greenbelt towns were hardly to be compared with either Soviet or American revolutionaries. While some American planners looked longingly at the Soviet Union's engineered society,[56] the same was not true of the average American architect, who was generally a white, Anglo-Saxon conservative.[57] The great majority of the architects and engineers who directed the greenbelt town program were Republicans. Their enthusiasm was not solely philanthropic; it was also sparked by the technical challenge of the program. Lansill remembers that several of the chief architects and town planners remarked to him that while they could make far more money in private practice when prosperity returned, they would remain in the Suburban Division forever if they could continue planning more greenbelt towns.[58] They were inspired by a program which became the most significant American experiment with garden city building the nation had ever seen. Will Alexander says, "They were sure this Resettlement Administration was going to revolutionize things."[59] Marquis Childs recalled the enthusiasm of the planners who kept the lights burning far into the night at the MacLean mansion—"They thought they were planning a new world."[60]

1. John S. Lansill Papers, from files in his personal possession, Lexington, Kentucky (hereafter cited as Lansill Papers, personal files).

2. "Summarized History of Greenbelt Project," John S. Lansill Papers, Suburban Division files, 1935–38, University of Kentucky Library, Lexington, Kentucky (hereafter cited as Lansill Papers, official files).

3. Memo from Wallace Richards to John Lansill, March 25, 1935, Lansill Papers, personal files.

4. Draft report on future policies of the Division of Land Utilization from Richards to Lansill, April 10, 1935, Lansill Papers, personal files.

5. Memo from Richards to Lansill, March 25, 1935, Lansill Papers, personal files.

6. Memo from Richards to Lansill, April 11, 1935, Lansill Papers, personal files.

7. U.S., Resettlement Administration, *Interim Report of the Resettlement Administration*, p. 18. Interview with Warren J. Vinton, Washington, D.C., November 25, 1964.

8. Unsigned memo to John Lansill, April 12, 1935, Lansill Papers, personal files.

9. Roosevelt Papers, O.F. 79. Also Tilford E. Dudley, "Report of Land Section, Suburban Division, Resettlement Administration" (manuscript copy in Wesleyan University Library, Middletown, Conn.).

10. Interview with Warren J. Vinton, Washington, D.C., November 25, 1964.

11. For a brief description of this project, see Paul K. Conkin, *Tomorrow a New World*, pp. 107–8.

12. "The Resettlement Administration and Its Work," Roosevelt Papers, O.F. 1568.

13. R. J. Wadsworth, "Summary Description of the Greenbelt Project" and "Summarized History of the Greenbelt Project," Lansill Papers, official files.

14. U.S. Resettlement Administration, *Interim Report*, pp. 26–31. For a description of the Hightstown project, see Conkin, *Tomorrow a New World*, pp. 256–76.

15. Letter from administrator of Resettlement Administration to comptroller general, October 9, 1935, Lansill Papers, personal files.

16. Rosenman, *Public Papers and Addresses*, 4:21–22.

17. Harold L. Ickes, *The Secret Diary of Harold L. Ickes*, 1:428.

18. National Association of Housing Officials, *Housing Yearbook*, p. 40.

19. Interviews with Lansill and C. B. Baldwin.

20. Searle F. Charles, *Minister of Relief: Harry Hopkins and the Depression*, pp. 210–24; Robert E. Sherwood, *Roosevelt and Hopkins: An Intimate History*, p. 70.

21. John Morton Blum, *From the Morgenthau Diaries: Years of Crisis, 1928–38*, p. 239.

22. Ickes, *Secret Diary*, 1: 436–37.

23. Blum, *From the Morgenthau Diaries*, p. 245.

24. Franklin D. Roosevelt to director, Bureau of Budget, and administrator of Rural Resettlement, September 12, 1935, and Daniel Bell to Franklin D. Roosevelt, September 23, 1935, Roosevelt Papers, O.F. 79.

25. U.S., Resettlement Administration, "Weekly Progress Report No. 34," February, 1936, p. 3, National Archives, Record Group 16. Dudley, "Report of the Land Section." Lansill, "Notes on Origins of Suburban Program," n.d., Lansill Papers, personal files.

26. Interviews with Lansill and Dudley.

27. "Summarized History of Greenbelt Project," Lansill Papers, personal files.

28. Conkin, *Tomorrow a New World*, p. 263.

29. Dudley, "Report of Land Section."

30. Allocation request by Franklin D. Roosevelt to Secretary of the Treasury Morgenthau, September 23, 1935; and Bell to Roosevelt, September 23, 1935, Roosevelt Papers, O.F. 79.

31. "Summary of Resettlement Administration Funds," December 15, 1935, p. 1. Roosevelt Papers, O.F. 79.

32. Interview with C. B. Baldwin.

33. Letter from the administrator of the Resettlement Administration to comptroller general, October 9, 1935, Lansill Papers, personal files.

34. Notes from Lansill Papers, personal files.

35. Interview with Warren J. Vinton.

36. *Washington Star*, October 11, 1935.

37. *Washington Herald*, October 12, 1935, and *Washington Post*, October 11, 1935.

38. Interview with Warren J. Vinton, *Washington Post*, October 12, 1935. *Washington Star*, October 12, 1935.

39. U.S., Resettlement Administration Press Release, October 11, 1935, Roosevelt Papers, O.F. 1568, pp. 2–3.

40. Administrative Personnel Record, Lansill Papers, personal files.

41. Interview with C. B. Baldwin.

42. Wadsworth, "Summary Description of the Greenbelt Project," February, 1938, Lansill Papers, official files.

43. Administrative Personnel Record, Lansill Papers, personal files.

44. Interview with C. B. Baldwin.

45. The final plan for Greenbelt reduced the streets to six miles. See Rexford G. Tugwell, "Magical Greenbelt Is Rising: Model Maryland Community," *Work: A Journal of Progress*, October, 1936, p. 4.

46. Interviews with Tracy Augur, Warren Vinton, John S. Lansill, and C. B. Baldwin, Washington, D.C., January 12, 1965. See Henry S. Churchill, *Greenbelt Towns: A Study of the Background and Planning of Four Communities for the Division of Suburban Resettlement Prepared from Official Records* (manuscript copy in Lansill Papers, official files), chap. 3, pp. 1–2. Also see "Greenbelt Towns," *Architectural Record* 80 (September, 1936): 221.

47. Raymond Unwin to Tugwell, November 18, 1935, Lansill Papers, personal files. See also Carl Feiss, "Unwin's American Journeys," *Town and Country Planning*, December, 1963, p. 424.

48. The Construction Division, officially separated from the Suburban Division on December 1, 1935, completed the planning and construc-

tion of the Hightstown project. It also completed the construction of twenty-two other former subsistence homesteads. The funds for this work came from a $7,000,000 allocation made specifically for this purpose. See U.S., Resettlement Administration, "Weekly Progress Report No. 16," October 5, 1935, pp. 16–17; "Weekly Progress Report No. 21," November 9, 1935, p. 6; and "Weekly Progress Report No. 22," November 16, 1935, p. 1.

49. Administrative Personnel Record, Lansill Papers, personal files.

50. Ibid.

51. In 1925, John Nolan introduced Ebenezer Howard to President Calvin Coolidge. Nolan, serving as president of the National Conference on City Planning, was host to Howard, Unwin, and many other European planners at the 1925 International Town, City, and Regional Planning Conference which was meeting in Washington, D.C. See *The American City* 32 (June, 1925): 634.

52. "Architectural Contracts," *Architectural Record* 74 (July, 1933): 57. U.S., Department of Commerce, Bureau of the Census, *Historical Statistics of the United States from Colonial Times to 1957*, pp. 379–80.

53. U.S., Resettlement Administration, *Greenbelt Towns*, p. 32.

54. Suburban Division Planning Staff, "Reasons for Excessive Costs in Developing the Program," October 20, 1936, Lansill Papers, personal files.

55. "Alphabet Soup in a Washington Mansion," *Literary Digest* 120 (August 31, 1935): 10–11. *Washington Star*, January 10, 1937. The Lansill Papers, official files, contain a series of striking photographs of the Suburban Division offices.

56. Charles S. Ascher, "Public Tools for Regional Planning," *The Survey* 68 (October 1, 1932): 472.

57. John Burchard and Albert Bush-Brown, *The Architecture of America: A Social and Cultural History* (Boston: Little, Brown and Co., 1961), pp. 310–11, 334.

58. Interview with Lansill.

59. Will W. Alexander, *Oral History Memoirs*, p. 396.

60. Marquis Childs, *I Write from Washington*, p. 11.

4

🍁 LAND ACQUISITION

In August, 1935, Warren Vinton wrote from the Blackstone Hotel in Chicago:

> Ted [Tilford] Dudley and I have been moving through the country preparing to buy land in the grand manner. In Cincinnati I laid out a tract of some 20,000 acres. . . . We will stop back on Wednesday and narrow down the area. I'm delighted with the good results we are getting, but I find a good deal of initial difficulty in getting cooperation. The country has been run to death with project planning followed by nothing thereafter, and the people are sick of it.[1]

The deadine stipulated by the president greatly increased the chance that the greenbelt town projects would become another New Deal plan that died aborning. While the Land Section had

begun operations at each of the five project sites, only at Beltsville, Maryland, had substantial progress been made.

The Land Section of the Suburban Division played only a
small role in the acquisition of land for Greenbelt, Maryland,
because most of it had been optioned by the Land Utilization
Division of the Federal Emergency Relief Administraton and
the Subsistence Homesteads Division of the Interior Department.[2] The Suburban Division of the Resettlement Administration inherited the previously optioned land and added to these
properties until a total of 12,189 acres had been purchased by
September, 1935.[3] Most of this land was ultimately transferred
to the Agricultural Research Center. The Resettlement Administration retained 3,371 acres which were purchased at a cost of
$556,632.15, or an average price of $165.00 per acre.[4] The R.A.
advertised a land cost figure of $91.00 per acre, and this has
been accepted by scholars,[5] who failed to note that the figure
was an average of the entire 12,189 acres rather than the portion
of this tract which the R.A. retained as the site for Greenbelt.[6]

The prospects of purchasing enough land for the other four
towns at a reasonable price appeared dim. The Land Section
staff was very small considering the fact that it was responsible
for the purchase of thousands of acres of land scattered across
a thousand miles of the nation. Only seven full-time negotiators
were available to cover the five sites. These men were aided by
a small staff of clerical workers and professional land appraisers.[7] Tilford Dudley attempted to build a larger staff of negotiators and appraisers by raiding the Farm Credit Administration; but the F.C.A. complained to Tugwell, and Dudley was
forced to use only the few he had.[8] This necessitated the use of
private real estate firms to negotiate the options. While this had
certain advantages, it placed a great responsibility on people
whose only interest in the greenbelt town program was a financial reward. The government negotiators were compelled to act
as a reserve force for these local firms. The Washington staff,
aided by the use of a TVA airplane, attempted to be everywhere at once. Dudley in particular spent most of his nights

sleeping on railroad trains or in the airplane as he shuttled back and forth between Washington and the five project sites.[9]

In St. Louis the reluctance of the local real estate agency to act promptly contributed to the failure of the entire project. Dudley believed that this firm—the largest in St. Louis at the time—was not in need of extra work and therefore gave honest but leisurely service. By November when the acquisition programs at the other sites were nearly completed, the St. Louis firm had hardly begun. Dudley decided to hire another firm and continued optioning through his own negotiators, but precious time was lost. A second agency was found late in November, but it was not until January that it completed the optioning program. By that time the R.A. officials decided that sufficient funds were not available for the St. Louis project anyway, and it was abandoned. The loss of this project was not a severe blow to the Suburban Program, for no work had been done on town planning and the $24,438.11 consumed in obtaining options and clearing the titles comprised only .08% of the Suburban Division's allotment.[10]

In Cincinnati the R.A. was extremely fortunate in securing the services of the Walter Schmidt Real Estate Company. It was the largest in Cincinnati, and Schmidt was a national figure in the real estate business as an officer and later president of the National Association of Real Estate Boards. Schmidt had publicly opposed the federal housing program but was tactfully approached by Dudley and several other R.A. officials, who explained the entire concept of the greenbelt town project to him emphasizing its experimental and limited nature. Schmidt accepted the commission, and a week after the funds came through from Hyde Park, twelve of his negotiators were in the field collecting options.[11]

Two smaller real estate firms were selected in Milwaukee; but what they lacked in size, they compensated for in diligence. The agents began work on August 29, but on September 18 Tugwell informed Dudley that the project was about to be canceled. The R.A. had decided that Milwaukee's needs for low-rent housing were not as severe as those in most other cities, especially since the P.W.A. had begun a housing project there.[12] Also, the R.A. did not wish to appear to be competing with Secretary Ickes's program. In the middle of October the decision was reversed, and there was very little time left to gather the options. The local agents, aided by as many negotiators as the Washington office could spare, "worked with a white heat of intensity."[13] The agents labored round the clock to take options, clear titles, and complete the many other steps in assembling land for the federal government. They worked from early morning until late evening in the field seven days a week, coming back to the office where another staff collated the material during the night.[14] The optioning was supposed to have been completed by November 20, but Dudley got a five-day extension. The last option was taken on the twenty-fifth, whereupon Dudley gathered up all the options along with the appraisals, title records, and other information, and rushed by train to Washington where they were presented to Tugwell and Lansill, who gave approval the following day.[15]

The land optioning, in all cases, had to be kept secret, for as Dudley and other federal land purchasers had found, "land owners take a special delight in holding their government up for high prices."[16] The Housing Division of the P.W.A. was forced to give up major projects in St. Louis and Chicago during 1935 because land prices skyrocketed when news of the plans reached the public.[17] Nor could the Land Section force the sale of land. Condemnation proceedings would take too long and had not been sustained by the federal courts.[18]

The real estate agents in Cincinnati were making rapid progress when the *Cincinnati Enquirer* came out on October 2 with a premature announcement of the Resettlement Administration project.[19] The leak had occurred in Washington, and the Land Section was naturally furious; but the negotiators were told to discount the story and tell everyone that "it was simply another rumor . . . and that they did not know anything except that they were working for the Schmidt Company and under orders from their superiors."[20] The newspaper was not able to follow up with further information, and options continued to flow into the Schmidt offices. At the same time, R.A. officials began to inform key figures in the Cincinnati area to line up their support when the project would be officially announced.

The site originally selected included land belonging to a number of stubborn German farmers and days went by before they were convinced to sell. The R.A. in Washington told the negotiators that if optioning could not be completed by October 15, the project might have to be given up. One individual named Muehlenhard proved unshaking in his desire to keep his land. When Harold Gelnaw, the Land Section's "high pressure ace," was flown in from Milwaukee to convince Muehlenhard, he was chased from the property with a three foot corn knife. Finally, Dudley was able to induce the man to visit the Schmidt Company offices where the full story of the project was presented to him. He was first exhorted to help the children of the slums through which the R.A. had driven him on the way to the office. Later he was threatened with condemnation proceedings.[21] After five hours the exhausted man signed an option and handed it to an equally exhausted staff which quickly gathered this and the other options and caught a train for Washington. They were due to report the next morning, October 17, on the completion of the optioning program.[22]

In Washington the entire plan was reviewed, and it was decided to shift the tract slightly to the south: this entailed further optioning. By the time the agents were back in the field, news of the project was well known in the area. An attorney for the Cincinnati Building and Loan League had even been meeting with land owners urging them not to sell out to the federal government. This action simply raised the price of the properties remaining to be optioned. Tugwell thought these prices were too high and ordered the negotiators to begin taking options to the north, thus playing one group of property owners off against the other. By the time this game was finished, the R.A. had options on 11,860 acres, which stretched for several miles along the edge of the Mill Creek Valley in Hamilton County.[23]

On December 3, 1935, Tugwell, Lansill, Dudley, Vinton, and the chief planners for Greenhills met to decide where to locate the town. Vinton said that the southern-most site was the best because it was closer to the factories in the valley where many of the residents would be employed and closer as well to Cincinnati. The further away the town was, the higher the transportation cost would be. Tugwell overruled him, however, saying that the land was too expensive. The northern location was chosen.[24] Premature publicity and lack of local cooperation, then, did not destroy the Cincinnati project, but did force the R.A. to build on a less advantageous site.

In Milwaukee the R.A. had taken the extra precaution of keeping its identity hidden from the real estate agents during the early weeks of land optioning. Information was, however, again inadvertently leaked by the federal government. In early December a group of R.A. officials checked into a leading hotel in Milwaukee and "stupidly . . . talked in the lobby and in the open rooms about the Milwaukee project."[25] Optioning was almost completed, but the first reaction of the press and public was one of skepticism and suspicion. This reaction could have had serious consequences had the R.A. not previously established a close relationship with the city and county officials. Immediately after the site had been selected, Vinton and Dudley explained the entire program to Milwaukee's popular Socialist Mayor Daniel W. Hoan and several other local officials. They were pleased with the willingness of the Resettlement Administrators to seek their support. More importantly, they were enthusiastic about the project itself.[26] Therefore, when the official announcement of the project was made on December 15, 1935, Mayor Hoan, U.S. Congressman Raymond J. Cannon, and a host of other Milwaukee area officials gave it their approval.[27] Harold Gelnaw, who headed the Milwuakee land acquisition program, told reporters that the R.A. received better cooperation in Milwaukee than in any other city.[28] He may still have been thinking of his encounter with the knife-wielding Mr. Muehlenhard.

Some apprehensions persisted, particularly among real estate groups and building and loan companies, but an attempt was made to win even their support. Lansill, Vinton, Jacob Crane (one of the chief architects), and several others went to Milwaukee and explained the project to these two groups.[29] Not everyone was convinced. There were continual reports that some of the building and loan groups and other individuals were about to seek court action to block the project, but no case was ever presented. The building and loan people may have been restrained from their action by the continued "solemn backing" of the local political leaders and the pressure that these leaders may have exerted on them.[30]

Rexford Tugwell was anxious to have the greenbelt towns demonstrate "the advantage of locating in suburban areas where land prices are lower."[31] He also hoped that the public would compare the slum clearance projects—built on higher priced land—with the spacious greenbelt towns.[32] He was, therefore, most anxious to buy land at the lowest possible price, and in this regard the land acquisition program was an unquestionable success.

Land prices at the three towns bore a direct relation to the distance of the tract from the central city. The land at Greenbelt, located approximately twelve miles from downtown Washington, was $165.00 per acre. The land for Greenhills, Ohio (5,930 acres), lay approximately four and one-half miles from Cincinnati and was purchased for an average price of $268.58 per acre.[33] The 3,410 acre tract[34] for Greendale, Wisconsin, was located only three miles southwest of Milwaukee and thus the most expensive—$372.50.[35] At Greenhills and Greendale the purchase price was below the value estimated by independent appraisers who set the Greenhills land at $268.58 per acre and the Greendale land at $412.52.[36] Most striking was the contrast between the land prices paid by the R.A. and the P.W.A. The P.W.A. at this time was paying an average of $.44 per square foot for their slum real estate which amounts to a cost of $19,166.40 per acre.[37]

In contrast to the land acquisition programs at Greenbelt, Greenhills, and Greendale, the attempt to purchase land for Greenbrook, to be located outside of New Brunswick, New Jersey, ended in failure after a long bitter fight which almost destroyed the entire greenbelt program. This was a tragic loss. The Greenbrook planning staff was the most distinguished team of architects assembled by the R.A., and the town most closely resembled the classic garden city. The story of Greenbrook reveals a small, but highly instructive, episode in the history of the New Deal and in the development of public attitudes towards a host of political, social, and economic questions connected with the government's housing program. Therefore, it will be discussed in some detail.

Little difficulty was experienced in initiating the program to purchase a site for the new town. On September 17, Dudley and Theodore Pellens, the project supervisor, arrived in Bound Brook, New Jersey, to select a real estate broker to collect land options for the R.A. The town was located about three miles from the proposed town site and was the home of several real estate brokers. The largest broker, a Mr. Fetterly, was currently the Republican candidate for mayor of Bound Brook. The second broker was a prominent Democrat. The third, a Republican, was Thomas D. Van Syckel, apparently the only broker giving his full attention to business. Van Syckel was checked for his honesty and general reputation in the community before being approached with the project plans.[38] Van Syckel liked the idea and, as time went on, developed an intense interest in the greenbelt town concept. He argued the R.A.'s case with as much sincerity and fervor as any of the project planners. Although he and the R.A. occasionally disagreed, there was no one so despondent over the failure of the project. Possibly, he regretted the loss of an opportunity not only to make money but to play a major role in a great enterprise—to make a lasting contribution to his community and the nation.[39]

The negotiators hired by Van Syckel did not all share his zeal, but the money earned was sufficient to keep most of them active in the field late into each evening. The R.A. concealed the true purpose of the optioning, as was the practice at the other sites. This was more difficult at Bound Brook since the township of Franklin, in which the project was to be built, had no property map and the R.A. was forced to construct an ownership map from the tax rolls. This raised the suspicion of the township tax assessor, C. I. Van Cleef, who began to inquire about the sharp increase of optioning. Van Cleef himself owned a large farm in the township and was approached in early October by Van Syckel and Pellens. It is not clear whether Van Cleef knew the reasons for the optioning, but he realized that whoever was buying land had a great deal of money. When approached again by Van Syckel and Dudley, he offered to sell for twice the value of his land saying that "his cooperation was worth much more than the difference in price and that he could give a great deal of valuable help to the buyer if won over to the proper side."[40] When the R.A. refused to buy at Van Cleef's price, he began persuading fellow landowners not to sign options.

A more serious problem was the purchase of five hundred acres on an estate belonging to John W. Mettler, president of the Interwoven Stocking Company. He was wealthy, politically powerful in the state of New Jersey, and a conservative Republican. Mettler was approached with caution by Dudley and Pellens, who interpreted their plans to him and solicited his land and his support. Dudley reported that Mettler "was coldly hostile, suspicious, and noncommittal."[41] He asked for time to have his land assessed and think over the proposal.

The negotiators left the Mettler tract alone for the time and concentrated on the rest of the project site. They found that many small tracts were owned by recent immigrants who had built up a modest truck farming industry but who were subsisting on low market prices. Many of them clung tenaciously to their little plots. The negotiators hired interpreters and spent long hours explaining the advantages of selling the land. Another group which balked at selling its land included local citizens whose families had owned the same land since colonial days and resented both the intrusion of the immigrants and the federal government.[42]

Near the end of October the R.A. realized that Mettler was stealthily moving against them. The local office began receiving calls from a real estate firm connected with Mettler. Next, one of the most prominent negotiators, Mr. Van Voorhees, said he would have to cease collecting options until after the November election in which he was running for reelection to the Somerset County Board of Freeholders.[43] On October 24, the Franklin Township Committee held an emergency meeting—its members having learned the whole story of the Resettlement Administration project. The New Brunswick *Daily Home News* broke the secret the following day, reporting also that the township committee planned a protest.[44] R.A. negotiators were caught unprepared and refused to make any statement. They deliberately brushed aside all the stories as mere rumors just as the Cincinnati group had done at the beginning of the month. This proved a poor policy as the rumors grew faster in the absence of specific information from the R.A.

On October 28, Franklin Township Attorney Clarkson Cramner telephoned the R.A. office in Bound Brook to notify them that in the evening a public meeting would be held at a local school to consider the project and that he, as chairman, wanted a government spokesman there to answer questions. The local R.A. people were taken unawares. They called Washington, and Lansill promised to send Isaac McBride, one of the R.A.'s most effective representatives. Emotions ran high at the meeting; the tone of the audience was described as "running a rout so stormy as to be only a step removed from open disorder."[45] Questions were asked about who was going to live in the new town, how it would pay taxes, and what the effect would be on local property values. One local resident, hearing that the project was for low-income families, shouted, "We don't want the scum of the earth brought in here."[46] State Representative Charles A. Eaton told the audience, "The Federal Government has no more right to come into this township and cram this proposition down its throat than has the government of Germany."[47] McBride answered questions as well as he could but was forced to hedge on the point of taxation. He tried to assure everyone that however the community was planned, the township and county would not be compelled to supply services without deriving an equal income. He summarized by saying,

> I simply am asking you as intelligent people to withhold your judgement and not proceed to condemn this project without knowing what you are condemning. Nobody is coercing you. This is a free country. Not one of you has to sell his property unless he wants to sell it. . . . The government is not going to resort to condemnation.[48]

The meeting voted to send a five man committee to talk with the R.A. in Washington. Later Cramner appointed five additional members—including Mettler—to what came to be called the Committee of Ten.[49]

The meeting was followed by a barrage of newspaper editorials on the project. The small *Somerset Messenger Gazette* asked its readers what the effect would be of erecting numerous "cheap houses" and filling them with "recent slum dwellers."[50] The New Brunswick *Daily Home News*, the largest local paper, criticized the secretiveness of the R.A. but reserved judgment on the project itself. The R.A. officials admitted that the *Daily Home News* presented the news "with complete fairness throughout the controversy."[51]

On November 1, the Somerset County Board of Freeholders voted to condemn the project because the federal property it would withdraw from the tax rolls would decrease local revenues and increase service costs sharply. In addition the board was "without definite information as to plans, purposes and scope of this project."[52] Two days later the R.A. officials announced that the tax problem would be solved by the transferal of the property to private hands as soon as the town was completed. This did not satisfy the *Daily Home News* or many of the local residents. The newspaper expressed the opinion of "many substantial Republicans" who believed the whole project was "the product of a deep laid plot to turn this staunchly Republican township and the equally staunchly Republican county of which it is a part, Democratic at the crucial 1936 election."[53] Bishop Alma White of the Somerset Pillar of Fire Church reported that "divine inspiration" had called her back from London, England, in time to fight the Resettlement Administration's attempt to buy land which her church held on the proposed project site.[54] Dudley and the R.A. concluded that it was not God who was directing the attack on the project, but John W. Mettler.

Mettler's position was published in a long interview for the November 17 issue of the New Brunswick *Sunday Times* (the Sunday edition of the *Daily Home News*). He said that the town would require more services than collectable taxes could support, that it was located too far from surrounding factories, and that it covered 6,000 to 8,000 acres while the entire city of New Brunswick covered only 2,500. His "greatest objection," however, was allegedly to the architectural style which he said "will undoubtedly be used—the pre-fabricated cement-type box-shaped house or the multiple-family packing-box type house without cellars and with flat roofs." He thought it "hopeless" to expect the "Colonial style house to be built in the project which, of course, would make it a very different proposition. No person would object to the right kind of houses which would bring a more desirable class of people than can be expected to occupy the pre-fabricated, flat roof, slab-type house."[55] There was no suggestion that his opposition stemmed from his political views, but Mrs. Mettler remembers that the fundamental objection of her husband was that the project was sponsored by the New Deal. She also recalled that he was afraid the proposed project would be similar to the one already under construction in Hightstown, New Jersey.[56]

For whatever reasons, Mettler remained an implacable foe

of the Suburban Division, and his position on the Committee of Ten was preeminent. The committee spent November 6 in Washington where they talked with Lansill, Vinton, and Bigger, who described the project and promised that future tax problems would be solved in a manner satisfactory to all. The R.A.'s efforts were in vain, for at a second meeting of 1,000 residents on November 13, 1935, the committee reported 8–2 against the project.[57] The R.A. campaigned to win local support while pressing the optioning. Albert Mayer, one of the Greenbrook architects wrote an article for the *New York Times Magazine* describing the greenbelt town program with special emphasis on Greenbrook.[58] Further contact with Mettler showed him willing to end his opposition if the town could be moved farther from his property—even offering the assistance of a real estate agent to secure the new options![59] Dudley conferred with Albert Mayer and Henry Wright, who agreed it could be shifted somewhat, but not as far as Mettler suggested. The next week was spent hounding the owners of the few remaining tracts needed and continuing the campaign for support.[60] On November 21 the R.A. held a meeting of nearly one hundred "interested Franklin Township residents" who voted 85–16 to support the R.A. after hearing a talk by Fred W. Ehrich, chairman of the New Jersey State Housing Authority. He affirmed that the new town would pay local taxes, be constructed in a "conventional style of architecture," and pay union wages to all those employed to build it.[61]

By November 27 the Land Section had optioned enough land to begin construction. On December 5, the *Daily Home News* was finally able to publish sketches of Greenbrook along with a detailed description of the development of the garden cities and the precise type of housing, streets, and other facilities to be built.[62] This was followed by an announcement that construction would soon begin. The *Daily Home News* now urged that Somerset County unemployed be given priority for the new jobs.[63] Local businessmen approved as over one hundred employees moved into the area to begin construction.[64]

Two days later the opposition asked the Federal District Court in Newark to issue an injunction restraining the R.A. from continuing their project. The action was undertaken on behalf of the Franklin Township Committee, the School Board, and four property owners, one of whom was C. I. Van Cleef. They were represented by Merritt Lane of Newark, who was a prominent Republican and one of the organizers of the Liberty League.[65] The Bill of Complaints charged that the Emergency Relief Appropriation Act of 1935 was unconstitutional, that the Executive Order creating the R.A. was also unconstitutional, and the entire action was an unlawful invasion of state's rights.[66]

This added a new and dangerous dimension to the struggle. The R.A. might win overwhelming local support only to be defeated in the courts. The fact that the project had just been endorsed by the Building Trades Councils of Somerset, Middlesex, and Union Counties was overshadowed by the news from Newark. On December 12, the Franklin Township Committee was petitioned to withdraw from the case.[67] On December 17, the Bound Brook Town Council endorsed the project after learning that the R.A. intended to build a new grade school and possibly a high school.[68] Other local residents applied for homes in Greenbrook.[69]

Dudley took over as director of the Bound Brook project in order to exert more pressure on Mettler, the local Republican machine, and opponents of the project. Mass meetings were held. A former option collector, Van Voorhees, became a leading heckler at these meetings. Dudley accused Freeholder Voorhees of being "evasive, weaseling and squirming" and of making "statements which reveal a gross ignorance of the facts."[70]

On December 22 Attorney Merritt Lane presented the case of the Franklin Township Committee before District Judge Clark in Newark. He noted that an R.A. pamphlet, printed upside down, was proof of an error "typical of the government," which caused Judge Clark to remark that Lane showed "a certain lack of patriotism." Lane heartily agreed. Judge Clark decided that the plaintiffs were in the wrong court and should take the case to the Supreme Court of the District of Columbia where the injunction would be filed against the officers of the R.A. instead of the local officials in Bound Brook.[71] This was done, and the case was taken over from Lane by none other than Dean Acheson, who sought to enjoin Lansill, Tugwell, Secretary of the Treasury Henry Morgenthau, Jr., and Comptroller General J. R. McCarl.[72] The struggle was now not only a local political fight but also a national legal contest with strong political undertones. The District of Columbia Supreme Court dismissed the injunction on January 3. Acheson appealed and was granted a temporary injunction, which was not even modified to allow the R.A. to accept land options which were expiring.[73] The case was argued on February 12 and the decision rendered on May 18. Lansill recalls the "superb" case presented by Acheson and the poor case presented by Lee Pressman's lawyers, Ralph S. Boyd and Allan Jones (Pressman did not even attend the trial). Lansill surmised that the government would be permanently enjoined.[74]

Meanwhile the local conflict moved into high gear with the R.A. launching "an intensified program of education" in the county with speeches, posters, articles, and pictures describing the project and its benefits to the local communities.[75] The R.A. stressed the many additions to the facilities of Franklin Township: the schools, roads, parks, and, of course, the houses—"A Garden Home You Can Call Your Own," as the title of an R.A. pamphlet announced. To the surrounding residents, the R.A. held out the promise of immediate "rush business" for the local construction firms and thousands of jobs for the unemployed. The town itself would bring a long-term increase in trade with the future residents of Greenbrook.[76]

The Somerset County Board of Freeholders remained opposed to the project with two Republicans consistently outvoting Frank J. Schubert, the lone Democrat.[77] A poll of Franklin Township tax payers was suggested, and Mettler at first agreed. The questionnaires were printed. Then, at the last moment, he backed down saying the poll would have no "legal standing."[78] The R.A. took its own poll which showed seventy-five percent favoring the project, fifteen percent opposed, and ten percent having no opinion.[79] Slowly, local support emerged. On January 20, the mayor and Town Council of Plainfield endorsed the project.[80] On February 17, the Franklin Township School Board withdrew as a plaintiff from the court case.[81] On the 25th a petition with 700 signatures was presented to the Franklin Township Committee asking that it withdraw from the suit and endorse the project.[82]

The day after the petition was presented to them, the three members of the committee were scheduled to meet with R.A. officials in Washington. Frederick Bascom, the chairman, refused to go, but the other two, Conrad Icke and John Amsler, went, accompanied by Clarkson Cramner, the township's attorney. They spent the afternoon with Lansill, Clarence I. Blau, the acting general counsel for the R.A., and Major John O. Walker, chief of the Management Section. Lansill reassured them that the R.A. was currently drawing up papers to divest itself of ownership as soon as the town was completed. Blau added that this had already been done for Greenbelt. When questioned about the bill introduced by Senator Bankhead providing the payment-in-lieu-of-taxes by the R.A. projects, Blau replied that this would only apply to the R.A. projects in Atlanta. Apparently, the committee members feared the Bound Brook project would become tied up and lay uncompleted as seemed to be the case in Hightstown. They wanted a written statement that Greenbrook would be completed by the R.A. Lansill replied that they would gladly sign such a statement, saying, "I'll give almost anything to get this through."[83] Tugwell also wrote a letter to the committee assuring them that the project would not only be completed, but that upon completion, "the Federal Government will divest itself of ownership so that the property embraced within the project will be subject to the same burden of taxation as all the other property within the state of New Jersey."[84]

The R.A. convinced the committee members that the tax

question was settled, but this failed to end the suit. The five property owners who were also plaintiffs announced they would continue the suit. The Franklin Township Committee withdrew from the case as a result of the conversations in Washington but was enjoined from doing so by a New Jersey Supreme Court judge. The injunction came after Merritt Lane presented an affidavit by C. I. Van Cleef stating that Mr. Amsler, one of the committeemen, had voted in favor of the project because he had been offered a seventy-five-dollar-a-week job on it.[85]

While bribery charges were being debated in Trenton, New Jersey, Senator W. Warren Barbour introduced in the Senate a resolution to investigate the entire program of the Resettlement Administration. It would authorize the establishment of a special committee, financed with a $25,000 budget and empowered to subpoena witnesses. A resulting report would indicate

> 1) the nature and extent of all expenditures made or proposed to be made by such Administration, 2) the nature and extent of projects undertaken by it, and the advisability of undertaking future projects, 3) the effect of each such project in State and local taxation and on local real estate values, 4) the extent to which such projects have benefited and will benefit labor, and 5) the circumstances relating to the securing of persons as tenants or purchasers in connection with such projects, and the effect on such persons of becoming such tenants or purchasers.[86]

In a statement to the press Barbour said the general purpose of the investigation would be to determine if the R.A. was doing a good job and should be supported, or if it was "heading for a dead-end smash-up and should be stopped before the wreck occurs." He also urged immediate investigation of the bribery charge leveled against the R.A.[87] The resolution failed but was reintroduced without the investigative machinery, making it merely a Senate request for information. While discussing his second resolution, Barbour specifically attacked the two R.A.

projects in New Jersey. He characterized the Hightstown project as "a chaotic mudhole with a few tin houses to glorify the money that has been spent." Concerning Greenbrook he conceded that the R.A. "paints a fine picture of the future development," but considering "the failure of the other project at Hightstown," he had little confidence in the success of Greenbrook.[88] He also quoted from the series of articles in the *Washington Post* by Felix Bruner which were highly critical of the Resettlement Administration and the community projects.[89]

Comparison of Greenbrook to the Hightstown project was damaging not only because of the real errors made at Hightstown, but because its particular character subjected it to vicious attacks in the press. The *Philadelphia Inquirer*, for example, published an article on the project entitled, "Tugwell Hands Out $1,800,000 for N.J. Commune." The community was described as a "model of a Russian Soviet Commune . . . for the immigration of two hundred Jewish needleworkers . . . headed by a Russian-born little Stalin who will be running their 'co-operative' full blast not fifty miles from the birthplace of American Democracy."[90] On May 8, the day after this article appeared, the Senate approved Barbour's resolution by a voice vote.[91]

Ten days later, on May 18, the United States Court of Appeals for the District of Columbia handed down a sweeping decision which not only forbade the Bound Brook project, but assailed the very foundation of the New Deal. Acheson's bill of complaint accused the project on two major counts: first, that it was unnecessary as opportunities for employment in the township were sufficient, and second, that it was detrimental to the local community by introducing "industrial workers of low income from the congested areas" into an area where "the bulk of the population is . . . rural in character." Further, the township would lose one-fourth of its taxable land while the new town would increase public service costs but not contribute sufficiently to defray them. Local autonomy would be affected, and "since 1735 the Township has protected and fostered the

interests of its inhabitants in the security of its lands, property
and persons and in the development and character of the community." The R.A.'s town would cause this protection and control to be "virtually destroyed," and "the whole character of the
community may and will be changed contrary to the wishes of
the inhabitants and solely in accordance with the wishes of the
officers of the United States." The complaint stated that one of
the five property owners who rented a house on her land would
suffer a depression of rental value. Finally, the complaint said
the project was illegal because it was financed with funds from
the Emergency Relief Appropriation Act of 1935 and administered by an agency financed with funds from this act. The act,
it continues, "is an effort to delegate to the President legislative
power in contravention of Article I, Sec. 9, Clause 7; and Article
II, Sec. 1 of the Constitution of the United States." These articles outline the powers granted to the Congress and to the president. The contention of the five Franklin Township Appellants
was that the E.R.A.A. of 1935 granted legislative powers to the
President which he in turn granted, through a series of executive orders, to the Resettlement Administration and other agencies receiving funds from it.[92]

The three-to-two decision of the court was delivered by Associate Justice Van Orsdel. First, the court made it clear that if
the state of New Jersey undertook the Bound Brook project,
the township government could not maintain its suit in the
courts, but that the five property owners could do so even if the
state government were financing and administrating the project. Since the U.S. government was the agent, however, both
the property owners and the township government had a right
to bring suit. Second, turning to the Emergency Relief Appropriation Act of 1935, the court declared that in this case it was
"a clearly unconstitutional delegation of legislative power" to
the president and the R.A. The court found nothing in the
terms of the act which would give the president guidelines for
legal uses of the funds. It left him, in fact, "virtually unfettered"
as to how the money should be spent and was an example of

what Supreme Court Justice Cardozo had recently called "delegation running riot."[93] The court was fearful of such powers in the hands of the president and his agents as were granted by the E.R.A.A. "without path or program" to circumscribe his actions.

> Obviously, if the President were so disposed, he could use the entire sum appropriated in building houses exclusively for our colored population, or on the other hand, he could just as well exclude that portion of the population from any benefits whatever. . . . The houses for which this vast sum of money is to be spent may be rented or sold, at a profit or at a loss. They may be constructed in cities where there is no demand, or in the country to create and build a new city in its entirety. Indeed, they may be built and left unoccupied; and while, as a practical matter, this may be said to be a mere fancy, the principle is none the less involved, for that principle demands that in the appropriation of the public moneys the congressional mandate shall include a reasonable limitation on the discretion of the executive in their use. . . . The fundamental question involved is the total lack of constitutional power on the part of Congress to put into operation through legislation a project such as is here contemplated; and this can be ascertained, not from any possible determination of fact, but from the very terms of the statute itself.[94]

The two dissenting justices, Groner and Stephens, agreed that a permanent injunction should be granted to halt the Bound Brook project but thought that the decision concerning the unconstitutionality of the entire Emergency Relief Appropriation Act of 1935 was unnecessary and should not have been attempted until the facts of the case were more fully presented. Thus the entire court shared the opinion that a permanent injunction should be issued and the dissenters were not flatly ruling out future concurrence with the majority concerning the E.R.A.A.[95]

Reaction from federal officials was confused. Tilford Dudley in Bound Brook confidently predicted that the government would appeal to the Supreme Court "right away," while in Washington Attorney General Homer S. Cummings issued a statement that in his opinion the decision affected only the single project in New Jersey. He did not mention an appeal to the Supreme Court.[96] President Roosevelt told his press conference that same day that, while he had not read the decision, he agreed that it applied to Bound Brook only. He too remained silent on the question of an appeal.[97] The next day both Tugwell and Solicitor General Stanley Reed issued statements saying they agreed with Cummings and that, while there were no immediate plans to appeal, no final decision had been made.[98]

Resettlement officials, on the advice of Cummings, decided not to appeal the case fearing that further litigation might halt all the projects, which, they believed, could be completed without going to court.[99] Since the object of the Relief Appropriation was to employ workers as quickly as possible, the Resettlement officials were forced to announce "the suspension, if not the abandonment of further efforts" at Bound Brook.[100] The offices were closed, the employees dismissed, and the options allowed to lapse. "The project was dead," commented Tilford Dudley in June.[101] Tragedy was added to the heartbreak of the project planners when Henry Wright, chief architect and planner of Greenbrook, died suddenly on July 9, knowing that his most ambitious attempt to house the underpriviledged in a beautiful community had been destroyed.

Opponents of the Bound Brook project and the New Deal were naturally pleased with the court decision and the abandonment of Greenbrook. Frederick Bascom, one of the five plaintiffs, commented on how fortunate those residents were who gave options to the government because "the next few years will certainly bring increased values for land in Franklin Township," and added that "this is the logical way for the township to develop."[102]

The *Milwaukee Journal* believed the decision was a blow to

the constitutionality of any federal housing program and asked its readers if they really wanted a "sweeping and largely arbitrary authority over the housing of people."[103] The *Washington Post* believed the decision "a powerful indictment of the sloppy legislative habits into which Congress has fallen" which allows the executive branch to engage in such "vast experimental projects."[104] Similar views were expressed by the *St. Louis Star-Times* and the *Baltimore Sun*.[105] The *St. Louis Globe-Democrat* and the *New York Times* thought the entire question should be taken to the Supreme Court.[106] The *Albany Evening Press* questioned the narrow application of the decision which canceled only one R.A. project and left the agency and its appropriation untouched. "If the government does not respect the spirit of the law, how can it expect its citizens to do so?"[107] The National Association of Real Estate Boards was pleased with the court action because "it sets a precedent which will bring a flock of similar suits" on all public housing projects, including those of the P.W.A. It was concerned, however, that such decisions might lead to passage of a broad housing bill which would not be to the advantage of real estate agencies.[108] The *Harvard Law Review* disagreed with the decision. Not only would the project be a legal delegation of congressional power, but the greenbelt towns would be an enormous aid to the well-being of the nation and could only be financed by the federal government.[109]

In Milwaukee a group of building and loan firms announced plans to file suit in the Federal District Court to halt both the P.W.A. and the R.A. housing projects in Milwaukee County. Fortunately for the R.A., the land was already in its possession and therefore, by the terms of the Bound Brook decision, was immune to injunctions on any count save the constitutional one.[110] The Milwaukee group actually filed a suit in late August, 1936, but the case was never argued.[111]

During the summer and fall of that election year, anti–New Deal papers pointed to the Bound Brook episode as an example of the sinister, bungling New Deal housing efforts. The New

York *Sun* believed the project had been impractical and (failing to note the court decision) declared that Greenbrook had "collapsed of its own weight." Again, on October 2, *The Sun* decried the secret efforts of the federal government to ruin "a high class productive farming area" with a "low cost housing slum clearance project," and championed local residents who formed a "militant opposition" which ultimately destroyed the plan.[112]

The real story shows how a small group of local political officeholders, real estate dealers, and residents in combination with a wealthy and politically powerful landowner were able to prevent a project, which by the spring of 1936 was favored by a majority of the local citizens. On May 18, the day of the court decision, Tilford Dudley published the results of a survey conducted by the R.A. which showed 75 percent of the 2,390 people polled approved of the project.[113] This poll is corroborated by the 200 vote majority President Roosevelt received in Franklin Township in November, 1936.[114]

The judicial attack on the R.A.'s suburban town program had far-reaching ramifications for the future federal housing program. The P.W.A. housing projects were experiencing similar troubles with local residents and hostile courts. Two months before the Greenbrook decision, the federal government acquiesced to a lower court decision which prohibited a P.W.A. housing project in Louisville, Kentucky. In addition, the attorney general refused to take it to the Supreme Court for fear of losing all authority to spend money for housing projects.[115] At this same time the New York State Supreme Court upheld the right of the New York City Housing Authority, a local rather than a federal agency, to obtain land through condemnation and build a public housing project.[116] This impelled the federal government to seek a program which would be locally controlled and federally financed. This was enthusiastically endorsed by many housing reformers and written into the Wagner Housing Act of 1937 and repeated in the Housing Act of 1949. Even though the courts later upheld direct federal construction of housing projects, local housing authorities have remained rather naturally reluctant to give control back to the federal government. The result has been that suburban areas have effectively blocked low-income housing projects by refusing to establish housing authorities or constituting them with directors opposed to low-income housing.[117]

1. Vinton to Lansill, August 5, 1935, Lansill Papers, personal files.
2. Dudley, "Report of Land Section"; and U.S., Resettlement Administration, *Interim Report*, p. 19.
3. There are conflicting reports on this figure. The figure of 12,345 acres is given in the U.S., Resettlement Administration, "Weekly Progress Report No. 80," May 20, 1937. R. J. Wadsworth, one of the architects of Greenbelt, gives a figure of 13,044 acres in his "Summary Description of the Greenbelt Project," February, 1938, Lansill Papers, official files. The figure accepted by this author is 12,189 cited by John S. Lansill in his "Final Report on the Greenbelt Town Program," June, 1938, Lansill Papers, official files. The introduction to this report was reprinted as an introduction to George A. Warner's *Greenbelt: The Cooperative Community*, pp. 13–21.
4. A small portion of this money ($22,625.68) came from funds allocated under the Subsistence Homesteads Program of the Interior Department under Title II of the National Industrial Recovery Act of 1933. See U.S., Congress, House Subcommittee of the Committee on Appropriations, *Hearings on the Agriculture Department Appropriations Bill for 1942*, 77th Cong., 1st sess., 1941, pt. 2:118–19. The $556,632.15 cost of the 3,371 acres at Greenbelt cited by the House subcommittee is in substantial agreement with the figure of $556,464.12 published by the Farm Security Administration in its "Final Report of Project Costs" (Greenbelt, Maryland, National Archives, Record Group 96, p. 10).
5. See Clarence S. Stein, *Toward New Towns for America*, p. 127; and Albert Mayer, "Greenbelt Towns Revisited," *Journal of Housing* 24, no. 3 (April, 1967): 151.
6. U.S., Farm Security Administration, "Progress Report No. 103." April, 1938, National Archives, Record Group 96, p. 27.
7. Dudley, "Report of Land Section."
8. Unsigned memo to Dudley, October 5, 1935, National Archives, Record Group 96 (general correspondence).
9. Interview with Tilford E. Dudley.

10. Dudley, "Report of Land Section."

11. Brice Martin, "Analysis of Cincinnati Land Acquisition," February 8, 1937, Lansill Papers, personal files.

12. Parklawn, the P.W.A. project in Milwaukee, is described in Michael W. Straus and Talbot Wegg's *Housing Comes of Age*, p. 212.

13. W. L. Mellette, "Analysis of Milwaukee Land Acquisition," November 1, 1937, Lansill Papers, personal files.

14. Interview with Dudley.

15. Mellette, "Analysis of Milwaukee Land Acquisition."

16. Dudley, "Report of Land Section."

17. Irving R. Brant, "Policies of Local Housing Authorities," for the Third Conference on Slum Clearance and Low Rent Housing (Washington, D.C., 1936), mimeographed copy in Library of Congress.

18. The attempt of the P.W.A. to condemn land in Louisville, Kentucky, for one of its housing projects was declared illegal by the Supreme Court in *U.S.* v. *Certain Lands in City of Louisville*, 78 F (U.S.) 684 (1936). For background of this case, see *New York Times*, March 6, 1936.

19. *Cincinnati Enquirer*, October 2, 1935.

20. Martin, "Analysis of Cincinnati Land Acquisition," February 8, 1937, Lansill Papers, personal files.

21. John S. Lansill, "Notes on Greenbelt Town Project," Lansill Papers, personal files.

22. Dudley, "Report of Land Section."

23. Martin, "Analysis of Cincinnati Land Acquisition."

24. Ibid. Alas, this northern tract did not include the Meuhlenhard property.

25. Frank H. Osterlind to R. G. Tugwell, n.d. (received by Tugwell, December 12, 1935), Records of the Office of the Administrator, Housing and Home Finance Administration, Washington, D.C., Drawer 536. These records contain some of the working papers of members of the Suburban Resettlement Division, the Legal Division of the R.A., and the Management Division of the Public Housing Administration, the agency to which the greenbelt towns were transferred in 1942. These records were located in a government warehouse in Washington, but have been removed to the National Archives where they are awaiting cataloging. They will be cited hereafter as R.O.A., H.H.F.A.

26. "Public Relations," Greendale Project Book, Lansill Papers, official files.

27. *Milwaukee Sentinel*, December 16, 1935.

28. *Milwaukee Journal,* December 16, 1935.

29. *Milwaukee Journal,* January 3, 1936.

30. The R.A. was informed who the opposition leaders were and how pressure might be brought against them through city, county, state, and federal agencies. It was even suggested that the Internal Revenue Service might check their past income tax forms. See Frank H. Osterlind to Victor Rotnem, General Counsel's Office, Resettlement Administration (received by V. R. on January 16, 1936), R.O.A., H.H.F.A., Drawer 535.

31. Tugwell, N.B.C. Radio Address, December 2, 1935, Roosevelt Papers, O.F. 1568.

32. Tugwell, "The Meaning of the Greenbelt Towns," *The New Republic* 90 (February 17, 1937): 43.

33. The figure given by Dudley, "Report of Land Section," conflicts slightly with that given in Lansill, "Final Report on the Greenbelt Town Program," June, 1938, that 5,931 acres were purchased. The appropriations bill for 1942 states that 5,944 acres were purchased for a total price of $1,619,528.00, which is $272.48 per acre; see U.S., Congress, House, Subcommittee of the Committee on Appropriations, *Hearings on the Agriculture Department Appropriations Bill for 1942,* 77th Cong., 1st sess., 1941, pt. 2: 118–19.

34. The figure of 3,410 acres is taken from Lansill, "Final Report . . . ." Lansill Papers, official files. A figure of 3,491 acres is cited in Dudley, "Report of Land Section." A figure of 3,403 acres is cited in U.S., Congress, House, Subcommittee of the Committee on Appropriations, *Hearings . . .* , 77th Cong., 1st sess., 1941, pt. 2: 118–19. The community manager of Greendale stated that the tract was 3,400 acres; see Walter E. Kroening, "The Story of Greendale," April, 1944 (mimeographed copy in possession of the author).

35. The price is taken from Dudley, "Report of Land Section." An average price of $361.25 per acre is cited in U.S. Congress, House, Subcommittee of the Committee on Appropriations, *Hearings . . .* , 77th Cong., 1st sess., 1941, pt. 2: 118–19.

36. Dudley, "Report of Land Section."

37. Strauss and Wegg, *Housing Comes of Age,* p. 96.

38. Dudley, "Report of Land Section."

39. Interview with Dudley.

40. Dudley, "Report of Land Section."

41. Ibid.

42. Interview with Dudley.

43. Dudley, "Report of Land Section."

44. *The Daily Home News* (New Brunswick, New Jersey), October 25, 1935.

45. *Somerset Messenger Gazette*, October 29, 1935.

46. Ibid.

47. *Trenton Times*, October 29, 1935.

48. *Somerset Messenger Gazette*, October 29, 1935.

49. *Trenton Evening Times*, November 14, 1935.

50. Editorial in *Somerset Messenger Gazette*, October 29, 1935.

51. "Summary History of Greenbrook Project," Lansill papers, official files.

52. *Daily Home News*, November 3, 1935.

53. Ibid., November 2, 1935.

54. Ibid., November 6, 1936; letter to author from Arthur K. White, bishop and president of the Pillar of Fire, October 26, 1964.

55. *The Sunday Times*, November 17, 1935.

56. Interview with Mrs. John W. Mettler, Bound Brook, New Jersey, October 9, 1964.

57. *Trenton Times*, November 14, 1935.

58. Albert Mayer, "Greenbelt Towns for the Machine Age," *New York Times Magazine*, February 2, 1936.

59. Dudley, "Report of Land Section"; *Daily Home News*, November 19, 1935.

60. Dudley, "Report of Land Section."

61. *The Record* (Kingston, New Jersey), November 22, 1935; *Daily Home News*, November 22, 1935.

62. *Daily Home News*, December 5, 1936.

63. Ibid., December 6, 1935.

64. *The Sunday Times*, December 8, 1935.

65. *New York Herald Tribune*, December 11, 1935; Dudley, "Report of Land Section."

66. *Daily Homes News*, December 11, 1935.

67. Ibid., December 12, 1935.

68. Ibid., December 18, 1935.

69. *Somerset Messenger Gazette*, December 20, 1935.

70. *Daily Home News*, December 19, 1935; *Plainfield Courier News*, December 20, 1935.

71. *New York Times*, December 22, 1935.

72. Transcript of Record, United States Court of Appeals for the District of Columbia, October Term, 1935, No. 6619, *Township of Franklin et al.* v. *Rexford G. Tugwell et al.*

73. "Summarized History of the Bound Brook Project," Lansill Papers, official files.

74. Interview with John S. Lansill.

75. Dudley, "Report of Land Section."

76. "A Suburban Housing Project in Franklin Township: A Garden Home You Can Call Your Own," U.S. Resettlement Administration handbill, n.d. (copy in possession of author).

77. *Daily Home News*, December 28, 1935.

78. Ibid., January 3, 1936.

79. Dudley, "Report of Land Section."

80. *Piscataway Chronicle*, January 23, 1936.

81. *Daily Home News*, February 19, 1936.

82. Ibid., February 25, 1936.

83. Transcript of conference in Lansill's office, February 26, 1936, Lansill Papers, official files.

84. U.S., Resettlement Administration, Press release for publication, March 3, 1936, Yale University Library.

85. *Daily Home News*, March 4, 7, 9, 12, 15, 23, 1936.

86. U.S., *Congressional Record*, 74th Cong., 2d sess., 1936, 80, pt. 6: 6194.

87. *New York Times*, March 12, 1936.

88. *Congressional Record*, 74th Cong., 2d sess., 1936, 80, pt. 6: 6266–67.

89. The articles were written for the *Washington Post* by Felix Bruner under the general title "Castles in the Air" and appeared in the *Post* beginning on February 24, 1936. They were widely reprinted as, for example, in the *Daily Home News* beginning March 13, 1936. They will be discussed in chapter 8.

90. *Philadelphia Inquirer*, May 7, 1936.

91. *Congressional Record*, 74th Cong., 2d sess., 1936, 80, pt. 6: 6894.

92. Transcript of Record, United States Court of Appeals for the District of Columbia, October Term, 1935, No. 6619, *The Township of Franklin, et al.* v. *Rexford G. Tugwell, Administrator of Resettlement Administration et al.*, Appeal from the Supreme Court of the District of Columbia.

93. *Schecter* v. *United States*, 295 U.S. 495 (1935).

94. *Franklin Township* v. *Tugwell*, 85 F (App., D.C.) 208 (1936).

95. Ibid.

96. *Daily Home News,* May 19, 1936.

97. "Press Conferences," 7: 261, Roosevelt Papers, O.F.

98. *New York Times,* May 20, 1936.

99. Will W. Alexander, *Oral History Memoir,* p. 408; interview with Eugene Agger, New Brunswick, New Jersey, October 9, 1964, and C. B. Baldwin, August 17, 1967.

100. Eugene Agger (special assistant to Tugwell) to Elmer B. Boyed, publisher of the *Daily Home News,* in *Daily Home News,* May 22, 1936; and interview with Eugene Agger.

101. Dudley, "Report of Land Section."

102. *Daily Home News,* May 19, 1936.

103. *Milwaukee Journal,* May 19, 1936.

104. *Washington Post,* May 19, 1936.

105. *St. Louis Star-Times,* May 20, 1936; *Baltimore Sun,* May 21, 1936.

106. *St. Louis Globe-Democrat,* May 20, 1936; *New York Times,* May 20, 1936.

107. Albany *Evening Press,* May 28, 1936.

108. National Association of Real Estate Boards, "Weekly Confidential Letter," May 25, 1936.

109. "The Constitutionality of Federal Relief Measures," *Harvard Law Review* 50 (March, 1937): 803, 812–13.

110. This was the opinion of the Department of Agriculture's legal staff as stated in a memo from Irving J. Levy (assistant general counsel) to Monroe Oppenheimer (acting general counsel of the Resettlement Administration) May 21, 1936, R.O.A., H.H.F.A., Drawer 528.

111. *New York Times,* September 1, 1936.

112. *The Sun* (New York), July 11, 1936, and October 2, 1936.

113. *Daily Home News,* May 18, 1936.

114. Ibid., July 4, 1937.

115. *U.S.* v. *Certain Lands in Louisville, Kentucky,* 78 Fed. 2d 648 (July 15, 1935); appeal dismissed 297 U.S. 726 (March 30, 1936).

116. *New York City Housing Authority* v. *Muller,* 270 New York 333 (March, 1936).

117. Charles Abrams, *The City Is the Frontier* (New York: Harper & Row, Publishers, 1965), pp. 242–48.

5

 PLANNING OF THE GREENBELT TOWNS

The decision of the Resettlement Administration to build complete garden suburbs rather than housing projects greatly complicated the task of the Suburban Division. In the face of many limitations—early deadlines, reduced funds, relief labor, and federal red tape—the division could have met its primary responsibility by merely constructing a large number of simple dwellings. However, the enthusiasm of the staff centered around the challenge of planning complete suburban communities containing a full range of the same physical facilities found in the typical American town. Since the R.A. had obtained land at a very low price, the planners hoped the savings gained thereby could be matched by those accruing from the planning techniques and together fulfill their own prophesies about superior communities created at a lower cost through large scale preplanning.[1]

Under the direction of Thomas Hibben, a report was drawn up on August 1, 1935, cataloging a long list of facilities which were to be constructed and administered as "public utilities." All streets, sidewalks, bridges, and underpasses were to be planned with the aim of segregating pedestrian and vehicular traffic. Comprehensive water, gas, and electrical systems were suggested including water reservoirs, gas storage tanks, and electrical power plants. Housing units were to vary in size and design. A wide variety of nonresidential buildings was suggested, including schools, administration buildings, offices, warehouses, markets, hospitals, fire and police stations, auditoriums, fairgrounds, stores, and "industrial buildings" for "production" and for "processing and handling of agricultural and other commodities."[2] Other facilities could be parks, playgrounds, swimming pools, fish ponds, game conservation areas, airports, gardens, forest preserves, and farms. While not stated in the policy paper, it seems clear that these lists were only to serve as indicators of the possibilities open to the planning staff rather than actual specifications. The chief contributions of Frederick Bigger and his new staff of architects were to establish more clearly the objectives of the towns and to improve the quality of site planning. Shortly after he became planning head, Frederick Bigger described the purposes of the greenbelt town program.

The principal objective of this Division of Suburban Resettlement, so far it concerns the four major projects now being planned, is as follows:

(a) To secure a large tract of land, and thus avoid the complications ordinarily due to diverse ownerships; in this tract to create a community, protected by an encircling green belt; the community to be designed for families of predominantly modest income, and arranged and administered (managed) so as to encourage that kind of family and community life which will be better than they now enjoy, but which will not involve subjecting them to coercion or theoretical and untested discipline; the dwellings and the land upon which they are located to be held in one ownership, preferably a corporate entity to which the Federal Government will transfer title, and which entity or corporation will rent or lease the dwellings but will not sell them; a municipal government to be set up in character with such governments now existing or possible in that region; coordination to be established, in relation to the local and state governments, so that there may be provided those public services of educational and other character which the community will require; and, finally, to accomplish these purposes in such a way that the community may be a tax paying participant in the region, that extravagant outlays from the individual family income will not be a necessity, and that the rents will be suitable to families of modest income.

(b) To develop a land use plan for the entire tract; to devise, under the direction of the Administrator, a system of rural economy coordinated with the land use plan for the rural portions of the tract surrounding the Suburban community; and to integrate both the physical plans and the economies of the rural area and the Suburban community.[3]

The freedom given the greenbelt town planners is almost unique in the history of public housing in America. In the 1950s Clarence S. Stein contrasted this freedom with the restrictions placed on subsequent public housing architects. He concluded that drab plans are bound to result when "the essential abilities of architects—imagination, invention and ingenuity—are dried up and negated."[4] However, numerous unsolicited suggestions were offered the greenbelt planners on how they should proceed.

Frank Lloyd Wright presented John Lansill with his model of Broadacre City and suggested that the Resettlement Administration scrap its plans, add $70,000,000 to its $30,000,000 allocation and allow Wright to construct "the finest city in the world."[5] The great architect further stipulated that there must be no interference with his direction of the project. Lansill does not believe Wright was serious about the suggestion since the conditions he demanded were obviously beyond reason. Had Wright been willing to work within the liberal guidelines imposed on the rest of the planning teams, the R.A. would have considered Broadacre City. As it was, he reacted to Lansill's rejection with a denunciation of all public and private housing in America and never again communicated with the Suburban Division.[6]

A more obscure architect, Edgar Chambless, suggested his plan for urban America. He called it "roadtown." The idea came to him in 1893 as he sat penniless on a hill overlooking Los Angeles trying to understand why his savings, invested in railroad stocks, had disappeared in the crash. He envisioned an extension of the row house idea—stretching for hundreds of miles through the countryside with three levels of subways linking the homes, factories, and stores. Roadtown, said Chambless, "will be a line of city through the country. . . . It will give the suburbanite all that he seeks in the country and all that he regrets to leave in town."[7] Chambless sent letters and telegrams to Roosevelt, Wallace, Tugwell, and many other New Deal officials.[8] He even received some support from the National Grange.[9] In late 1935 or early 1936 he explained his idea to Lawrence Hewes, one of Tugwell's special assistants. Hewes looked at the drawings but never considered the project seriously.[10] Chambless was equally unsuccessful in his attempt to interest the New York World's Fair Committee. In the last week of June, 1936, he committed suicide in his small furnished room on East Forty-ninth Street in New York.[11]

President and Mrs. Roosevelt were also deeply interested in the towns, but did not follow the planning closely or suggest major changes. The president reviewed the plans for Greenbelt, Maryland, on April 30, 1936, but no changes were made by him.[12] Mrs. Roosevelt visited Greenbelt, Maryland, several times with Mrs. Henry Morgenthau.[13] She hoped to convince the secretary of the treasury, through his wife, that the greenbelt towns were not as bad as he thought they were.[14] Morgenthau, after all, had "broad control over the financing of the projects."[15] Mrs. Roosevelt also visited Greendale, Wisconsin, in

November, 1936, and criticized the residential architects for locating the basement laundry next to the coal bin.[16] Lansill was diligent in keeping R.A. officials away from the planning offices and project sites where they would occasionally arrive and begin issuing orders.[17] Tugwell was too busy to give serious attention to the physical planning of the towns, although he kept informed on their progress.[18]

Beyond the guidelines established in October, 1935, Frederick Bigger imposed none of his own ideas on the planning staff. This was commendable. As the only senior administrator with technical competence in architecture and city planning, he could easily have dictated the town plans. Albert Mayer, an advisor to the Suburban Division in 1935–36 and one of the architects of Greenbrook, New Jersey, said that Bigger chose to serve primarily as an advisor and coordinator.[19] A separate staff was assigned to each town and worked independently of the other town planning staffs. This was necessary since each town site was different in topography, population, economy, and legal structure. Each planning staff had three departments: town planning, architecture, and engineering. Subsections were established to plan electrical and heating facilities, utilities, and landscaping. Special sections rendered drawings and scale models, made detailed records, and conducted field research. The planning staff was headed by one or two men designated as chief town planner, chief architect, or chief engineer; but the group was collectively responsible for the whole project. All four staffs had a regional coordinator whose responsibility was to keep the planning staffs and the R.A. administrators informed.[20]

A number of people involved in the planning remarked on the high degree of dedication and cooperation among the planners, most of whom had never worked on a project calling for daily teamwork and compromise.[21] Hale Walker, the town planner of Greenbelt, said he had never seen a more cooperative group of people: "Everyone seemed to recognize that the problem was town building. Interdepartmental criticism was freely given and taken in good spirit."[22] For example, if the heating section decided to use coal for fuel instead of oil, it would necessitate changes in the house plans to allow for a coal bin and a change in the site plan and street plan to allow coal trucks to deliver directly into the coal bin. The planning staffs worked with almost every department of the government. In his annual report, Lansill expressed gratitude to twenty-eight federal agencies, technical associations, corporations, and foundations for their cooperation.[23] There is no evidence to support a claim of rivalry between the four staffs as reported in the New York *Sun*.[24] Conflicts which might have arisen over pay scales were minimized by C. B. Baldwin, who asked John A. Overholt of the Civil Service Commission to draw up classifications and pay scales for all jobs in the R.A. The Resettlement Administration was not under Civil Service, but Baldwin found it more desirable and equitable to follow Overholt's recommendations than to involve himself and other R.A. officers in salary disputes.[25]

The most serious design problems resulted from a lack of experience in the construction of low-cost towns. Few architects had designed low-cost homes. Few members of the American Institute of Planners were trained in town planning. Most were engineers or landscape architects.[26] "Some of the early studies," commented Clarence Stein, "looked as though they were meant for the Westchester villas of young bankers."[27]

Information about the needs, desires, and financial limitations of low-income groups was badly needed to determine proper distribution of funds among the four towns.[28] Initially it was assumed that a total of 5,000 housing units would be constructed with the $31,000,000 allocation.[29] By February, 1936, when the four planning teams met with Lansill, Bigger, and Budget Director Diggs to decide on a "definite" allocation for each town, the total number of housing units was reduced to 3,500 as follows:[30]

Towns	Units	Cost
Greenbelt, Md.	1,000	$6,950,000
Greenhills, Ohio	1,000	8,750,000
Greendale, Wisc.	750	7,050,000
Greenbrook, N.J.	750	7,150,000

Most of the planners felt this was not enough money. Roland Wank said they had a chance of reaching their goal "if nothing unforseen arises, but I must say that it would be an unforeseen circumstance if nothing unforseen occurs."[31]

It was decided to proceed with the intention of constructing the highest quality facilities consistent with a "reasonable first cost." The alternative would have been to construct inexpensive facilities of inferior quality.[32] As Tugwell explained to the Regional Planning Commission of Hamilton County, Ohio, in 1936,

> It is our belief that the highest standards of construction are essential to genuinely low-cost building. . . . We are asking ourselves most searchingly not "what is the first cost?" but rather; "what do the forty-year costs add up to?"[33]

The planners hoped the towns would provide a yardstick against which architects and builders could measure similar projects. For this reason detailed technical and cost reports were filed in the Suburban Division Library. They represented the most comprehensive record of planning techniques ever made in America.[34]

Fortunately, the Suburban Division had acquired large enough tracts of land to allow the planners great latitude in blocking out the towns. The tracts were well beyond built-up urban areas so few roads or structures hindered the development of comprehensive town plans. The only preexisting physical factor in planning the town layouts was the topography of each tract. At Greenbelt, Hale Walker laid out a sweeping, crescent-shaped town along a beautifully wooded ridge with the open end of the crescent facing prevailing summer breezes. Greenhills was built along the crest of a number of small ridges cut by ravines and resulted in a somewhat irregular town pattern.[35] It is situated high above the "grimy but busy" Mill Creek valley affording its residents a spectacular view of the countryside.[36] Justin Hartzog, the chief planner, said one emerged from the smog in the valley "to burst suddenly out into sunlight and take a deep breath from the upper strata."[37] Greendale is laid out on very gently rolling land, but the tract is cut by Dale Creek, which runs through its very center and empties into the Root River which flows along the western edge. The two courses meet at the southern end of the town. Instead of using Dale Creek as a convenient drainage ditch, it was incorporated into the town plan as a lovely park.[38] Greenbrook was to have been built on almost flat terrain. The chief problem in planning the town would have been a branch line of the Pennsylvania Railroad which ran through the southern edge of the tract and was to have been the center of an industrial park.[39]

The planners had to determine the ultimate size of each town. The basic question was how large a community must be to support adequate public and commercial facilities, amortize the mortgage, and still retain a sense of "community." Clarence Stein was asked to prepare several studies one of which explored the financial aspects of this question. He said that if the average resident had an annual income of $1,250, the towns would each require a minimum population of 4,000 to pay for maintenance and administration alone, excluding amortization of the mortgage. Each of the 4,000 residents would cost the town $79.09 per year or $316.36 for a family of four. If the breadwinner's income was $1,250 he would have to pay twenty-five percent of it in rent to cover this cost. Stein believed twenty-five percent was too high for families in this income group. However, if the population was increased the maintenance cost per person would decline so that a town of 7,000 would require $72.02 per person.[40] The dilemma presented by Stein's report was serious. Unless each of the four towns had slightly over 1000 housing units (research at Greenhills indicated the average family size of potential residents to be approximately 3.7 persons), the towns could not afford to maintain services; but 4,000 units were more than the Suburban Division could afford. The solution was to build as many units as possible and plan for the construction of the remaining number of units in the future. In the spring of 1936 the Suburban Division reported that all four towns were planned for populations of between 4,000 and 6,000 families.[41] With continued cutbacks in the number of units, the whole question of the ultimate size became somewhat academic and no clear plans were made for the projected development of the towns with the exception of Greendale. Hartzog spoke of a town of 7,000 people at Greenhills, while the planners of Greenbrook envisioned a total population of 15,000 to 20,000 residents. Greendale's staff set its final number at 12,000. No definite proposal was made for the ultimate size of Greenbelt although Hale Walker mentioned a population of 30,000.[42]

Low residential density was considered desirable for all the towns. In the residential area of Greendale there were approximately five families per acre. At Greenhills there were 8.5 families per acre and at Greenbelt four families per acre.[43] There is no comparison between the population densities of the Greenbelt towns and any urban housing projects undertaken by the federal government. The P.W.A. projects, built on land costing anywhere from $50,000 to $350,000 per acre, included as many as eighty-two housing units per acre as in the Harlem River Houses of New York.[44]

The unique planning feature of the greenbelt towns was, of course, the greenbelt. Its purpose was to separate the town from surrounding built-up areas, to provide a land reserve for expansion of the community to its predetermined limit, and to provide a rural environment for the townspeople. The rural use of the greenbelt was given more attention in Resettlement Administration publications and reports than by the planning staffs who generally looked on the greenbelt as an open space buffer area and land reserve. It may be that its possibilities for agricultural use were publicized to satisfy the comptroller that the towns were in part a rural rehabilitation project and entitled to funds from the Emergency Relief Appropriation.[45] The land at Greenbelt was unsuitable for profitable farming, and the planners of Greenhills and Greenbrook gave little attention to agricultural uses of the greenbelt.[46] At Greendale, however, Elbert Peets and Jacob Crane made a detailed recommendation for the creation of what was actually a collective farm on the greenbelt with all the farmers employed on a salary basis with a share in the profits.[47] Both Bigger and Lansill liked the idea, but it was not executed. The planners remodeled some existing farms on the greenbelt and leased them to tenants. All of the towns did make use of an idea advocated by perspective residents—to plan individual flower and vegetable gardens on the greenbelt. An overwhelming majority of families questioned indicated such a desire.[48] Allotment gardens were planned which could be rented for a small annual fee. The gardens became particularly important during World War II when fresh vegetables were difficult to obtain.

The question of the most suitable width for the greenbelt was given careful attention by Tracy Augur. He thought it ought to be at least half a mile wide except where some other physical barrier such as a ravine would make crossing the greenbelt equally difficult. This would direct "the daily contacts of its citizens inward toward the center rather than outward into nearby developments."[49] Augur expanded his ideas:

> The width of the protective belt should be such that persons living at the edge of the community will not be tempted to walk across it to shopping facilities which may spring up in the surrounding territory, but will instead find it more convenient to go to their own shopping centers within the community. It should be wide enough and open enough in character that persons crossing it by automobile will distinctly realize that they have left one community and entered another. It should be so wide that private subdividers

of adjoining land can not make a plausible demand that their tracts be connected with the water and sewer lines and streets of the community. It should be so wide that it would from a natural boundary between school districts so that there would be no temptation to place part of the new community in the same school district with unorganized areas outside.[50]

It is unfortunate that none of the greenbelt towns will be able to test the idea. All of them have lost most of their greenbelts.

Initially both Greenbrook and Greendale were to have industrial sites for private businesses. Greenbrook was an obvious choice for a major industrial park. This had been one of the reasons for selecting the site and the subsequent growth of industry in the Bound Brook–New Brunswick area indicates the accuracy of that judgment.[51] After the Greenbrook project was abandoned, the possibility of establishing a ten-acre industrial park at Greendale was investigated and rejected. First, no money was available to assist the industries in moving to Greendale and they would not relocate without help. Second, in most of the local factories, half the employees were earning less than the proposed minimum income ($1200) needed for residence in Greendale. However, an area was reserved for future light industry.[52] In 1962 a small (fifty-two acres) industrial park was initiated and another one hundred acres have since been proposed for industrial use.[53] The inclusion of industry in the original towns might have solved the commuting problem and broadened the town tax base.

The streets and pedestrian walks were laid out to provide safety, convenience, and a physical setting for social contacts. At Greenbrook and Greenbelt the curvilinear streets were designed to form superblocks intended to form a physical basis for the development of neighborhoods—as had been done at Radburn and several other towns.[54] The superblocks at Greenbelt are fourteen to eighteen acres. They would have varied from nine to slightly over thirty acres at Greenbrook.[55] The homes face the center of the block in which a large common play area is provided. The streets at Greenhills, running along the crests of the ridges, form a kind of natural superblock. The homes again face inward. The superblock also lowered construction costs. At Greenbelt it was calculated to have reduced by thirty percent the cost of streets, sidewalks, and utility lines which would have been built for an equal number of homes laid out in the traditional gridiron block pattern.[56]

Greendale planners rejected the superblock as well as curvilinear streets. Elbert Peets, the town planner, was attracted to traditional architectural styles, particularly that of colonial Williamsburg which had opened shortly before he was hired by the Suburban Division. Peets said it "was not quite an accident that in its skeleton organization the plan of Greendale is much like the plan of Williamsburg."[57]

Careful attention was given to traffic safety in planning the streets and walkways. In each town the street system was constructed so that traffic would not be able to use residential streets for passing through the community, but would travel around it on a peripheral highway. A major arterial highway was planned to cut through the center of Greenhills, but the R.A. convinced the Hamilton County Regional Planning Commission to relocate it outside the town.[58] At Greendale most residential streets ended in cul-de-sacs. Traffic circulation streets were kept at a minimum and intersections were designed to give drivers wide vision of approaching vehicles and pedestrians. All residents could reach the town center by crossing only one traffic circulation street. Everyone could reach a park or playground without crossing a single street.[59] Pedestrian underpasses were planned where walkways crossed major traffic streets. The Greenbelt planners designed many of them; but the expense was too great, and only a small number were constructed.[60] The other town plans, perhaps because of the cost at Greenbelt, did not include underpasses.

The focal point of each community is the town center. It was agreed that the center should be "more than the usual commercial store center—rather a gathering place and part of the cultural life of the town."[61] Questionnaires sent to local residents helped determine the facilities included in each center. Families in the Washington, D.C., area expressed strong preferences for a library, a swimming pool, and a community hall. In the Milwaukee area (where in 1936 there was a tavern for every 300 persons) citizens wanted a tavern along with the library and community hall.[62] Standard shops and stores such as groceries, drug stores, variety shops, beauty parlors, and gasoline stations were planned in every town. Greenbelt and Greendale each had a theater. Greenbelt was to have had a small inn to house guests of the town or the Agricultural Research Center. It would have contained a tap room and a 150-seat dining room overlooking the lake for community group dinners.[63] Naturally local fire, police, and administration offices were located in the town center. One main building was used for the school by day, a meeting place in the evening, and a church on Sunday. All the town plans had areas set aside for independent church structures though none were built until the 1950s.[64]

The schools were planned on the basis of studies made of local systems and costs. The Suburban Division considered it unwise to ask local county school districts in the project areas to provide educational facilities for the sudden influx of children. Therefore, each town was planned to provide twelve grades of instruction for its children. At Greenbelt planners arranged with Prince George's County officials to construct the high school independent from the grade school–community center. It would become a regional consolidated high school. Greenhills high school consolidated five small rural districts and undoubtedly improved the level of secondary education for the area. Greendale's school was intended to be used for all twelve grades, but it was too small; the high school students attended school outside the town.[65]

The Suburban Division hoped to demonstrate the economy of installing all utilities at the same time. On the other hand, local utility companies hoped to charge high rates for their services thus offsetting the original savings. The town of Green-hills, for example, began negotiations in May, 1936, with the city of Cincinnati for the purchase of water, but the city wanted twenty-four cents per thousand cubic feet. The Greenhills planners considered this far too expensive, noting that water was sold within the city for only sixteen cents. The R.A. began negotiating with Hamilton County for the right to drill wells in the Mill Creek Valley. Options were taken on well sites, and test wells were drilled. At the last minute, however, the Board of County Commissioners refused to issue the permits apparently due to fears of industries in the valley and neighboring towns that the wells would lower the water table—a possibility the planners denied. In May, 1937, a tripartite agreement between the city of Cincinnati, Hamilton County, and the R.A. allowed water to be supplied through a federally financed water main, but the cost in time and money was great.[66] Fewer utilities would have been purchased from local companies if the Suburban Division had been able to afford independent services. In the spring of 1936 the Suburban Division planners discussed building an electrical generating plant at Greenbelt thereby creating an "all electric" community with rates comparable to the TVA rates, but the Potomac Electric Power Company provided electricity at a good wholesale rate. The fact that the three towns were all electric (lighting, cooking, and hot water) was coincidental as a separate consideration was made for each town. Greenhills would have used gas had it not been offered a lower rate on electricity. Had Greenbrook been built, it would have used gas.[67]

The continued reduction in the number of homes to be constructed at each of the towns obviously complicated the task of planning utilities. The result was that utilities were laid for many more housing units than were actually constructed. At Greendale all the streets, walks, water, and sewer lines were laid for a town of 1,200 families; but the final construction budget allowed only 572 homes to be completed. Utilities at Greenhills were built to serve 1,000 units of housing while only 676 were built. Greenbelt built utilities for 2,000 homes and constructed only 890. Some of the major trunk sewer and water lines were built with a capacity to handle even larger populations.[68]

Heating systems for each town caused much debate between planners and engineers. Essentially, the question was whether to install individual heating systems or build central systems making it a public utility. Studies of the installation and operating costs of five different heating systems indicated that central systems were less costly. Other factors, however, complicated the issue. The proponents of individual heating systems argued that (1) the tenant would have more independence and could save money by using less heat, (2) the tenant could burn lower grades of coal or even wood (in a coal-fueled system), (3) operation of the individual system would cost only time to the tenant but a management would have to employ operators which would raise rents, and (4) the cost of laying heating pipes to a large number of small units or to units spread out for a great distance from the heat source would be too expensive. Advocates of central heating answered that (1) underheating of one unit of a multifamily dwelling would rob neighboring units of heat through the walls; (2) the use of low-grade coal or wood would ruin the equipment, whereas professional maintenance of central equipment would result in fewer repairs and greater savings to the tenants in the long run; (3) central heating would allow the use of oil furnaces, which could become a cheaper fuel as was already seen in Washington, D.C., and Bound Brook, New Jersey; (4) paternalism would be no more threatening than in centrally-heated private apartment buildings and is a problem created by management not the physical plant; and (5) in coal-fueled housing central heating would eliminate the extra cost of ash collection and free the site planner from the limitations imposed by individual coal delivery. Each planning staff made its own decision on the heating system, and only Greendale provided individual coal furnaces for the tenants.[69]

The most important feature of any community is its homes: they usually represent the most valuable physical property in the town (overwhelmingly so in residential suburbs) and are the buildings in which most of the family living is done. The planning of the homes for the greenbelt towns reveals the only fundamental divergence among the planning teams. An attempt was made to formulate a general policy for home planning in October, 1935, when the three staffs from the Greenbelt, Greenhills, and Greenbrook projects (no staff for Greendale had been selected at this time) met with the Suburban Division directors and special advisors Henry Wright, Clarence Stein, and Catherine Bauer. It was decided to go on the assumption that "they were planning a long term investment for a perpetual entrepreneur" which would justify "increased capital investment if it produces lowered maintenance and operation costs."[70] They also agreed that while one or two types of dwellings might appear to be superior, each community should have a variety of plans and the architects should be allowed "to indulge somewhat (but not too much) in experiments as to type plan."[71] Finally, every effort should be made to determine what type of housing was preferred by potential residents.

Each staff sent questionnaires to potential residents concerning their living accommodations at the time—what facilities, rooms, home arrangements (i.e., detached, row, or apartment homes) they would prefer.[72] At least two staffs sent field researchers out to gain more detailed knowledge which was supplemented by census information on family size and composition prepared by the Research Section.[73] Results of the questionnaires revealed striking differences in housing preferences of would-be residents. In the Washington area only thirty-two percent desired a detached house while sixty-eight percent in the Cincinnati area and seventy-four percent in the Milwaukee area indicated that desire. Only in Washington did more families (forty-five percent) choose a row house over a detached house. Also in Washington, twenty-two percent wanted apartments while almost no one did in either Cincinnati or Mil-

waukee.[74] Field research at Cincinnati indicated a close relationship between income and housing preference. The poorer
families assumed that a detached house was out of the question
for them even in a government project built for moderate and
low incomes. They generally picked row houses which were
certainly better than the overcrowded apartments in which they
lived.[75]

Most planners agreed that row houses were the only type
of dwellings economically feasible for moderate incomes. Henry
Churchill's statement that the average American's desire for a
detached house "is a sentimental idea without much to recom-
mend it" reflects more than a pure cost analysis, and it also
represents the thinking of the Greenbrook, Greenhills, and
Greenbelt staffs.[76] At Greendale, however, Elbert Peets disagreed. He felt that a detached house was far superior to a row
house which had been accepted by "sophisticated planners,
largely on the English precedent."[77] He thought each house
should stand apart with its own fenced yard around it. It was
hoped a useful cost comparison could be made between the
detached houses at Greendale and the row house units at the
other projects, but the task became impossible and only a rough
estimate can be made of per unit costs. Greendale's detached
houses at $10,814 per unit compare favorably with Greenhill's
row houses at $10,872 per unit and were not a great deal more
than Greenbelt's row houses and apartments at $9,909 per unit.[78]
Ultimately the Greendale staff had to be content with only 274
detached houses and 298 multifamily units completed the town.
Greendale remains the only public housing program which
built the detached houses most Americans apparently prefer.

One of Clarence Stein's studies for the Suburban Division
indicated that seventy percent of the tenants would have automobiles. A similar study by the Research Section for Greenhills
showed that ninety percent would have them. Some planners
thought both figures were much too high.[79] Naturally, all three
greenbelt towns today suffer from the large number and increased size of automobiles; though less so than most other

American towns built before the Second World War. Only Greendale and Greenbrook attempted to plan for a sizable number of individual garages. At Greendale, Peets designed the house, driveway, and garage so the resident has complete privacy going between his car and home. In this respect, he consciously tied the home and the outer world together with the automobile and most accurately anticipated the home building trend of the future.[80]

The homes in each town were designed in a wide variety of floor plans.[81] The number of rooms planned for each of the living units was determined by the Research Section's analysis of family size and composition in each project locality. As originally planned the majority of units in each project were to have two or three bedrooms.[82] Only Greenbelt with thirty-five percent of its units containing one bedroom planned to accommodate as many single persons and older couples as corresponded to their population in the local area. Greenbrook, Greenhills, and Greendale planned a small number of four bedroom units approximating the number of families in the locality needing such rooms.[83] The house designs, therefore, prescribed that the greenbelt towns would be populated primarily by young families with one or two children.

Experiments were made in combining the dining and living rooms as well as in planning the living room for use as a bedroom at night. At Greenbrook field researchers found that local residents treated the living room as a "parlor," using it only on special occasions. One house plan placed the stairway to the second floor in the living room in an attempt to force more use of this room. Windows were situated to give maximum light and air circulation.[84] In this last respect the relationship of one building to another was as important as proper placing of windows. Scale models of each project enabled the architects to see more accurately the relationship of each building and each room and each window to its surroundings. The use of scale models was still new and the use of the "helidon"—a light positioned to show the shadow pattern for any time of the day over a con-

tour model of the site with its trees and buildings—was just
being tested by Henry Wright at Columbia University.[85]

The Special Skills Division of the Resettlement Administration, under the direction of Adrian Dormbush, employed artists
to design furniture for the tenants and sculptured pieces for
each of the town centers. The furniture was produced under
contract by private companies. It could be purchased at cost by
any tenant of the greenbelt towns through the Treasury Department.[86] It was made of oak and an entire house could be
furnished for $300 to $400.[87] Like the housing at Greenbelt and
Greenhills, it was functional and very sturdy. The furniture was
well received in both trade and popular journals. The home
furnishing edition of *Retailing* praised the R.A. for its high quality, inexpensive designs and also for allowing private firms to
manufacture it.[88] *House Beautiful* was even more enthusiastic
in a short paragraph lauding the designs as splendid examples
of the functional theory of art:

> There is a welcome absence of "gingerbread" so often found
> on inexpensive furniture and used primarily to cover up struc-
> tural defects. The beauty of the Resettlement furniture is not
> the self-conscious "arty" type, but functional and therefore
> living and real. Its freshness and simplicity have grown out
> of the very limitations imposed upon the designers.[89]

The statuary designed for the three town centers is indica-
tive of the Resettlement Administration's desire to create towns
in the pattern of the traditional small town, for there is hardly a
community in the nation without at least one statue. The pieces
were designed by the Special Skills Division and executed by
artists obtained through the W.P.A. The results range from an
attractive group of figures cut by Alonzo Hauser for Greendale
to a ponderous statute of a mother and child by Lenore Thomas
in Greenbelt's central plaza.[90] Greenhills never received its
statues. The W.P.A. sculptor, Seth Velsey, began cutting four
figures out of twenty tons of rock in the yard of a Dayton, Ohio,

stone company and had completed two of the figures by May, 1942, when the W.P.A. fired him. In April, 1948, the stone company wrote the Greenhills town manager asking for six years of storage fees on the stones. The request was sent to the comptroller's office in Washington, but nothing was done about it.[91] Greenhills has not yet received its statuary.

With all the thought and debate that went into the green-belt towns, the exterior design of the buildings is generally disappointing. Henry Churchill, an advisor to the Suburban Division and vigorous supporter of the program admitted that the exteriors were "competent and undistinguished."[92] At Greenbelt one of the architects said, "There was no conscious effort to follow any set precedent in the design of the buildings"; and if one had to label the style, it could be called "functional" or "contemporary."[93] Greenbelt's row houses and apartments look like solidly-built boxes pierced with windows; their appearance is redeemed only by their placement in the landscape. The units at Greenhills are similar except for an unsuccessful attempt to hide the box-like skeletons with several types of exterior trim. One explanation for the cinder block, flat-roofed buildings at Greenbelt was that more complex structures would require more skilled labor than could be drawn from the relief rolls.[94] Greenbelt's architecture is an example of what the designers of the 1930s regarded as the "New Tradition" (now called the International Style) in architecture—a reaction against the ornamentation and sentimental traditionalism of Victorian styles which held their own in the United States through the 1920s. In Europe the Bauhaus architects created "functional" buildings of which the Greenbelt and Greenhills structures are but poor reflections.[95] The harsh conclusion of two eminent architectural historians is that the level of all the New Deal architecture "was almost as low as the level of its painting and considerably less amusing."[96]

That conclusion is certainly not true of Greendale, which, from an aesthetic point of view, is the most interesting greenbelt town. Elbert Peets was the only planner to unashamedly concern himself with "civic art." In 1922 Peets had collaborated with architectural historian Werner Hegemann on *The American Vitruvius: An Architect's Handbook of Civic Art*. They hoped to emphasize the "art" side of architecture and city planning because they felt the profession was "drifting too strongly in the directions of engineering and applied sociology."[97] American colonial traditions provided the inspiration for Greendale's architecture. Peets seemed to take literally the injunctions of men like Stein, Churchill, and Mayer to re-create the closeness of the colonial village. Greendale's houses are set in the American colonial and European village pattern—close to the street with small fenced yards on the side and rear. While all the towns are green and spacious, only Greendale has charm and atmosphere. As the towns grow older, the homes at Greenbelt and Greenhills will require more modern facing materials, whereas the houses at Greendale will look more authentic with each new coat of paint. Greenbelt and Greenhills are recognizable as institutional type structures while Greendale, even with row houses, looks like a collection of individual homes which happened to grow together into a lovely village.

No description of the towns can equal a short stroll through them. While better materials, more efficient shopping centers, and better house plans have since been developed, community planning—the integration of all these elements—was not seriously attempted again in America until the 1960s. The planners of the greenbelt towns showed remarkable imagination and thoroughness in the face of great pressures. Tugwell, Lansill, and Bigger had the courage to act on Daniel Burnham's directive to "make no little plans."[98] Possibly the best tribute to the greenbelt town planners came from the National Association of Real Estate Board's *Confidential Weekly Letter* which, between its denunciation of all government housing programs, praised the three towns for their "excellent design."[99]

1. U.S., Resettlement Administration, *Greenbelt Towns*, pp. 3, 16, 24–27; and Lansill, "Final Report on the Greenbelt Town Program," Lansill Papers, official files.

2. "Policies of the Division of Suburban Resettlement," August 1, 1935, Lansill Papers, personal files.

3. "Statement of General Policies and Objectives of Suburban Resettlement Administration," October 1, 1935, Lansill Papers, personal files. This statement also appears in U.S., Resettlement Administration, *Greenbelt Towns*, p. 1.

4. Clarence S. Stein, *Towards New Towns for America*, p. 120.

5. Interview with John S. Lansill.

6. Ibid.

7. Edgar Chambless, *Roadtown*, pp. 17–18.

8. Telegram from Chambless to Roosevelt, September 22, 1935, Roosevelt Papers, O.F. 503.

9. L. J. Taber, master of the National Grange, to Louis M. Howe, July 26, 1933, Roosevelt Papers, O.F. 503.

10. Lawrence I. Hewes, *Boxcar in the Sand*, p. 72.

11. Bruce Bliven, "Suicide of a Dreamer," *The New Republic* 87 (July, 1936): 238–39.

12. "Summarized History of Greenbelt Project," Lansill Papers, official files.

13. Timothy McDonnell, *The Wagner Housing Act: A Case Study of the Legislative Process* (Chicago: Loyola University Press, 1957), p. 91.

14. Interview with Warren J. Vinton.

15. *New York Times*, May 2, 1935.

16. *Milwaukee Sentinel*, November 14, 1936.

17. John S. Lansill to W. W. Alexander, October 14, 1935, National Archives, Record Group 96; and interview with John S. Lansill.

18. Interview with Albert Mayer, New York, October 5, 1964.

19. Ibid.

20. "Project Planning Organization," Memorandum No. 1, October 18, 1935, Lansill to Technical Principals, Lansill Papers, official files.

21. Interviews with John S. Lansill, Tracy Augur, Albert Mayer, and Warren Vinton.

22. Hale J. Walker, "Some Minor Technical Problems Encountered in the Planning of Greenbelt, Maryland," *The Planners' Journal* 4 (March-April, 1938): 34.

23. U.S., Resettlement Administration, *First Annual Report*, p. 43; and Frederick Bigger, "Site Planning," *Housing Monograph No. 3*, pt. 2 (Washington: U.S. Government Printing Office, 1939), p. 20 (mimeographed).

24. *The Sun* (New York), July 11, 1936.

25. Interview with C. B. Baldwin.

26. Charles Cheney, "Urban Development: The Pattern and the Background," *The Planners' Journal* 1 (November-December, 1935): 35.

27. Stein, *Towards New Towns for America*, p. 120.

28. Henry S. Churchill, *Greenbelt Towns* (manuscript copy in Lansill Papers, official files), chap. 1, pp. 30–31.

29. U.S., Resettlement Administration, Press Release, October 11, 1935, Roosevelt Papers, O.F. 1568.

30. R. W. Diggs to Finance Director Burton D. Seeley, April 4, 1936, R.O.A., H.H.F.A., Drawer 527.

31. Minutes of Project Principals Conference on Allocations, February 7, 1936, Lansill Papers, personal files.

32. Henry S. Churchill, "Report on Federal Housing Administration Low Cost Housing" (unpublished report for the Suburban Division), June 11, 1936, Lansill Papers, personal files.

33. Tugwell, Address to the Regional Planning Commission of Hamilton County, Ohio.

34. Unfortunately, there is no complete set of reports and recommendations remaining since the disappearance of the Suburban Division Files. The largest collection is in the Lansill Papers, official files.

35. U.S., Resettlement Administration, "Weekly Progress Report No. 32," January 25, 1936, p. 2.

36. Justin R. Hartzog, "Planning of Suburban Resettlement Towns," *The Planners' Journal* 4 (January–February, 1938): 29.

37. Ibid.

38. For a brief discussion on the preservation of streams in subdivisions, see Christopher Tunnard and Boris Pushkarev, *Man-Made America: Chaos or Control*, pp. 140–41.

39. Albert Mayer, "Greenbelt Towns: What and Why," *The American City* 51 (May, 1936): 60.

40. Stein, "Report on Operation-Maintenance Costs at Suburban Resettlement Communities," National Archives, Record Group 96, Box 308, December 5, 1935.

41. "Summary Information Reports for Greenbelt, Greenhills, Greenbrook, and Greendale," Lansill Papers, personal files.

42. Hartzog, "Planning of Suburban Resettlement Towns," p. 31; Mayer, "Greenbelt Towns: What and Why," p. 60; "Ultimate Development of Area," Reports and Recommendations, Greendale, Wisconsin,

prepared by Greendale Planning Staff, Book 1, p. 3 (in Public Housing Administration Library, Washington, D.C.); and Walker, "Some Minor Technical Problems," p. 35.

43. "Summary Information Reports for Greenbelt, Greenhills, Greenbrook, and Greendale," Lansill Papers, personal files.

44. "Report on W.P.A. Housing Division Projects," September, 1937, Lansill Papers, personal files.

45. Letter from administrator of Resettlement Administration to comptroller general, October 9, 1935, Lansill Papers, personal files.

46. Comments on town planning by Russell Black, Tracy Augur, and Henry Wright, Greenbrook Project Book (copy in possession of Albert Mayer, New York).

47. Elbert Peets and Jacob Crane, "Program for Agricultural Planning at Greendale," Reports and Recommendations, Greendale, Wisconsin, Book 2, and memo from Lansill, September 2, 1936, attached to above.

48. Greenhills Project Book, Lansill Papers, official files.

49. Memo from Tracy Augur to Frederick Bigger, January 21, 1936, Lansill Papers, personal files.

50. Ibid.

51. Interviews with Warren J. Vinton, Albert Mayer, and John S. Lansill.

52. "Report on Industrial Development," Reports and Recommendations, Greendale, Wisconsin, Book 1.

53. Greendale Woman's Club, *Greendale . . . thru 25 Years . . . 1938–1963* (prepared by the Greendale Woman's Club for Greendale's 25th anniversary), p. 10.

54. Roy Lubov, "New Cities for Old: The Urban Reconstruction Program of the 1930's," *Social Studies* 53 (November, 1962): 203–13.

55. Churchill, *Greenbelt Towns*, Chap. 4, p. 12; Walker, "Some Minor Technical Problems," p. 36; and O. Kline Fulmer, *Greenbelt*, p. 7.

56. Fulmer, "Superblock v. Gridiron," *The American City* 55 (July, 1940): 72–73.

57. Elbert Peets, "Greendale," in *City Planning Housing*, by Werner Hegemann, 2: 415.

58. "Report on Street and Road System," Greenhills Project Book, Lansill Papers, official files.

59. Jacob Crane, "Safety Town," *Public Safety* (August, 1937), 28–29.

60. U.S., Resettlement Administration, "Weekly Progress Report No. 27," December 21, 1935, p. 10.

61. Walker, "Some Minor Technical Problems," p. 37.

62. *Washington Post*, February 18, 1936; "Report on Business Center," Reports and Recommendations, Greendale, Wisconsin, Book 2. Several of the questionnaires are in the National Archives, Record Group 96, Box 308.

63. U.S., Resettlement Administration, Press Release, February 1, 1936, National Archives, Record Group 96, Box 230. A drawing of the proposed inn appears in John Drier's "Greenbelt Planning," *Pencil Points* 18 (August, 1936): 406.

64. U.S., Resettlement Administration, *Information for Greenbelt Applicants* (Washington: U.S. Government Printing Office, 1936), pamphlet in Vertical Files of Public Housing Administration Library, Washington.

65. L. Livingston Blair, "Schools in Greenbelt Towns," Lansill Papers, official files; Research on Schools for Projects, prepared by the Research Division, National Archives, Record Group 96, Box 308; *City of Greenbelt, 25th Anniversary, 1937–1962* (brochure prepared under the auspices of the Silver Anniversary Committee, from material provided by the *Greenbelt News Review*, with the assistance of local organizations), pp. 27–28; *Cincinnati Post*, April 2, 1940; and *This Is Greendale* (brochure privately published in 1948), p. 15.

66. Churchill, *Greenbelt Towns*, pp. 28–31; Legal Division Reports, 1936–37, Resettlement Administration Legal Division Records, R.O.A., H.H.F.A.; *Cincinnati Post*, December 15, 1936; and U.S., Resettlement Administration, "Weekly Progress Report No. 81," June, 1937, p. 24. No attempt will be made to discuss the technical aspects of the utilities for the greenbelt towns. The utility system of Greendale is outlined in Walter E. Kroening and Frank L. Dieter, "Utility Planning for Greendale, Wisconsin," *Civil Engineering*, February, 1938, pp. 94–98.

67. U.S., Resettlement Administration, "Weekly Progress Report No. 45," April, 1936, p. 6; Churchill, *Greenbelt Towns*, pp. 32–34.

68. "Expansion of Present Greendale Village," Reports and Recommendations, Greendale, Wisconsin, Book 1; Greenhills Project Book, Lansill Papers, official files; and U.S., Resettlement Administration, *Interim Report*, p. 11.

69. Churchill, *Greenbelt Towns*, pp. 48–54.

70. Memo from Frederick Bigger, October 23, 1935, Lansill Papers, personal files.

71. Ibid.

72. Housing questionnaire prepared for the Resettlement Administration, National Archives, Record Group 96.

73. Memo from Frederick Bigger, October 23, 1935, Lansill Papers, personal files.

74. Churchill, *Greenbelt Towns*, pp. 38–40; and John O. Walker, "Greenbelt Towns," *Shelter* 3 (January, 1939): 20–25.

75. Milton Lowenthal, "Report on Characteristics, Customs, and Living Habits of Potential Tenants of the Resettlement Project in Cincinnati," Greenhills Project Book, Lansill Papers, official files.

76. Churchill, *Greenbelt Towns*, p. 36.

77. Elbert Peets, "Greendale," in *City Planning Housing*, ed. Werner Hegemann, 2: 410.

78. The unit cost figures are determined by dividing the total expenditures at each project for housing by the number of units constructed. The figures are based on what the author believes are the most authoritative—those given by the Farm Security Administration to the Cooley Committee in 1943; see U.S., Congress, House, Select Committee of the Committee on Agriculture, *Hearings to Investigate the Activities of the Farm Security Administration*, 78th Cong., 1st sess., 1942–43, pp. 1118–19.

79. Stein, "Report on Operation-Maintenance Costs"; Lowenthal, "Report on Characteristics . . . in Cincinnati."

80. Peets, "Greendale," in *City Planning Housing*, ed. Werner Hegemann, 2: 410.

81. Greenhills has thirty-three different interior designs; Greenbrook was to have had nineteen; Greendale has seventeen; and Greenbelt, thirteen. The only extensive collection of house plans are found in the project books of the four towns and in other papers of the Lansill official files. The best published selection of house plans and exterior elevations is found in "Comparative Architectual Details in the Greenbelt Housing," *American Architect and Architecture* 149 (October, 1936): 20–36.

82. The figures for the towns are as follows: Greenbelt, sixty-five percent; Greenbrook, seventy-five percent; Greenhills, seventy-eight percent; and Greendale, eighty-one percent. See Churchill, *Greenbelt Towns*, pp. 37–39.

83. Ibid.

84. "Greenbrook Specifications," Greenbrook Project Book; Churchill, *Greenbelt Towns*, p. 42; and "Comparative Architectual Details in the Greenbelt Housing," pp. 20–21.

85. "Site Planning and Sunlight Developed by Henry Wright," *American Architect and Architecture* 149 (August, 1936): 19–22; and Albert Mayer, "Site Planning," *Four Papers on Housing Design* (Chicago: National Association of Housing Officials, 1942), pp. 30–31.

86. U.S., Resettlement Administration, *First Annual Report*, pp. 90–91.

87. "Cooperative Corners: Greenbelt, Maryland," *Literary Digest* 124 (October 16, 1937): 16.

88. "Low Cost Furniture," *Retailing,* July 26, 1937, p. 31.

89. "Low Cost Furniture," *House Beautiful* 79 (April, 1937): 131–33. (This article contains photographs.)

90. *Greendale Review,* December 1, 1938; and *City of Greenbelt, 25th Anniversary, 1937–1962,* pp. 19, 41.

91. Lawrence Tucker to John R. Lynch, April 13, 1948, R.O.A., H.H.F.A.

92. Churchill, *Greenbelt Towns,* p. 45.

93. Fulmer, "Greenbelt Architecture," *Greenbelt Cooperator,* December 1, 1937.

94. Fulmer, "Why Some Greenbelt Houses Have Flat Roofs," *Greenbelt Cooperator,* January 5, 1938.

95. Alan Gowans, *Images of American Living: Four Centuries of Architecture and Furniture as Cultural Expression* (Philadelphia: J. B. Lippincott Co., 1964), pp. 443–44.

96. John Burchard and Albert Bush-Brown, *The Architecture of America: A Social and Cultural History,* p. 399.

97. Werner Hegemann and Elbert Peets, *The American Vitruvius: An Architect's Handbook of Civil Art,* p. 4.

98. Christopher Tunnard and Henry Hope Reed, *American Skyline: The Growth and Form of Our Cities and Towns,* p. 153.

99. National Association of Real Estate Boards, *Confidential Weekly Letter,* August 30, 1937.

6

🍁 UNEMPLOYMENT RELIEF:

CONSTRUCTION OF THE TOWNS

Construction began even before the creation of the Construction Division, which was organized on December 1, 1935. It had previously been under the direct control of the Suburban Division.[1] The commencement of work at Greenbelt started "a spectacular race between the architects and the construction engineers. . . . Plans were rushed to the blueprinters almost before the last lines were drawn—in order to keep ahead of the surveyors and steam shovels."[2] Since the entire greenbelt program was geared to the employment of relief workers, the hiring schedule set the pace for the entire program—if drawings or materials failed to arrive when the hiring schedule called for the employment of several hundred workers, the men were given make-work projects absorbing thousands of dollars each day.[3]

George E. Allen, the District of Columbia W.P.A. administrator, turned the first spade of dirt at Greenbelt on October 12, 1935, and told reporters that the project solved "the greatest single relief problem which the District Government faces."[4] The problem was indeed great. The District housed approximately 1500 transient men at five locations. The men were unskilled, diseased, and hopeless. There was constant "fighting, drinking, gambling, and dope peddling in the transient lodges."[5] Conditions were worse for the several hundred Negroes who were housed and fed separately in a warehouse at 12th and N Streets.[6]

The Suburban Division took over the transient lodges and began to move the able-bodied men out to Greenbelt. A number were suffering from venereal diseases and were shipped to Fort Eustis, Virginia, for treatment. Over six hundred of the men were unable to perform manual labor, but there is no record of whether the Suburban Division continued to house them or sent them back to another relief agency.[7] To pay for lodging and meals the other nine hundred were employed 136 hours per month instead of the usual eighty-eight hours. However, the cost of room and board was considerably more than the extra 48 hours of labor. A remarkable improvement was observed in the morale of the transients. Most of the violence and disorganization in the lodges disappeared. The Negro lodge underwent a renaissance. The men formed their own policing system and lodge council. They organized sports teams, purchased equipment for the lodge, and even put on a vaudeville show. It was estimated that the transients were at least seventy-five percent as efficient as regular wage workers—far more than the Suburban Division expected. Some of the men worked only until their first paycheck and then disappeared, but most stayed with the project until its completion.[8] At Greenbelt the transients began work two weeks before road and street plans were available. They were first used to clear trees and excavate the site for a man-made lake. They continued to be used primarly for pick and shovel work. This may have been why a proposal for a C.C.C. camp at Greenbelt was dismissed.[9]

While there was no group comparable to the D.C. transients in the Cincinnati or Milwaukee areas, there were substantial numbers of unemployed men who were hired before they were needed. Greenhills and Greendale were begun in December. The Greenhills planners did not even receive the topographical survey of the site until December 30 and thus were not able to submit any road plans until the end of January. The plans were further revised after a field study at the site, and construction on the first streets and residential units did not begin until March, 1936. From the inception of construction on December 15 until early March, between one and two hundred laborers were employed each day, but there was very little useful work for them to perform.[10] At Greendale between eighty and one hundred men were employed through the winter, but little could be accomplished because the original topographical survey (made through tenfoot snow drifts) proved to be inaccurate and streets could not be redrawn and staked out until late April.[11]

Once blueprints reached the field, the R.A. substantially increased the number of employees. From March, 1936, to November, 1938, the payrolls for the three projects never fell below 3,000. During the six peak months of 1936–37 over 8,000 were employed. A total of over 13,000 people worked at Greenbelt making it one of the largest single projects built during the New Deal.[12]

Employment policies of the Suburban Division were determined primarily by C. B. Baldwin, who was an assistant administrator of the R.A. However, he was required by the president's original allocation letter to obtain written approval from the Works Progress Administration affirming that there was a sufficient number of unemployed laborers on relief to warrant funding of the project from the emergency relief appropriations. The W.P.A. also had to consent, in each instance, to the hiring of laborers from outside the relief group.[13] Approval to begin the projects was quickly obtained, but the hiring of nonrelief labor caused some conflict between the R.A. and the W.P.A.

Harry Hopkins was interested in employing as many relief workers as possible, so efficient use of labor was of little interest to him. The R.A. hoped that ninety percent of its laborers could be taken from the relief group, but this proved to be impossible. Therefore, whenever the R.A. found it necessary to hire skilled labor from outside the relief group, the W.P.A. would approve only on the condition that a larger number of unskilled relief workers be hired at the same time. The unemployed men were willingly taken on, but R.A. officials regretted that there was often little productive work for them to do, particularly in the latter stages of construction.[14]

As construction progressed, more skilled labor was needed, and the Suburban Division was forced to seek it from local labor markets. At Greenbelt, for example, only forty-five of the one thousand laborers were nonrelief workers in November, 1935. In May, 1936, the R.A. hired 650 skilled workers from the nonrelief group.[15] By February, 1937, forty percent of the two thousand laborers were drawn from outside the relief rolls; this figure rose to sixty percent by June, 1937. While detailed figures are not as complete for the other two towns, the same approximate ratio had been reached by the summer of 1937.[16] The R.A. was forced to undermine its preferential policy for relief laborers for two reasons. First, the R.A. refused to use unskilled men to do skilled union jobs and rapidly absorbed all the local union construction workers on relief, leaving no alternative but to seek nonrelief union men. Second, training unskilled workers to perform complex jobs would have increased costs and risked the building of inferior facilities. The priority goal was to reduce future maintenance and replacement costs by building high quality structures in the beginning. For these reasons, the Greenhills community building and most of the utilities were built under competitive private contracts. In the case of the community building, the contractor substantially underbid the R.A.'s own Construction Division.[17] The community building at Greendale was also built under private contract, but the installation of utilities was done by R.A. laborers.[18] The construction of the Greenbelt water system was accomplished by the Washington Suburban Sanitary Commission under a special contract.[19]

Local labor practices regarding job classifications were adopted.[20] All hourly wage rates followed prevailing local pay scales for each trade. Wage rates varied considerably at the three projects. At Greenbelt skilled laborers earned as much as $1.75 per hour while at Greenhills the maximum was $1.37. Unskilled workers classified as "common laborers" received sixtynine cents per hour at Greendale, and at Greenbelt they received fifty-one cents (which later rose to fifty-seven cents).[21] The R.A.'s work rules and wage policy were heartily endorsed by organized labor.[22] The unions had failed to obtain a mandatory prevailing wage policy for federal relief projects.[23] In sharp contrast, the Federal Housing Administration did not require union work rules or prevailing wages on F.H.A. financed construction, and W.P.A. projects in Prince George's County paid far below the rate at Greenbelt.[24] The W.P.A.'s "security wage" was below the R.A.'s wage at every level of skill. Unskilled laborers at Greenbelt made $44.88 per month compared to $35.00 a month for the W.P.A. unskilled laborer. Also, all R.A. laborers worked only 88 hours per month for their wages while W.P.A. laborer worked 130 hours. R.A. skilled laborers who drew the highest hourly rate ($1.75) made $154.00 per month compared to $52.00 for the skilled W.P.A. laborer.[25]

In spite of the R.A.'s beneficient policies, the wages for unskilled laborers were low considering that the men were only allowed to work eighty-eight hours per month so that more individuals could be employed.[26] If the Resettlement project was the only source of income for the laborers and they were only able to work eighty-eight hours per month, only those who earned $1.15 per hour could meet the $1200 minimum income requirement for residency in the very towns which the government labeled "low income" housing. There is evidence to indicate that some of the laborers secretly took outside work to supplement their $700–$800 annual income. The average annual income of skilled laborers working on the greenbelt towns was estimated by an R.A. labor relations official to be almost $1,900.[27]

Naturally, local politicians were eager to obtain what they considered for their fair share of the jobs for their unemployed constituents. Senator Tydings protested to Tugwell that not enough Maryland laborers were being used at Greenbelt.[28] A rumor that the Greenhills, Ohio, project might be abandoned brought immediate and strong response from a host of Cincinnati and Hamilton County officials.[29] There was also the danger with so large a program that unscrupulous R.A. officials would use their positions to political or private advantage. Only one case of political pressure was discovered. The assistant superintendent of the Greenhills Construction Division was soliciting funds and forcing employees to attend local Democratic Party meetings. The individual was immediately dismissed.[30] At Greenbelt a truck driver was fired for "loan sharking," and, in a more serious case, the supervisor of Labor Management at Greenbelt withheld paychecks from five hundred employees until they paid personal debts to him or to several stores in Washington which allegedly hired him to collect bills. Both individuals were investigated by the Justice Department.[31] These appear to be the only cases of graft connected with the greenbelt towns. No other charges appear in the existing government records or in the local press.

To give more men jobs, hand labor was often preferred over machines. When relief laborers at Greenbelt were forced to use shovels instead of bulldozers, Tugwell reportedly infuriated Roosevelt by suggesting the president might like them to use spoons.[32] Even horsedrawn wagons were used for hauling at the Greendale site.[33] R.A. officials, and particularly the planners, felt some frustration watching their funds drain away. John Lansill, however, accepted it philosophically, noting that the funds were, after all, allocated primarily to make jobs.[34]

Provision of transportation for the worker put a further strain on the budget. Men working at Greenbelt were bussed

from Washington and Baltimore. But when their numbers increased, special trains took them to Branchville, Maryland,
where trucks picked them up for the last two miles of the jour-
ney. The cost of the trains was sixty cents per man per day.[35]
At Greenhills the Cincinnati Street Railway Company lodged
a formal protest to the Ohio Public Utilities Commission complaining that the R.A. was transporting people from Cincinnati
without a license and illegally competing with the C.S.R.[36] At
Greendale a spur rail line was built into the project site over
which men and materials arrived from Milwaukee.[37] Again, in
contrast to the R.A., the W.P.A. did not provide for the transportation of its employees to its projects.[38]

Impending deadlines necessitated the purchase of materials
before planning was completed. It was impossible to estimate
correct quantities accurately but to wait for blueprints would
have left hundreds of laborers without work. The engineering
section's unfamiliarity with procedures resulted in delivery of
some items that were wrong in size and quantity. Orders were
processed for through a "ponderous" federal purchasing system
designed for longer-term projects.[39] The Procurement Division
of the Treasury Department had to advertise for bids on each
item—a process that usually took four weeks. Often separate
bids on component parts of the same item were accepted and
the parts were found to be slightly unmatched.[40] Some companies bid so low as to be unable to deliver the goods. Other
firms found that government building contracts were not as
profitable as private ones in 1936–37 when the price of construction materials was rising.[41] Notwithstanding, the quality of materials was "the best money could buy."[42] No experimentation
was done with materials, but the concrete and cinder block
structures in the three towns will last a century or two.[43]

In the winter and spring of 1935–36 even the weather con-
spired against the construction of the towns. Progress was
slowed at Greenbelt by "one of the worst winters in Washington's history."[44] In January and February frost penetrated to a
depth of fourteen inches delaying the digging of foundations

and the pouring of cement. Nevertheless, the R.A. kept all its 1,122 workers on the payroll. Several hundred men were employed at Greenhills, Ohio, clearing the site; but deep snow and below-zero weather greatly reduced their efficiency.[45] During several weeks in February no work at all could be done in surveying and clearing the site at Greendale, Wisconsin, because the snow stood eight to ten feet deep. It took several days to clear even a single road into the project. No workers were laid off during the stoppage. In March the winter broke at Greenbelt. The ice turned to water and heavy rain fell. The roads to the project became impassable, and 250 men were put to work trying to improve them.[46] During the summer Greenbelt made great progress, and after a year of work, 838 dwelling units were underway and over half were under roofs. At Greendale and Greenhills work was proceeding rapidly, but no units had been roofed. The winter of 1936–37 was not particularly cold, but very heavy rains fell. At Greenbelt the rain delayed delivery of materials though interior work continued. All work stopped at Greenhills in mid–January, 1937, while the 2,000 workers and their equipment help clean up the city of Cincinnati after the disastrous flood in the Ohio and Miami River valleys. The project site, located on high ground, was not inundated by the flood; but there was no electric power, water, or adequate transportation.[47] The towns were finally completed—Greenbelt in the fall of 1937, Greenhills and Greendale in June, 1938—three years after the organization of the Resettlement Administration.[48]

The relief function of the greenbelt town program ended in June, 1938; altogether it had provided jobs for 20,000–30,000 men.[49] However, the cost to the R.A. was high. At Greenbelt (for which the only detailed figures are available), labor costs comprised 67.8 percent of land development and construction compared to the average thirty to forty-five percent in private industry.[50] In February, 1936, the total costs were estimated at $29,900,000, but that figure was subject to drastic revision. Prediction of labor costs was hampered by the force account system of hiring which required direct hiring of day laborers instead of letting contracts for the job to be done.[51] During the spring of 1936 when construction began on a large scale, planners were able for the first time to project fairly accurate total-cost figures. They were compelled to reduce the total number of dwellings for each town. Consequently, by June, 1936, Greenbelt was to have 1,300 units; Greenhills, 1,000 units; and Greendale and Greenbrook, 750 apiece.[52] The number of units was further decreased until the final figures were substantially lower than planned: Greenbelt contained 885 units plus five farm houses (547 row houses in two-story units, 306 units in four-story apartment buildings, and five prefabricated, detached houses); Greendale contained 572 units plus sixty-five farm houses (274 detached houses, ninety semidetached houses, and 208 units in two-story row houses); Greenhills contained 676 units plus fifty-six farm houses (152 apartments, 500 units in two-story row houses, and twenty-four detached houses).[53] The sad fact for planners and architects was that only forty percent of the dwelling units envisioned in the fall of 1935 were actually constructed. Not only had many hours of planning been wasted, but all original calculations for stores, schools, and other facilities were undone by a severely decreased population. The cost of operating schools and commercial establishments would be extremely high if the standards set for the larger towns were retained. Even with the elimination of Greenbrook and 1,400 units from the other three towns, the total development cost was over $36,000,000.

Since much of the criticism leveled at the greenbelt towns was based on the high costs, an explanation of how these figures were calculated is helpful. The federal government published confusing and, at times, conflicting cost figures. For example, at Greenbelt the most detailed cost figures are listed in the Farm Security Administration's *Final Report of Project Costs: Greenbelt, Maryland* and set the total cost of the project at $14,016,270.61. However, that figure includes two items outside the cost of the town itself—"Farm Improvements" which amounted to $30,172.04 and was not computed in the R.A.'s per-unit cost of the Greenbelt dwellings, and $122,309.33 for household furniture which was sold to the residents. Deducting those two items lowers the total cost of Greenbelt to $13,863,789.24.[54] In 1940 the Farm Security Administration listed Greenbelt's total development cost at $13,394,406.00.[55] Yet again, in 1943 during the Cooley Committee hearings on the R.A. and F.S.A., the cost was cited as $13,701,817.00.[56] As for cost per unit, the F.S.A. *Final Report* adds the cost of house construction ($7,361,269.35) to overhead ($624,476.68) for a total of $7,985,746.03 or $8,972.00 per unit.[57] The F.S.A. pamphlet of 1940 and the figures given to the Cooley Committee in 1943 cite $8,819,732.66 as the total cost of Greenbelt housing which is $9,909.00 per unit.[58] This last is the figure Tugwell accepted as the cost per unit at Greenbelt.[59]

Another way of computing the unit cost would be to divide the total project cost (houses, roads, community buildings, schools, rural lands, etc.) by the 890 units constructed—a per-unit cost of approximately $15,000 if the $13,701,817.00 total cost is used. Figures on the other two towns, based on the Cooley Committee hearings, are $11,860,627.00 total for Greenhills ($8,012,917.00 for housing or $10,872.00 per unit) and $10,638,465.00 total for Greendale ($6,601,376.00 for housing or $10,314.00 per unit).[60] The cost of the three greenbelt towns together amounted to $36,200,909.00. The number of housing units of the three towns combined is only one-seventh of the total number built by the R.A. and F.S.A. However, the total cost of the three towns comprised slightly over one-third of the $104,895,624.00 expended by the two agencies on all 193 of their communities.[61]

1. Wadsworth, "Summary Description of the Greenbelt Project," Lansill Papers, official files.

2. O. Kline Fulmer, *Greenbelt*, p. 17.

3. Wadsworth, "Summary Description."

4. *Washington Star*, October 12, 1935.

5. Greenbelt Labor, Lansill Papers, personal files.

6. Ibid.

7. Ibid.

8. Memo from Wallace Richards to Lansill, April 6, 1937, Lansill Papers, personal files; and Fulmer, *Greenbelt*, p. 16.

9. White House memo, n.d., Roosevelt Papers, O.F., 1568.

10. "General Historical Analysis: Greenhills Project," Lansill Papers, official files; and U.S., Resettlement Administration, "Weekly Progress Report No. 32," January 25, 1936; "Weekly Progress Report No. 33," February 1, 1936; "Weekly Progress Report No. 40," March 21, 1936.

11. U.S., Resettlement Administration, "Weekly Progress Report No. 40," March 21, 1936; "Weekly Progress Report No. 42," April 4, 1936; "Weekly Progress Report No. 45," April 25, 1936.

12. The employment totals can be located in U.S., Farm Security Administration, "Progress Report No. 103," April, 1938, p. 27. The Greenbelt figure is in U.S., Resettlement Administration, "Monthly Progress Report No. 49," September, 1936, p. 31. (The "Monthly Progress Report" replaced the "Weekly Progress Report," but consecutive numbering was continued.) The 13,000 figure is in a memo from Wallace Richards to Lansill, April 6, 1937, Lansill Papers, personal files.

13. Letter from Roosevelt to Tugwell, September 23, 1935, and quoted in U.S., Resettlement Administration, "Weekly Progress Report No. 18," October 19, 1935; and interview with C. B. Baldwin.

14. "Summary Information Reports"; and interview with C. B. Baldwin.

15. *Baltimore Sun*, May 6, 1936.

16. U.S., Resettlement Administration, "Weekly Progress Report No. 25," December 7, 1936; "Weekly Progress Report No. 74," February 25, 1937; "Weekly Progress Report No. 81," June, 1937.

17. "General Historical Analysis: Greenhills Project."

18. Walter B. Kroening and Frank L. Dieter, "Utility Planning for Greendale, Wisconsin," *Civil Engineering*, February, 1938, p. 94.

19. U.S., Resettlement Administration, Press Release, June 4, 1936 (located in Yale University Library, New Haven, Conn.).

20. U.S., Resettlement Administration, *First Annual Report*, pp. 103–4.

21. U.S., Farm Security Administration, "Final Report of Project

Costs Including Analysis of Actual Construction Costs from Inception of Project to June 30, 1938," August 30, 1939, National Archives, Record Group 16 (mimeographed); *Washington Star*, September 7, 1936; and *Milwaukee Journal*, September 17, 1936.

22. U.S., Congress, Senate, *Resettlement Administration Program*, 74th Cong., 2d sess., 1936, Senate Doc. 213, p. 21.

23. Ray W. Bronez, "Interest Groups and Public Housing Policy" (Ph.D. dissertation, University of Chicago, 1958), pp. 110 n., 125–26.

24. "Reasons for Excessive Costs in Developing Program" (memo approved by Suburban Division Planning Staff), October, 1936, Lansill Papers, official files.

25. *Washington Post*, October 23, 1935; and Donald S. Howard, *The W.P.A. and Federal Relief Policy*, pp. 213, 860.

26. "Reasons for Excessive Costs," Lansill Papers, official files.

27. Mercer G. Evans, "Labor and the Cost of Housing," *Housing Monograph No. 3, Pt. V* (Washington: U.S. Government Printing Office, 1937) (mimeographed).

28. *Washington Post*, May 26, 1936.

29. *Cincinnati Enquirer*, June 6, 1936.

30. *New York Times*, October 10, 1936, and October 16, 1936. Hewes recalls the man in question rushing into his office "in a towering rage" saying, "I was only trying to help Roosevelt! Why should you get mad?" (Lawrence I. Hewes, *Boxcar in the Sand*, p. 91).

31. U.S., Department of Justice, Report (files on George R. Hackett and Charles Meredith), R.O.A., H.H.F.A., Drawer 528.

32. Cleveland Rogers, *Robert Moses: Builder for Democracy*, p. 131 n.

33. *Milwaukee Journal*, April 4, 1937.

34. Lansill, "Final Report on the Greenbelt Town Program."

35. Memo from Wallace Richards to Lansill, n.d., Lansill Papers, official files; and U.S., Resettlement Administration, Press Release, May 12, 1936 (located in Yale University Library, New Haven, Conn.).

36. Letter from Harold W. Starr, regional attorney for U.S.D.A. to the solicitor, U.S.D.A., January 27, 1937, R.O.A., H.H.F.A.

37. Kroening and Dieter, "Utility Planning for Greendale, Wisconsin," p. 94.

38. Donald S. Howard, *The W.P.A. and Federal Relief Policy*, p. 204.

39. Lansill, "Final Report on Greenbelt Town Program."

40. "Reasons for Excessive Costs," Lansill Papers, official files.

41. Felix Belair, Jr., "Greenbelt: An Experimental Town," *New York Times Magazine*, October 10, 1937, p. 21.

42. U.S., Congress, House, Committee on Banking and Currency, *Hearings on H.R. 2440*, 81st Cong., 1st sess., 1949, p. 47.

43. Tugwell, Address to Regional Planning Commission of Hamilton County, Ohio. Officials at all three towns told the author the structures would last at least 100 years—several believed they would stand much longer.

44. *Baltimore Sun*, March 31, 1936.

45. U.S., Resettlement Administration, "Weekly Progress Report No. 33," February, 1936.

46. U.S., Resettlement Administration, "Weekly Progress Report No. 35," February 15, 1936; "Weekly Progress Report No. 37," February 29, 1936; "Weekly Progress Report No. 40," March 21, 1936.

47. U.S., Resettlement Administration, "Weekly Progress Report No. 72," January 27, 1937; "General Historical Analysis: Greenhills Project"; and U.S., Resettlement Administration, Press Release, January 25, 1937 (located in Yale University Library, New Haven, Conn.).

48. The original construction schedule called for the completion of Greenbelt in December, 1936, while the other three towns were to be ready for occupancy by February, 1937. See the "Summary Information Reports for Greenbelt, Greenhills, Greendale, and Greenbrook."

49. Wallace Richards estimated that 13,000 people were employed at Greenbelt. The other two towns each maintained payrolls two-thirds the size of Greenbelt and did so for approximately the same number of months as Greenbelt. Therefore, it can be assumed that approximately 8,500 people were employed at each of the other two towns making a grand total of 30,000. Richard's estimate, however, may be inaccurate. During the period of peak employment (October, 1935, to January, 1938), an average of approximately 5,000 people were working on the three towns each month. To achieve the total figure of 30,000, each job had to turn over six times. No records of job turnover have survived, nor have the actual payroll records. The R.A. weekly and monthly progress reports give only the total number of men at work on each town at the end of each month.

50. The Greenbelt figure is from U.S., Farm Security Administration," Final Report of Project Costs. . . ." The figure for private industry is from U.S., National Resources Planning Board, *Housing: The Continuing Problem*, p. 38.

51. Lansill, "Final Report on the Greenbelt Town Program." For a brief explanation of the force account system, see Josephine C. Brown, *Public Relief 1929–1939*, p. 168 n.

52. U.S., Resettlement Administration, "Monthly Progress Report No. 47," July, 1936.

53. Walker, "Life in a Greenbelt Community" (Greenbelt, Maryland), *Shelter* 3 (December, 1938): 21. "Greenbelt Towns" (Greendale, Wisconsin), *Shelter* 3 (January, 1939): 23; and "A Demonstration in Community Planning" (Greenhills, Ohio), *Shelter* 3 (February, 1939): 30.

54. U.S., Farm Security Administration, "Final Report of Project Costs . . . ," p. 10.

55. U.S., Farm Security Administration, *Greenbelt Communities* (pamphlet in files of the Public Housing Administration Library, Washington, D.C.), p. 10.

56. U.S., Congress, House, Select Committee of the House Committee on Agriculture, *Hearing to Investigate the Activities of the Farm Security Administration 1942–1943*, 78th Cong., 1st sess., 1943, pp. 1118–19 (hereafter cited as Cooley Committee, *Hearings*).

57. U.S., Farm Security Administration, "Final Report on Project Costs . . . ," p. 10.

58. Cooley Committee, *Hearings*, pp. 1118–19; U.S., Farm Security Administration, "Greenbelt Communities," p. 10.

59. Tugwell, "The Meaning of the Greenbelt Towns," *The New Republic* 90 (February 17, 1937): 42. Neither Tugwell or any other R. A. official published an estimate of the excess cost arising from the inefficiency of the relief labor used at Greenbelt. The *New York Times*, however, quoted an unnamed R. A. official who said it increased the cost by $4,902,000. See *New York Times*, October 10, 1937.

60. Cooley Committee, *Hearings*, pp. 1118–19.

61. U.S., Congress, House, Subcommittee of the Committee on Appropriations, *Hearings on the Agriculture Department Appropriations Bill for 1942*, p. 108.

7

❧ THE DECISION TO RETAIN
FEDERAL OWNERSHIP

Contrary to its original intention, the Resettlement Administration retained ownership of the greenbelt towns. This arrangement greatly encumbered the towns' political, economic, and social institutions, and ultimately jeopardized the entire program. The R.A. stated that it did not intend the greenbelt communities to be "federal islands," but rather "normal American communities in which every person has his full share of both duties and privileges."[1] From Tugwell to officials under him, it was firmly stated that the federal government would divest itself of ownership after the towns were complete.

> When the construction of each demonstration is completed, the entire property will be conveyed by the Federal Government to a nonprofit corporation or local housing authority. Thereafter, the only function of the Federal Government

will be to see that restrictions to preserve the original character of the development are carried out. . . . Each community will be a tax paying participant in the region.[2]

But preservation of the original character of the towns seemed
difficult to insure once they were transferred to private ownership and local political control. In part, R.A. officials decided by
default to keep the towns under federal ownership. They pro-
crastinated and debated on this and many other matters until
it was too late to do anything else.

Will Alexander states that there was considerable disagreement on the question of turning the towns over to a private
housing corporation. He suspected that a group of people surrounding Lee Pressman, the general counsel, had little faith
in the system of private ownership and was able to postpone
the question and keep the R.A. from making any clear-cut disposition plan. "Our difficulty," says Alexander, "was that we just
couldn't make up our mind. It was generally assumed that
sometime we would, but we never got it done."[3] This, Alexander
later said, was a serious error, because even though he, Tugwell, and C. B. Baldwin believed the greenbelt towns would
be better maintained with the land in public hands—"the belief
in the desirability of land ownership as a sound policy is so
deeply engraved in our people that when you go against it,
you can't maintain any such policy as that in Congress."[4] Alexander was correct in his suspicion. Both Pressman and Baldwin
opposed the transfer of the greenbelt towns to private ownership, and these two men were closer to Tugwell and to the
Suburban Division than was Alexander. However, they could
not seriously advocate federal retention of the towns until a
legal device was found by which the residents could be taxed
and operate a government within the state structures while the
town remained federally owned.[5]

On October 20, 1935, Lee Pressman recommended that the
Greenbelt, Maryland, project "should be entrusted to local
controls. . . . The forms of community organization should be

adapted to the normal conditions present in like communities in the vicinity."[6] To maintain the garden city concept of single ownership, the land and structures should be deeded to "some corporate entity created under the laws of Maryland."[7] If the project remained under direct federal ownership, not only would the state and local governments be unable to tax it, but Greenbelt citizens would "not be entitled to the ordinary rights and privileges of state citizenship."[8]

In view of the charges then being made by local citizens in Prince George's County, Maryland (Greenbelt), and Somerset County, New Jersey (Greenbrook), that the Resettlement towns would destroy the tax base, some action had to be taken. The R.A.'s early press releases and other publications indicated the towns would become normal, tax-paying communities. In December, 1935, Tugwell decided to transfer ownership of the towns to the people living in them. Residents would be citizens of the state, pay all state and local taxes, and retire their mortgage with the R.A. from rent payments to their own privately controlled housing authority.[9] It was contemplated that the housing authority would sign a contract whereby the R.A. would administer the projects "for a term of years."[10]

However, further analysis showed this plan to be financially unfeasible. Stein's report on operation-maintenance costs was based on a projected income level averaging $1,250 and indicated that the towns would have to have at least 1,000 units simply to pay maintenance costs. Mortgage payments were not included in this study. Another report on operating expenses submitted in February by Wallace Richards was also based on a town of 1,000 units. It projected operating costs at $353,663, which was very close to the actual expense at Greenbelt during its early years. Added to this amount, however, was an annual charge of $105,000 towards amortization of the mortgage. The mortgage was for $7,000,000 (the estimated total cost of Greenbelt) to be payed over sixty-seven years at one and a half percent interest.[11] Simply to meet operating costs, the average income of the tenants would have to be above $1,250 unless they paid more than twenty percent of their income for housing. As the total cost of Greenbelt rose, the planners tried to increase the number of units. In July, 1936, Greenbelt was raised from 1,000 to 1,300 units, but this was cut back the next month to 1,250.[12] During the fall it was reduced again to the 885 units then under construction. This put Greenbelt below Stein's figure for minimum pay-as-you-go services, not to speak of Greenhills with only 672 units and Greendale with 572.

The R.A. was caught in a dilemma. If the towns were transferred to a private housing corporation, rents would have to exceed the amount low- or moderate-income families could afford. This would not only contradict all the announced intentions of the Resettlement Administration but also might be an illegal use of the project funds under the executive order directing the R.A. to resettle "destitute or low income families."[13] On the other hand if the R.A. were to sell the towns at a price the residents could afford, the result would amount to a gigantic subsidy for a very small number of people. The third alternative was for the R.A. to retain ownership of the towns.

The Bankhead-Black Act (49 Stat. 2035, 40 U.S.C. 431) of June 29, 1936, made federal retention of the towns practicable. The act held that federal ownership of resettlement project property did not "deprive any State of political subdivision thereof of its civil and criminal jurisdiction in and over such property, or . . . impair the civil rights under the local law of the tenants or inhabitants on such property." The Resettlement Administration was additionally authorized to negotiate with local taxing units "for the payment by the United States of sums in lieu of taxes . . . based upon the cost of the public or municipal services to be supplied." Payments were to be taken from receipts derived from operation of the projects.[14]

Although the hearings were primarily concerned with the rural property held by the R.A., the greenbelt towns were mentioned briefly in regard to selling them when completed. Deputy Administrator W. W. Alexander affirmed that this was the plan.[15] The issue became confused when Representative Carl Vinson, appearing on behalf of William Bankhead, said the bill was intended to cover only those projects which were "strictly farming" and suggested a separate bill be introduced for the towns. Fortunately, R.A. officials had solicited the aid of Representative John McCormack, chairman of the committee, who ignored Vinson's suggestion.[16] McCormack made clear, however, that the act would only provide a temporary solution for the towns "until the whole matter is given further consideration."[17] Pressman agreed. McCormack then asked for a further definition of the taxation problem, and Pressman replied,

> With respect to the housing problem, particularly in suburban resettlement projects, if we do not make some arrangement with respect to our taxing problem we are undoubtedly going to be combatted by every single local taxing unit through lawsuits, local comment and local prejudice, and what not; and it is very difficult to estimate just what kind of a situation we are going to have if we do not satisfy the local governmental units and the people in those local communities. . . . [At Greenhills] they have asked us what arrangements we are going to make before the year is over. . . . Our answer has been that we simply cannot tell. We have no way of arranging it. . . . The indication is that probably they will start a lawsuit to enjoin us from going on with our project. That is the situation in every one of the other communities where we are acquiring land.[18]

Although the R.A.'s *First Annual Report*, submitted over four months after the passage of the Bankhead-Black Act, reiterated the intention of transferring ownership of the towns, the administrators were not fully committed.[19]

In January, 1937, Lansill inquired what legal problems would be involved "if Greenbelt is operated eventually by the Federal Government instead of being leased to a local corporation."[20] Neither possibility—leasing or directly operating the towns—had been mentioned to the congressional committee or otherwise publicized. Nevertheless, the solicitor of the Depart-

ment of Agriculture replied to Lansill that the Bankhead-Black
Act would allow the Resettlement Administration to become
landlord of Greenbelt.[21] Such action would still enable the
community to be incorporated and have a regular town government.[22]

Lansill's inquiries regarding Greenbelt were very likely oc-
casioned by the difficulties encountered in arranging the transfer of Greenbelt to a private housing authority. The major legal
problem was the necessity of obtaining enabling legislation in
the Maryland Assembly for the establishment of a Greenbelt
Housing Authority and a municipal charter. Prince George's
County political leaders headed by State Senator Lansdale
Sasscer at first opposed the entire town. They were concerned
about the taxes the town would pay, about the color of the residents, and whether they would become a burden on the county
relief rolls.[23] After meeting with R.A. officials in October, 1935,
however, Sasscer gave the town his endorsement.[24] Meeting
again in March, 1936, R.A. officials and leaders from Prince
George's County agreed on a municipal charter, but could not
agree on a housing authority.[25] It was decided to wait on both
issues until the next session of the Maryland Legislature in
1937 when "these matters could be given more thought."[26]

In April, 1937, the Prince George's County legislators introduced bills in the Maryland Assembly to incorporate Greenbelt
and establish a housing authority. The charter of incorporation
(House Bill No. 395) was passed by the assembly. It had been
jointly agreed upon by Prince George's County leaders and the
R.A.'s legal division. The charter provided for the first town
manager in Maryland history.[27] In establishing a housing authority, the Maryland Senate, under the leadership of Sasscer,
refused to cooperate with the R.A. On April 3, 1937, the Senate
passed a general housing authority enabling bill for Maryland
municipalities but specifically excluded Greenbelt from establishing an authority under the act.[28] Two days later the Senate
passed the Greenbelt Charter but amended it at the suggestion
of Sasscer to allow the establishment of "no other housing au-

thority than the one allowed in House Bill No. 155."[29] House Bill No. 155 regulated fireworks in Prince George's County, but attached to it was a rider establishing the Greenbelt Housing Authority. The housing authority was given sweeping powers. It could lease and determine the rents on all housing, repair the structures, and construct new ones. It could not only acquire new property, but "sell, lease, exchange, transfer, assign, mortgage, pledge or otherwise dispose of such real or personal property or any interest therein."[30] It would run all public services "without the necessity for any franchise from the Town of Greenbelt."[31] In sum, the housing authority controlled Greenbelt.

The foregoing power would be exercised by a board of governors composed of the chairman of the Prince George's County Board of Commissioners, the chairman of the Washington Suburban Sanitary Commission, the chairman of the National Capital Park and Planning Commission, the member of the National Capital Park and Planning Commission from Prince George's County, the president of the University of Maryland, the mayor of the town of Greenbelt, one resident of Prince George's County to be selected by the County Board of Commissioners, one resident of Greenbelt to be elected by the other residents, and one person to be appointed by the federal agency administering the interest of the federal government at Greenbelt. The unsatisfactory nature of the board is obvious. First, the residents of Greenbelt were allowed only two of the nine votes and even with the allowance of a quorum of four, the residents could never comprise a majority. The interest of the federal government was hardly protected with only one vote on the board. Who would control Greenbelt? It is difficult to believe that all the members would be able to regularly attend board meetings. The largest bloc of votes would be in the hands of the Prince George's County Board of Commissioners, which was itself represented by its chairman and which appointed two other members. The fireworks bill with its amendment passed the Maryland Senate unanimously on the evening of April 5, 1937—the last day of the session.[32]

As late as March 30, 1937, Monroe Oppenheimer told the solicitor of the Department of Agriculture that legislation was pending in the Maryland Assembly to incorporate the town of Greenbelt and "to establish a Greenbelt Housing Authority to which the project could be conveyed or leased or to which various phases of the administration of the project could be entrusted on a cooperative basis."[33] The day after the fireworks bill passed, Oppenheimer wrote to Solicitor White saying that the version passed by the general assembly "was never agreed to by the Resettlement Administration" and was passed "despite the opposition of the Resettlement Administration."[34] Unfortunately, there is no record of the R.A.'s proposal for the Greenbelt Housing Authority, but Oppenheimer closed his letter saying that the R.A. officials "feel that the constitution of the Authority is so obnoxious to them that they will probably never avail themselves of this legislation."[35] Faced with the opening of Greenbelt to residents in the fall, the R.A. gave up further attempts to transfer the towns to private ownership. The final arrangement at Greenbelt set the policy for the other two towns.

The planners of Greendale believed the town was too small to be self-sustaining and should not, therefore, be incorporated as an independent community. It should be merged, along with the other Milwaukee suburbs, into "one metropolitan city."[36] The Legal Division of the R.A. thought it best to leave the choice of independence or annexation up to the future residents of Greendale.[37] The Research Section of the Suburban Division never considered the possibility of annexation and recommended only that Greendale be incorporated as a separate village and not come under the jurisdiction of the neighboring town of Greenfield because local officials feared they would "be dominated by new electors added as a result of the development of the Milwaukee project."[38] By October, 1936, the R.A. had definitely decided to incorporate Greendale as an independent municipality with a village council–manager government.[39]

The establishment of a Greendale Housing Authority to which the federal government could transfer title was recommended by the Legal Division in December, 1935. Wisconsin housing corporation laws already in existence allowed this action, but the R.A. took no further movements in that direction.[40] Soon after the residents of Greendale moved into the town in 1938, the Farm Security Administration petitioned the State Circuit Court of Milwaukee for a charter of incorporation. It was submitted to a referendum and passed 312–142. The charter was filed with the Office of the Registrar of Deeds in Milwaukee on November 1, 1938, and on that day the project became an independent municipality known as the village of Greendale.[41]

The incorporation of the Greenhills, Ohio, project was no problem for the Resettlement Administration because Ohio law provided for municipalities with extremely broad powers. The Legal Division of the R.A. examined the possibility of deeding the project to a housing authority in Cincinnati, but there is no evidence that such a plan was ever given detailed consideration.[42] Greenhills was incorporated in the fall of 1939 with the same mayor–council–manager type of municipal government instituted at Greenbelt, Maryland.[43]

The three communities did have municipal charters, and the tenants could establish their own governments. All the R.A. administrators agreed that these should be chartered independently of the federal government. However, they would be necessarily subordinate to the landlord—the Resettlement Administration—which would maintain its own staff of administrators in each community.

The decision to retain the towns under federal ownership had a number of advantages. It kept alive the possibility of completing the towns if Congress appropriated funds at a later date. It prevented the extensive undeveloped lands from falling into the hands of private interests which might develop them without regard to the general town plans. It allowed the possibility of resettling increasingly lower income families in the towns after they became established in their localities as wholesome communities. The towns could, if Congress wished, become unique laboratories for experiments in housing, town planning, and community organization. Congress, of course, never gave any serious thought to this possibility during the decade and a half in which the towns existed as half-forgotten federal suburbs.

1. U.S., Resettlement Administration, *Greenbelt Towns*, pp. 30–31.

2. U.S., Resettlement Administration, *First Annual Report*, p. 44.

3. Will W. Alexander, *Oral History Memoir*, pp. 412–17; Wilma Dykeman and James Stokely, *Seeds of Southern Change: The Life of Will Alexander*, p. 219.

4. Alexander, *Oral History Memoir*, pp. 412–17.

5. Interview with C. B. Baldwin.

6. Interoffice Communication from Lee Pressman to Lansill, October 20, 1935, R.O.A., H.H.F.A., Drawer 527.

7. Ibid.

8. Ibid.

9. U.S., Resettlement Administration, *Interim Report*, pp. 24–25. The housing authority would be an independent public corporation with power to operate the project as well as finance and construct further additions. See National Association of Housing Officials, *Housing Officials Yearbook, 1937*, p. 160.

10. Clarence I. Blau to Lansill, December 30, 1935, National Archives, Record Group 96, Box 308.

11. Stein, "Report on Operation–Maintenance Costs at Suburban Resettlement Communities"; memo from Wallace Richards to Lansill, February 18, 1936, National Archives, Record Group 96, Box 98.

12. U.S., Resettlement Administration, "Monthly Progress Report No. 47," July, 1936, and "Monthly Progress Report No. 48," August, 1936.

13. E. O. 7027 cited in Samuel I. Rosenman, ed., *The Papers and Addresses of Franklin D. Roosevelt*, 4: 144.

14. U.S., *Statutes at Large*, 40, pt. 1: 2035–36.

15. U.S., Congress, House Subcommittee of Committee on Ways and Means, *Hearings on H.R. 12876, Payments in Lieu of Taxes on Resettlement Projects*, 74th Cong., 2d sess., 1936, p. 3.

16. Interview with Warren J. Vinton.

17. U.S., Congress, House, *Hearings on Payments in Lieu of Taxes . . .*, p. 38.

18. Ibid., pp. 38–39.

19. U.S., Resettlement Administration, *First Annual Report*, p. 44.

20. Letter from Lansill to Monroe Oppenheimer, January 26, 1937, R.O.A., H.H.F.A., Drawer 527.

21. Letter from Martin G. White, solicitor, U.S. Department of Agriculture, to Lansill, February 12, 1937, R.O.A., H.H.F.A., Drawer 527. On January 1, 1937, the Resettlement Administration was transferred to the Department of Agriculture by Executive Order 7530.

22. Ibid.

23. *Baltimore Sun*, October 16, 17, 1935.

24. *Washington Post*, October 17, 18, 1935.

25. Ibid., March 3, 1936.

26. Letter from Charles C. Marbary to Clarence I. Blau, chief of the Community Management Section, General Counsel's Office, March 16, 1936, R.O.A., H.H.F.A., Drawer 527.

27. Maryland, General Assembly, Senate, *Journal of Proceedings*, January, 1937, Session (Baltimore, 1937), pp. 1532–38.

28. Ibid., pp. 1456–57.

29. Ibid., p. 1456.

30. Ibid., p. 1457.

31. Ibid.

32. Ibid., pp. 1551–56.

33. Memo from Monroe Oppenheimer to Solicitor White of the U.S., Department of Agriculture, March 30, 1937, R.O.A., H.H.F.A.

34. Letter from Oppenneimer to Solicitor White, April 6, 1937, R.O.A., H.H.F.A.

35. Ibid.

36. "Report on Relationship of Greendale to Milwaukee Regional Planning," Reports and Recommendations, Greendale, Wisconsin, prepared by Greendale Planning Staff, Book 1 (April 14, 1937) (in Public Housing Administration Library, Washington, D.C.).

37. Clarence I. Blau to Lansill, December 30, 1935, National Archives, Record Group 96, Box 308.

38. U.S., Resettlement Administration, Research Section, "Report on Government and Taxes for the Greendale Project," April 4, 1936, R.O.A., H.H.F.A., Drawer 535.

39. Letter from the Public Service Commission of Wisconsin to Walter E. Kroening, R.A. community manager of Greendale, October 5, 1936, Reports and Recommendations, Greendale, Wisconsin, prepared by Greendale Planning Staff, Book 2 (in Public Housing Administration Library, Washington, D.C.).

40. Blau to Lansill, December 30, 1935, National Archives, Record Group 96.

41. "Incorporation File: Greendale," R.O.A., H.H.F.A., Drawer 535.

42. Memo from Blau to Lansill, February 10, 1937, R.O.A., H.H.F.A., Drawer 530.

43. U.S., Federal Public Housing Authority, "Greenbelt Communities," November, 1945, Washington, D.C. (mimeographed).

8

🍁 TENANT SELECTION

Every community is judged not only by its buildings and landscape, but by its residents—individually and as a society. Perhaps the most crucial aspect of the social and political planning of the greenbelt towns was the selection of the people who would live in them. The planners were certain they had created an outstanding physical environment, but none could accurately predict what would happen when hundreds of families were thrown together in the new communities. Would the residents like the town? Would they get along with each other, with the residents in neighboring towns, and with the federal government?

The Resettlement Administration took very few risks in selecting the families to live in the towns. Each new resident was carefully screened. There is no evidence that the R.A. considered housing a true cross section of moderate- or low-income families or that the need for better living conditions constituted the sole basis for selection. The choice of tenants was made from a very large number of applicants. Over 5,700 families applied for the 885 homes in Greenbelt, 2,700 for the 676 homes in Greenhills, and over 3,000 for the 572 homes in Greendale.[1] Frank H. Osterlinder, the R.A.'s regional attorney in the Milwaukee area, wrote, "It is interesting and pitiful to see the large number of applications of citizens who are desirous of becoming occupants of these government homes."[2] Reports on living conditions of several of the families admitted to Greendale give an indication of the need for better housing and neighborhoods:

> Young couple, one child: Present housing one room, serves as living room, bedroom and dining room. Poorly heated. Entrance on alley. Landlord will not allow the child to play in yard. . . .
> Couple, one child: Now pay 43 per cent of $1,650 income for rent. Will pay 25 per cent at Greendale.
> Childless couple: Now live in one furnished room and makeshift kitchen partitioned off in attic. Kerosene stove. Entrance through landlord's living room. Share bathroom with two other families.
> Couple, three children: Present house small and overcrowded. Kitchen in attic. Bathroom only source of water.

The letters of application also reveal the plight of those families seeking entrance to the greenbelt towns as evidenced in the following:

> We are a young married couple with no children, as yet, but are looking forward to Greenbelt to solve that privilege, as we have not, heretofore, felt that the high rent here in Washington gave us the right to have a child on our modest income.
>
> . . . .
>
> The expenses for my little girl's last two operations have handicapped me so that it is next to impossible to make ends

meet and I simply must have a decent, clean and healthy place for these youngsters which I cannot find in or around Washington for the amount of money I can afford to pay. . . . My need is desparate from the financial standpoint and also for my children's health sake. My salary being only $1,440 out of which I have $21 a month to pay for old hospital and doctor's bill . . . This you can readily see leaves me a very limited income to cover the little girl's care, rent, food, transportation and clothes.

.   .   .   .

I have looked for a place that we can afford until I am about on my last legs, and my husband told me something that scared me last night, too,—he said they told him when he filled out the questionnaire for Greenbelt that they didn't want "movers." Now, we don't want to be movers; it isn't in our blood to be. My husband was reared in the home his grandfather homesteaded in Kansas and I lived all my life in the same home in Tuscaloosa County in Alabama. My mother was reared in the same home her grandmother was and my grandfather's people were all home owners too. I'd almost think I was in heaven to live in a place like Greenbelt where my little boy could get in the sunshine in safety.[3]

It was initially announced that only families of "low income" would be selected as residents of the greenbelt towns.[4] This was defined by the government as $1,000–$1,999 income per year. Those who earned $2,000–$2,500 were defined as the "middle income" group, while those earning below $1,000 were labeled the "relief group."[5] Greenbrook, New Jersey, was planned with a goal to house families of 4.4 persons with an average annual income of $1,200, but included units for families with incomes as low as $1,000. Yet no way was found of cutting the physical facilities and maintenance costs to the point where families of 4.4 persons with $1,000 incomes could be housed. They would have had to pay more than twenty-two and one-half percent of their budget for rent (the percentage judged to be maximum for housing excluding utility costs), or the government would have had to subsidize their rent.[6] Clarence Stein's studies for the R.A. were based on an average family size of 4 persons with an average annual income of $1,250.[7] By the fall of 1936 the R.A. had to change the income range of prospective families to $1,200–$2,000 and began to call the future tenants "moderate income" families.[8] Actually the income and rental schedules were sliding ones depending on family size:

Number of Persons	Income
One	$ 800–$1,600
Two	$ 900–$1,650
Three	$1,000–$1,800
Four	$1,100–$2,000
Five	$1,200–$2,100
Six	$1,300–$2,200[9]

As of June 30, 1938, the average annual income for families in the three towns was: Greenbelt, $1,560; Greenhills, $1,771; and Greendale, $1,624.[10] The rent schedule was based on the assumption by the R.A. that each family should pay twenty-five percent of its income for rent and utilities charges (heat, water and electricity or gas).[11] Therefore the actual shelter rent on a one and a half room apartment was $18.00, but with the added charges for utilities the monthly rent was $21.00.[12] Because of this there appeared conflicting reports of the rent schedules in various publications. The original rent schedule, including the utility costs was:

Number of Rooms	Cost
1½ (apartment)	$21.00
2½	27.00
3	29.00
4 (row house)	31.00
5	34.50
5½	37.00
6	39.00
6½	41.00
4½ (single house)	45.00[13]

Almost as many families were probably too poor to enter the greenbelt towns as were too wealthy. Tugwell himself said that the majority of American city dwellers in 1936 earned less than $1,200 per year.[14] On the other hand rents at Greenbelt averaged $31.23 for all units while the District of Columbia Public Utilities Commission stated that there were "few houses fit for human habitation" in the District for under $35.00.[15] Rents in the greenbelt towns were approximately the same as P.W.A housing project rents. The average rent (including utilities) in the P.W.A. projects was $7.50 per room.[16] At Greenbelt the four and five room row houses (which are the most common) averaged $7.32 per room.[17] Rents at the other towns were slightly different. At Greenhills rents ranged from $18.00 to $42.00 and averaged $27.62. The range at Greendale was from $19.00 to $36.00 since it contained no six room units as did the other two towns.[18] Average rent at Greendale was $29.16 until 1939 when the Farm Security Administration lowered it to $27.95 to compensate for a drop in wages and employment in the Milwaukee area.[19]

More elusive than the income criteria were the standards designed to preclude families which might detract from the development of a wholesome, solid, and stable community. The first week after the announcement of the greenbelt town program, the R.A. reassured the doubting Senator Sasscer concerning the future residents. It was confirmed that they would be "chosen not from the relief rolls, but from among the low income workers in the Washington and Prince George's County area whose record proves them to be citizens of character and reliability."[20] Again in March, 1936, Wallace Richards was asked by a reporter about the fears of Prince George's County residents that Greenbelt would be populated with undesirable slum dwellers. "Prince George's County needn't worry," said Richards, "about a disreputable community. The Resettlement Administration will take no chances on the experiment failing because of being peopled by shiftless people."[21] John O. Walker, chief of the R.A.'s management division, stated in the *Interim Report* that, in the interest of low-cost maintenance, families would be selected to insure long-term occupancy. The families would need not only "economic security, but a reasonable, though adequate, educational and social development."[22] Walker stated elsewhere that families were excluded which posed "any exceptional social problems."[23] In short, the policy of the Family Selection Section of the Management Division was "to make sure, before any family is accepted, that it will fit into the proposed community with benefit both to itself and to the community."[24]

Each family filed an application form giving family size, income, present housing facilities, and other information which allowed the Family Selection Section to screen out those not meeting general requirements. Unfortunately, no copies of the form have survived to provide us with the bases on which 3,400 to 5,700 applicants to Greenbelt were eliminated.[25] Many applicants were rejected because their income was over the maximum allowable. One Greenbelt official said that "quite a few" had incomes over $5,000.[26] Families accepted for investigation were subsequently interviewed by a five-man family selection committee. Following this a social worker visited each family in its home and filled out a "rating sheet." Families were rated on the conditions of their present housing and also on personal habits and attitudes. Social workers were to determine whether a family in debt was trying to pay it off or was unconcerned, whether they were "neat and clean" or "very tidy," whether they were members of a "socially acceptable organization" or one "likely to conflict with project objectives," and whether they possessed "questionable family life and social attitudes" or were a "well integrated family group—normal, home loving, self-respecting."[27] A credit check was made and references from two landlords were reviewed. Finally, a physical examination was required for each family.

If the need of the applying family was desperate, its financial stability might not count so high on the application. Some of these families and others were favored because of their atti-

tudes towards community life in general and towards the greenbelt town in particular. At Greenbelt, in fact, some whose credit
was on the borderline were admitted because of their interest in
the greenbelt experiment and because of the inadequacy of
their other housing facilities.[28] Of all the "community participation" requirements, the one eliminating the most applicants prohibited wives of employed husbands to work. In the Washington
area one-third of all families were ineligible for consideration
because of this rule. Undoubtedly a number of these families
would have dropped below the $1,000 annual income require-
ment if the wife stopped working. This regulation later caused
some conflict between the greenbelt town residents and the
government.

Some effort was made to reflect the diversity of the metropolitan population within the income limitations, of course.
Greenbelt, in the first years, attempted to retain a religious ratio
of 30 percent Roman Catholic, 7 percent Jewish and 63 percent
Protestant, the same as the District of Columbia in the 1930
census. It was considered desirable to have one-third of the
families employed outside the federal government.[29] Selection was made without regard to political affiliations or views.
There were no charges that politics influenced the choice of residents. All three towns embraced citizens with political philos-
ophies from socialism to laissez faire capitalism.[30] Each of the
towns soon had both Republican and Democratic Clubs, although the latter outnumbered the former in the early years.
This may reflect the previous local party affiliations of families
in the moderate income strata. The selectivity of the R.A. may
overshadow this effort to assimilate diverse elements in the
towns, but Carlton F. Sharpe later recalled that the residents
of Greenhills were "a pretty good cross section of the moderate
income group despite the screening process."[31]

The most inflexible rule excluded Negro applicants. In June,
1936, during the early planning stages of Greenbelt, Maryland
(while it was still under the direction of the Subsistence Homesteads Division), the plan called for "a separate development
area, the Rossville Rural Development, which will be for Negro

families." It was to have included 800 acres—almost one-third of the entire Greenbelt tract which was then planned for 2,796 acres.[32] However, when the Greenbelt, Maryland, project was officially announced in October, 1935, eight months before the Rossville Development was planned, Will Alexander admitted "that there is little likelihood that any of the houses will be rented to colored tenants."[33] Actually, several Negro families lived on Greenbelt's farms, but they numbered only fourteen and played no part in the life of the community.[34] Cedric Larson, who studied the tenant selection policies and interviewed its directors, explained in 1938 that "Negroes were not admitted as residents, since they have their own low cost housing project in Northeast Washington . . . called Langston Terrace."[35]

This discrimination on the part of the Suburban Division is nowhere explained in the existing records of the Resettlement Administration, but it probably deferred to the local communities adjacent to the towns and to the prevailing views of Congress on integrated public housing. Local residents as well as the powerful State Senator Sasscer, it will be recalled, had strongly objected to the possible inclusion of Negro residents at Greenbelt.[36] There was no mandatory policy for federal housing projects to separate the races. In fact, Langston Terrace in Washington, built by the P.W.A., had a few white residents; and the P.W.A. project in Milwaukee, Parklawn, had both white and Negro residents in 1938. Still, these two were among only ten of the forty-nine P.W.A. housing projects that were racially integrated by 1938.[37] The inequity of this racial policy is immeasurable. In the opinion of Edith Elmer Wood, in an Interior Department study, the worst slums of Washington, Baltimore, Cincinnati, and Milwaukee were Negro slums.[38] It is not known how many applied and were rejected by the Suburban Division, but there was interest on the part of the Negro community in the suburban town program. A group in Toledo, Ohio, asked the R.A. about having a suburban community built outside Toledo; yet there is no record of any motion in that direction by the Planning Section.[39]

The racial exclusiveness of the greenbelt towns stands in

contrast to other R.A. (later F.S.A.) programs in which Negroes
were discriminated against, but were at least allowed entrance.[40]
Tugwell, for example, told the R.A.'s regional director in Illinois
and Missouri to see that Negroes were given an equal opportunity to receive aid from the R.A.[41] Will Alexander's long ca-
reer on behalf of Negro advancement speaks for itself, but apparently neither man intervened in this program. C. B. Baldwin
later regretted the segregation in the towns but added that at
the time there was no support for integration and they were
involved in controversy enough. Neither the N.A.A.C.P. nor
any other Negro group protested the segregation.[42] The R.A.'s
statement in its report to the Senate that the employees constructing the greenbelt towns "are prospective occupants," must
have rung with familiar hollowness to the many Negroes who
helped build those towns.[43]

The Resettlement Administration sought to insure the general success of the greenbelt towns, both as social and physical
experiments, by rigorously excluding those whose backgrounds
might create problems and inevitable bad publicity. This was
undoubtedly a policy dictated by practitioners of realpolitik. It
was unfortunately proven wrong by subsequent events. Even
with conservative tenant policies practically guaranteeing a social success, the greenbelt towns failed to influence either private developers or public housing policies. The towns would
have provided a much more useful social experiment had they
been opened to very low income groups to test the effect of *community* housing projects on a mixture of moderate- and low-
income families. Later public housing projects, containing none
of the physical features of the greenbelt towns and none of the
local autonomy, did admit low-income families and the result,
as is well known, was only the most negligible improvement of
the social structure. Perhaps the greenbelt towns would have
had little effect on the social structure of a true cross section of
the nation's poor, but that will never be known.

A true cross section of the poor, of course, would have included a sizable group of Negroes. The exclusion of this entire

group from the only suburban public housing projects ever built in this nation is tragically in line with the long history Negro exclusion from suburban areas. The boldness of the R.A.'s physical planning is hardly matched by the boldness or even the basic equity of the social planning.

1. Cedric A. Larson, "Educational Activities of the Federally Planned Community of Greenbelt, Maryland" (Master's thesis, George Washington University, 1939), p. 28; *Cincinnati Post*, February 24, 1937; and *Milwaukee Journal*, May 9, 1938.

2. Frank Osterlind to Victor Rotnem, n.d. [1938], R.O.A., H.H.F.A., Drawer 535.

3. The reports from Greendale were printed in the *Milwaukee Journal*, April 17, 1938; the letters are excerpts from those written by applicants for Greenbelt and are in the Lansill Papers, personal files.

4. U.S., Resettlement Administration, Press Release, October 11, 1935, Roosevelt Papers, O.F. 1568; and U.S., Resettlement Administration, *Interim Report*, p. 23.

5. For a discussion of New Deal income group definitions, see Carol Aronovici and Elizabeth McCalmont, *Catching Up with Housing*, pp. 22–26. The position of the R.A. is confused by the *Interim Report* which stated that both the subsistence homesteads and suburban projects "are intended for low-income workers, $1,600 per year is normally taken as the upper limit." U.S., Resettlement Administration, *Interim Report*, p. 23.

6. Memo from Henry Wright to Frederick Bigger, December 16, 1935, National Archives, Record Group 96, Box 308.

7. Stein, "Shopping Centers: A Report to the Resettlement Administration, 1935," in his *Towards New Towns for America*, pp. 162–64.

8. U.S., Resettlement Administration, *What the Resettlement Administration Has Done*, p. 13 (pamphlet); and U.S., Resettlement Administration, *First Annual Report*, p. 43.

9. Richard B. Hall, "Appraised Report and Valuation Analysis of Greenbelt, Maryland," R.O.A., H.H.F.A., Drawer 538, Part 1 (November 30, 1948), p. 4.

10. U.S., Farm Security Administration, *Annual Report: 1938* (Washington: U.S. Government Printing Office, 1938), p. 20.

11. Memo from Robert C. McManus to John S. Lansill, March 28, 1936, Lansill Papers, official files.

12. There was also a schedule for utility charges—the charge increasing with the size of the unit. See O. Kline, Fulmer, *Greenbelt*, p. 43.

13. Hall, "Appraised Report and Valuation Analysis of Greenbelt, Maryland," R.O.A., H.H.F.A., Drawer 538, Part I (November 30, 1948), pp. 5–6.

14. Rexford G. Tugwell, "Housing Activities and Plans of the Resettlement Administration," *Housing Yearbook, 1936*, p. 30.

15. *Baltimore Sun*, June 5, 1936.

16. Broadus Mitchell, *Depression Decade 1929–1941*, p. 333.

17. The figure is an average of the $7.75 per room rent in the four-room unit and the $6.90 per room rent in the five-room unit.

18. John O. Walker, "A Demonstration in Community Planning," *Shelter* 3 (February, 1939): 36; Walker, "Greenbelt Towns," *Shelter* 3 (January, 1939): 23.

19. *Greendale Review*, March 11, 1939.

20. *Baltimore Sun*, October 17, 1935.

21. *Washington Star*, March 18, 1936.

22. U.S., Resettlement Administration, *Interim Report*, pp. 23–24.

23. Walker, "Greenbelt Towns," p. 21.

24. U.S., Resettlement Administration, *First Annual Report*, p. 64.

25. The most complete discussion of family selection for Greenbelt, Maryland, is contained in Larson, "Educational Activities," pp. 27–30.

26. Fulmer, *Greenbelt*, p. 18.

27. Larson, "Educational Activities," p. 154.

28. Ibid., pp. 28–30; Fulmer, *Greenbelt*, pp. 18–19; and Wendall Lund, "Tenant Selection at Greenbelt," *Greenbelt Cooperator*, December 22, 1937.

29. Larson, "Educational Activities," pp. 29–30; Fulmer, *Greenbelt*, pp. 18–19; and William Form, "The Sociology of a White Collar Suburb, Greenbelt, Maryland" (Ph.D. dissertation, University of Maryland, 1944), pp. 61, 64.

30. In the presidential election of 1940, for example, Greendale's citizens cast 871 votes for Roosevelt, 196 for Wilke, 33 for Norman Thomas, and three for the Communist candidate, Earl Browder (*Greendale Review*, November 12, 1940).

31. Letter to the author from Carlton F. Sharpe October 22, 1964. Sharpe was the first community manager of Greenhills, Ohio.

32. U.S., Resettlement Administration, "Project Description Book: 1937," National Archives, Record Group 96.

33. *Washington Post*, October 12, 1935.

34. Form, "Sociology of a White Collar Suburb," pp. 63, 217.

35. Cedric Larson, "Greenbelt, Maryland: A Federally Planned Community," *National Municipal Review* 27 (August, 1938): 413–20.

36. *Baltimore Sun*, October 15, 16, 1935.

37. Robert C. Weaver, "The Negro in a Program of Public Housing," *Opportunity* 16 (July, 1938): 198–203.

38. Edith Elmer Wood, *Slums and Blighted Areas in the United States*, pp. 54, 64, 68–69.

39. Letter from Warren J. Vinton to Raymond C. Smith, director of Region No. 3, August 10, 1936, National Archives, Record Group 96, Box 229.

40. Baldwin, *Poverty and Politics*, pp. 196–97, 200–201.

41. Letter from Rexford G. Tugwell to R. C. Smith, director of Region No. 3, March 10, 1936, National Archives, Record Group 96, Box 229.

42. Interview with C. B. Baldwin.

43. U.S., Congress, Senate, *Resettlement Administration Program: In Response to Senate Resolution No. 295*, 74th Cong., 2d sess., 1936, Senate Doc. 213, p. 19.

9

🍁 FEDERAL MANAGEMENT

The management of the towns was part of a complex intergovernmental arrangement which functioned surprisingly well. The key figure in the administrative machinery was the federally appointed community manager in each town. In each case this individual also happened to be elected by the town councils to the local office of town manager.[1] His salary was paid by the federal government except in his capacity as town manager, for which he was paid a token salary of $1.00 per year by his respective town.[2] The R.A. was very fortunate to select three men who share equally the distinction of being directly responsible for creating the greenbelt communities. Roy S. Braden was the oldest and most experienced of the three. In 1940, during his tenure at Greenbelt, he was elected president of the International City Manager's Association. Sherwood Reeder, manager at Greendale, and Carlton Sharpe, manager at Greenhills, were both graduates of the Syracuse University School of Public Administration and the National Institute of Public Administration in New York City. Reeder had been assistant manager of Cleveland and Sharpe had been assistant manager of St. Petersburg, Florida. All three men left their positions with towns during the Second World War. Braden left to take another city manager position; Reeder and Sharpe both left to work on defense housing. Sharpe went on to a distinguished career as the city manager of Hartford, Connecticut, and Kansas City, Missouri. In spite of the short tenure of the three men, they provided able and experienced leadership to these new towns where few, if any, of the citizens knew any thing about running a local government.

In addition to the community/town manager, the town treasurer, the solicitor, the town clerk, and the director of adult education in each town, were paid directly by the federal government.[3] The balance of local employee salaries was paid by the towns with funds received annually from the federal government. The dual status of the community/town manager and other officials caused no serious problems in the early years because there was little friction between the locally elected town councils and the federal government. More complicated difficulties were encountered after 1945 under the stress of negotiations between the residents and the federal government over the dispossession of the towns.

Power over the local officials of the towns came from the Resettlement Administration—Colonel John O. Walker, chief of the Management Division, Administrator Will Alexander, and succeeding him, C. B. Baldwin. By the time the first residents moved into Greenbelt, of course, the Resettlement Administration had been absorbed by the Department of Agriculture. This was the first transfer of the greenbelt towns. By the end of 1947, they had been administered by five different agencies: Resettlement Administration (1935–37), Farm Security Administration (1937–42),[4] National Housing Agency (1942), Federal Public Housing Administration (1942–47), and the Public

Housing Administration (1947–54). Fortunately the towns had good friends in the Farm Security Administration. John O. Walker maintained close and friendly relations with the local town officials—particularly the community / town managers.[5] Will Alexander, C. B. Baldwin, and other F.S.A. officials were deeply interested in helping the residents develop their communities.[6] However, as Alexander himself later stated, the entire R.A. program was regarded with suspicion by the conservative element in the Department of Agriculture. Many members had opposed the merger of the two departments.[7]

The peculiar nature of the towns tended to blur jurisdictional rights. In 1937 and 1938 there was constant correspondence between the town solicitors and the F.S.A. regarding the legal power of the towns to perform such acts as insuring property or prohibiting hunting on the greenbelt. At Greendale, Sherwood Reeder asked permission to fumigate the tenants' furniture before it was moved into the new homes.[8] In these, as in most cases, the Department of Agriculture responded that the Bankhead-Black Act permitted such actions.[9] However, such a minor request as one to obtain land in the towns for new roads required the signed approval of the president under the same act.[10] A most ingenious arrangement was made to cut the grass at Greenbelt—a Kafkaesque example of intergovernmental accommodation. The town cut the grass next to the streets, and the F.S.A. cut it to everywhere else except for areas adjacent to the apartments where individual residents cut it.[11]

Some examples of the regulations imposed on the residents illustrate common concern for the success of the towns. At Greenbelt, Manager Roy S. Braden requested the people to keep off newly-seeded lawns, report contagious diseases, keep children from speeding through underpasses and roller skating near the houses after dark, refrain from making undue noise in the evening, and see that cars were parked in the spaces provided.[12] Rules governing the homes were the usual ones found in most private rental units. Repairs were to be made by the maintenance staff and interior alterations such as painting could be made with managerial permission.[13] Some rules made by the F.S.A.

and the town councils indicate an exaggerated regard for the physical appearance of the towns. Because of the "most unattractive appearance" of clothes hanging on the lines in Greenbelt, outside drying of clothes was prohibited after four P.M. on weekdays and all day Sunday.[14] In December of 1937 some residents of Greenbelt wanted the ban on owning dogs lifted so they could give their children puppies for Christmas. The F.S.A. refused; and, as in most other cases, the residents voted to uphold the decision by three to one.[15] In Greenhills the same issue was raised, and a referendum in 1940 indicated the majority of residents wanted dogs so the rule was changed.[16] Apparently the only rule which Greenbelt's people refused to obey was one dictated by their own town council. On June 26, 1939, an ordinance was passed prohibiting the wearing of bathing suits and shorts in the town center. It was ridiculed by the *Cooperator*, scorned by the Washington papers, and ignored by Greenbelt's sweltering citizens. After a few futile efforts the Greenbelt police also ignored it.[17] Generally, the record seems to show that the people of the towns were satisfied with the local administration of their communities in the early years of existence.[18]

Many problems were similar to those in any private housing project, except that the F.S.A. was more solicitous of the tenants. The tenants, in turn, were less prone to complain and generally obeyed regulations with good humor. The regulations were considered so complicated that it was difficult to understand them at Greendale, but no substantial grievances emerged.[19] There is some evidence that a few of Greenbelt's residents feared eviction if they complained, but this never occurred.[20] If it had, the town newspapers would have protested vigorously, and the national press would have used it as an example of the rigidity of regimentation. The only study made of residents who left the towns concerned the sixty-five families who left Greendale between 1938 and 1942. It was found that in no case did management pressure force them to leave. They were either incompatible with, and rejected by, the other residents, or they were unhappy living under the stigma of public housing.[21]

Two unique problems arose at Greenbelt. Due to the high

number of government employees there, the town government suffered from a lack of qualified people to serve. Government employees were covered by the Hatch Act of August 2, 1939, which, according to the Federal Civil Service, barred them from running for local offices or participating in local political affairs. In February, 1940, the *Greenbelt Cooperator* complained that the act "cheated the local governments of the best material."[22] In October of the same year the commissioner of Civil Service allowed government employees to hold elective offices in Greenbelt provided they remained nonpartisan and were not associated with any local, state, or national partisan organizations.[23]

The other problem involved relations with Prince George's County and the state of Maryland. At first, the residents of Greenbelt were not allowed to vote in any state or local elections or to participate in any of the state or county health services. Yet they were required to purchase Maryland driver's licenses and pay a state personal property tax.[24] In August, 1938, the Maryland attorney general ruled that Greenbelt was a part of the state of Maryland and therefore its residents were citizens of the state with all rights and responsibilities thus accruing.[25] Not until January, 1940, however, did the Maryland State Health Department agree to include Greenbelt in the Prince George's County health programs—even the vaccination plan.[26]

The initial suspicion and prejudice in the county was gradually overcome as the advantages of Greenbelt's high school, recreational facilities, hospital-clinic, and cooperative stores were recognized.[27] Moreover, payments-in-lieu-of-taxes for Greenbelt were always far above any tax rate for any other Maryland community.[28] The local Democratic leadership was not changed by the influx of new voters, in spite of the fact that Greenbelt immediately became the second largest community in the county and moved to first place in 1941.[29] Greenbelt citizens took an active interest in local affairs during the prewar years, but during the war the turnover was so high that few residents voted in the county elections. In 1943 only 200 out of 1500 eligible voters in Greenbelt registered for the local election.[30] Only after the sale of the town did residents resume an interest in local politics. Greendale and Greenhills experienced little or no difficulty assimilating with the local political structure.

Neither town planners nor government administrators made adequate provisions for commuting. When Greenbelt opened, there was no direct transportation to Washington, which was a distance of thirteen miles. Residents without automobiles had to find a way to Branchville, Maryland, several miles away, where a trolley would take them to Mount Rainier, and then another trolley would take them to the city. In November, 1937, the Greenbelt Citizens' Association formed a committee to study the problem. The F.S.A. agreed to finance bus service to Washington by contract with the Capital Transit Company of Washington. Lack of patronage caused a deficit of $10,000 during the first twelve months of service.[31] There seemed to be no profitable way to serve so small and distant a suburb, even at a weekly cost of $1.75 per person. In early March, 1939, the F.S.A. decided not to subsidize C.T.C. losses any longer. The company then announced that after April 7, direct bus service to Washington would end and service to the Mount Rainier trolley line would commence—at an increased cost of $2.00 per week. An overflow crowd at the next Citizens' Association meeting voted to protest to the Interstate Commerce Commission. The Capital Transit Company was accused of "inadequate service, questionable bookkeeping, and a general dictatorial attitude."[32] The direct bus service ended on schedule, the I.C.C. took no action, and Greenbelt residents bought twenty-six used cars in the first two weeks after the service ended.[33]

By the end of 1939 sixty-five percent of the Greenbelt families owned automobiles—a considerable financial sacrifice judging from the fact that only thrity-three percent even had telephones.[34] There was a short-lived attempt to operate shuttle station wagons to Washington, but most people either drove in car pools or spent an hour or two on busses and street cars.

Transportation was a continuing problem.[35] With the war came gasoline rationing and increased difficulty in using an automobile. The Capital Transit Company cited the war as a reason for terminating bus service to Mount Rainier in September, 1943, forcing residents to drive or ride to Branchville to get a trolley to Mount Rainier. The Greenbelters appealed to the Maryland Public Service Commission, the Federal Public Housing Administration, and the Federal Office of Defense Transportation. This time they won, and the Mount Rainier service was restored.[36] After the war the C.T.C. succeeded in cutting service back to Branchville and by 1949 raised the cost to $3.80 per week. In 1951, after the completion of the Baltimore-Washington Parkway reduced driving time from forty-five to thirty minutes, the C.T.C. ended all service to Greenbelt.[37] In 1965, with the opening of the Washington Beltway which runs through the center of the town, Greenbelt finally had a highway system linking it with the Baltimore-Washington metropolitan area.

At Greendale, the *Greendale Review* admitted in 1940 that its transportation problem was not as severe as that at Greenbelt. This gave little comfort to the commuters who sometimes spent over an hour traveling to work and another hour back home.[38] The needs of Greendale were complicated by the fact that, although Greendale was closer to the center of Milwaukee, many men worked at factories scattered throughout the area. When the Wisconsin Public Service Commission was approached for service in September, 1938, several different groups petitioned for different bus routes.[39] Bus service began in January, 1939, on a six month trial basis. At the end of the period the Midland Coach Lines reported losses due to low patronage, and service was ended with the approval of the Public Service Commission. A new company, the Milwaukee Electric Railway Company, furnished transportation to the end of the Milwaukee Transit System—and charged the same rate the first company had charged to go to the center of the city.[40] Service remained poor until the 1950s when Loomis Road, the main route between Greendale and Milwaukee, was widened into a limited access highway.[41]

Greenhills was located halfway between Cincinnati and Hamilton, Ohio, and residents worked in both places as well as in towns in between along the Mill Creek Valley. The Cincinnati Street Railway Company refused an R.A. request for service to Greenhills unless it could depend on a government subsidy.[42] During the first months there was no transportation for the public from Greenhills. Those traveling to Cincinnati drove to the end of the city bus line at North College Hill, approximately six miles.[43] A private bus company, the Greenhills Transportation Company, was formed in early 1939 its single antique bus made several trips per day into Cincinnati—when it was not overheating. The same year another bus company began service to Hamilton.[44] Obviously most residents relied on automobiles for transportation.

Attracting industry to the towns might have improved the commuting problem. At Greenbelt, however, little initial interest in that possibility was shown on the part of citizens or the government. Louis Bessemer, Greenbelt's first mayor, introduced a resolution in the town council in November, 1938, to ask the F.S.A. for $10,000 to survey the industrial potential of the town, but it was tabled. One council member said such a survey was not the responsibility of the Town Council, and another questioned the value of industrial development in Greenbelt. The following issue of the *Cooperator* stated that while a survey was a good idea, development of local agriculture and the processing of agricultural products would be "in keeping with the preconceived nature of Greenbelt."[45] At that time the majority of residents were long-term civil service employees and may not have had interest in industrial employment. But by the beginning of 1944 the situation had changed drastically. Although over eighty percent of the residents were government employees, many were in temporary wartime positions which would terminate at the end of the war. In January, 1944, the Citizens' Association invited Arthur S. Fleming to discuss postwar employment prospects for Greenbelt's federal employees.[46] The following month the town council unanimously passed a resolution to ask the Federal Public Housing Administration to allow the town to offer industrial sites along the Baltimore and Ohio tracks in the northwest corner of the town limits.[47] The Federal Public Housing Administration took no action and development of an industrial area waited until the 1960s.[48] Greendale did not develop an industrial area, which was called for in the original plans, until it was transferred to private control. Greenhills, built on rolling hills, is not suitable for the construction of industrial plants.

Income limitations on the residents led to continual reevaluation of their rights. Again, Greenbelt serves as the most detailed example of the problem. Families with incomes exceeding the maximum set figure were to be evicted from the town. This penalized those who were presumably rewarded by their employers and threatened to rob the town of some of its most educated and talented leaders. Further, it reinforced the belief of many residents that they were only temporary guests who would eventually be expected to move out and find a home of their own in a more permanent community. In 1939 the F.S.A. raised all income maximums by twenty-five percent but by the end of the year a number of families had exceeded the new maximum and faced eviction.[49]

A Special Committee on Community Life, which included George F. Warner, soon-to-be mayor of Greenbelt, Reverend Robert Kincheloe, pastor of the Community Church, and Walter Volkhausen, president of Greenbelt Consumer Services, was created. The committee requested an end to income limitations and a raise in rent for families with incomes exceeding the maximums. It noted that many government employees received raises which put them first at $2,300 and then to $2,600 push-them just $100 over the maximum for a family of four ($2,000 plus the twenty-five percent increase placed the maximum at $2,500).

You will not discover one family in Greenbelt which has a feeling of security of tenure which is the essence of home life and of community life because of the fear . . . that some day the family will get a raise and have to move.

This is the bed of sand on which we are attempting to build a more integrated community life. . . . This is the insecure foothold from which we are trying to better our relations with surrounding communities and establish our right to recognition by our county and our state.[50]

In mid–January, 1940, Alexander and John Walker agreed to allow families with incomes in excess of the revised maximum to pay more rent rather than be evicted.[51] This decision was reversed on November 1, 1941, and 300 families were told they would have to leave by March 31, 1942.[52] Again the F.S.A. changed the policy, and all families were allowed to stay at Greenbelt regardless of income.[53] At Greendale income limitation was not as severe a problem in the prewar years because a local recession in the Milwaukee area kept incomes generally lower than in other parts of the nation.[54]

A partial solution to the question of what to do with higher-income families residing in the towns was hoped for in some form of private home ownership. Respecting the desire of many families to own homes, the F.S.A. attempted to lease land to potential builders and to allow tenants to purchase the homes they inhabited.[55] These attempts were part of the basis on which cooperative homeowners' groups were formed.[56] However, all efforts towards private ownership in the towns were either tabled or aborted by the increasing demands of the war and the transfer of the towns to the Federal Public Housing Administration.[57] Most members of the homeowners' cooperatives built homes outside the towns.[58] Residents in Greendale had hoped the government might sell the entire town to a resident co-op, but as months passed without any action, they became exasperated and began leaving the town as soon as they saved enough money to purchase a house.[59]

The awkward position of the greenbelt towns, halfway between independent communities and government housing projects, created serious community problems. While stopping short of regimentation, federal management policies were intrusive enough to remind all residents that they remained in their new homes at the sufferance of a remote bureaucracy. This naturally lead to frustration and a feeling of impermanence. The failure of the Farm Security Administration to find a quick and simple method to allow the towns' residents to purchase their own dwellings or to build their own homes in the towns was a serious error. It was, unfortunately, only part of the general lethargy of F.S.A. in coming to grips with the fundamental purposes of the greenbelt town program. Engaged in far-flung and very controversial agricultural and rural development programs, it is not strange that the F.S.A. failed to respond to the original promise of its suburban stepchildren.

1. *City of Greenbelt, 25th Anniversary*, p. 13.

2. *Greenbelt Cooperator*, December 8, 1937, p. 2. When the towns came under the jurisdiction of the Federal Public Housing Administration in 1943, an attempt was made to clarify the dual status of its employees in the towns by requiring each town to pay these individuals at least $300.00 per year to signify their status as legal, full-time employees. See William Form, "The Sociology of a White Collar Suburb," p. 45.

3. Robert H. Shields to C. B. Baldwin, September 23, 1942, R.O.A., H.H.F.A., Drawer 527.

4. There was no change in the greenbelt administrative structure when the Resettlement Administration's name was changed to Farm Security Administration in September, 1937.

5. J. O. Walker to R. I. Nowell, April 28, 1937, National Archives, Record Group 96, Box 231.

6. Cedric A. Larson, "Educational Activities of the Federally Planned Community of Greenbelt, Maryland," p. 121.

7. Will W. Alexander, *Oral History Memoir*, p. 640–42.

8. Sherwood Reeder to John O. Walker, March 14, 1938, R.O.A., H.H.F.A., Drawer 536.

9. Mastin G. White, solicitor, U.S.D.A., to Major John O. Walker, July 18, 1938; and White to Alexander, November 25, 1938, R.O.A., H.H.F.A., Drawer 527.

10. Two such documents signed by President Roosevelt on January 13, 1936, and June 29, 1940, authorized the construction of roads at Greenhills, Ohio, R.O.A., H.H.F.A., Drawer 530.

11. Form, "The Sociology of a White Collar Suburb," p. 42 n.

12. Roy S. Braden to residents of Greenbelt, March 25, 1938 (mimeographed), Lansill Papers, official files.

13. *Greenbelt Manual* (1938), Records of the Public Housing Administration, Management Division, General Services Administration, Region 3 Records Center, Record Group 196, Accession Number 62A–651, Box 1 (hereafter cited as P.H.A., R.G. 196).

14. Braden to residents of Greenbelt, March 25, 1938, Lansill Papers, official files, p. 3.

15. *Greenbelt Cooperator*, December 22, 1937, February 23, 1938; and *City of Greenbelt, 25th Anniversary*, p. 39.

16. *Cincinnati Post*, April 3, 1940.

17. *Greenbelt Cooperator*, June 29, 1939; and *City of Greenbelt, 25th Anniversary*, p. 30.

18. Hugh Bone, "Greenbelt Faces 1939," *The American City* 54 (February, 1939): 59. William Form's extensive opinion polling at Greenbelt during 1942 and 1943 revealed that two-thirds of the residents found no fault with the federal administration of the community. See Form, "The Sociology of a White Collar Suburb," pp. 364–65.

19. *Greendale Review*, August 24, 1938.

20. *Greenbelt Cooperator*, March 23, 1939.

21. Douglas G. Marshall, "Greendale: A Study of a Resettlement Community" (Ph.D. diss., University of Wisconsin, 1943), pp. 54–57; and interview with Mrs. Ethel Shweer, Greendale, Wisconsin, February 4, 1965.

22. *Greenbelt Cooperator*, February 15, 1940.

23. Ibid., October 17, 1940.

24. Ibid., August 24, 1939; and memo to Alexander, March 30, 1939, R.O.A., H.H.F.A., Drawer 527.

25. *Greenbelt Cooperator*, August 3, 1938; and *New York Times*, August 28, 1938.

26. *Greenbelt Cooperator*, January 25, 1940.

27. Fulmer, *Greenbelt*, p. 36.

28. Hall, "Appraised Report and Valuation Analysis of Greenbelt, Maryland," R.O.A., H.H.F.A., Drawer 538, Part 1 (November 30, 1948), pp. 18–19; "Payments in Lieu of Taxes–Greenbelt, Maryland," P.H.A., R.G. 196, Box 14.

29. Milwaukee County includes the city of Milwaukee, and Hamilton County includes the city of Cincinnati.

30. Form, "The Sociology of a White Collar Suburb," p. 241.

31. *Greenbelt Cooperator*, November 24, 1937, August 3, 1938, September 21, 1938, and March 16, 1939.

32. Ibid., March 9 and 16, 1939, April 6, 1939.

33. *Greenbelt Cooperator*, April 27, 1939.

34. John O. Walker, "Life in a Greenbelt Community," *Shelter* 3 (December, 1938): 17; and Larson, "Educational Activities," p. 27.

35. *Greenbelt Cooperator*, September 9, 1940; and Philip S. Brown, "What Has Happened at Greenbelt?" *The New Republic* 105 (August 11, 1941): 184.

36. *Greenbelt Cooperator*, October 8, 1943.

37. Hall, "Appraised Report and Valuation Analysis of Greenbelt, Maryland," R.O.A., H.H.F.A., Drawer 538, Part 1 (November 30, 1948), pp. 2–3; and *City of Greenbelt, 25th Anniversary*, p. 6.

38. *Greendale Review*, December 15, 1938; May 1, 1940.

39. Ibid., September 23, 1938.

40. M. P. Frank to Mastin G. White, solicitor, U.S.D.A., March 29, 1941, R.O.A., H.H.F.A., Drawer 536.

41. Interview with John M. Kuglitsch, village manager, Greendale, Wisconsin, February 4, 1965.

42. Carlton F. Sharpe to Justin Hartzog, November 16, 1936, R.O.A., H.H.F.A., Drawer 530.

43. *Greenhills-Forest Park Journal*, Anniversary Edition, April 25, 1963.

44. Carlton Sharpe, "Progress Report of Greenhills Project," February 20, 1939, Lansill Papers, official files.

45. *Greenbelt Cooperator*, December 1 and 8, 1938.

46. Ibid., January 7, 1944.

47. Ibid., February 11, 1944.

48. An industrial park approximately a mile long and one-half mile wide along the B. & O. tracks was included in the Land Use Plan adopted by the Greenbelt City Council on March 8, 1965. *Annual Report 1964, City of Greenbelt, Maryland* (Greenbelt, Maryland, 1964), p. 5.

49. Brown, "What Has Happened at Greenbelt?" *The New Republic* 105 (August 11, 1945): 184.

50. *Greenbelt Cooperator*, January 11, 1940.

51. Ibid., January 18, 1940.

52. Ibid., November 7, 1941, March 13, 1942.

53. Ibid., March 13, 1942.

54. *Greendale Review*, March 6, 1940.

55. *Greenbelt Cooperator*, January 18, 1940, May 23, 1940, June 13, 1940, and July 25, 1940.

56. Ibid., March 28, 1941.

57. Ibid., July 25, 1941, December 19, 1941, January 30, 1942, May 8, 1942, and July 10, 1942.

58. Ibid., May 22, 1942.

59. *Greendale Review*, December 1, 1938, February 21, 1940, March 6, 1940, August 21, 1940, September 18, 1940, April 30, 1941; and Douglas G. Marshall, "Greendale," p. 34.

10

🍁 BUILDING A DEMOCRATIC AND
COOPERATIVE COMMUNITY

The creators of the greenbelt towns intended that the planned harmony of physical elements be paralleled by the development of political, social, and economic cooperation among the residents. Through face-to-face democracy residents would build a society in which there would be both individual freedom and mutual aid through cooperative institutions. The program was a mixture of the old New England town meeting, the mutual aid of the frontier towns, and the economic cooperatives of twentieth-century farmers—transformed to a suburban setting for white-collar and blue-collar consumers rather than agriculturalists. As a demonstration for the rest of the nation to follow, the greenbelt cooperative program was clearly more radical than the physical planning. The physical town could be imitated by the construction industry without major restructuring; but the spread of economic cooperation to a majority of consumers, not to mention manufacturers, would force a fundamental change in the American economic system. An editorial appearing when Greenbelt, Maryland, opened remarks that while the physical town was too costly to be of much value as a demonstration, the community of residents "will be the scene of a cooperative enterprise which the American people will watch with interest."[1]

The towns required a grass roots democratic structure not only to direct socioeconomic cooperation, but also to provide the normal services of an independent municipality. The federal government held all the land, but the residents held the keys to local political power through the charters of incorporation. Had these residents moved into a typical public housing project they would have noticed few changes beyond improved sanitation and prompt repairs. In terms of their socioeconomic existence, they would simply have traded one landlord, who was squeezing a profit, to another landlord who was not. By moving into one of the greenbelt towns, with all the physical, economic, and legal accouterments of an independent town, each resident achieved legal rights, political powers, and a common identity with fellow citizens that was quite impossible in a housing project. The further fact that the towns were without established patterns and institutions and were located several miles from the nearest community forced the first generation of residents to establish their own new society—a task which, for several years, transformed their lives.

The original residents took to heart Will Alexander's address to the first group entering Greenbelt, Maryland, in which he called them "pioneers . . . on a new frontier."[2] The pioneer motif stuck with the three towns in the prewar years. The Milwaukee *News-Sentinel* described the line of automobiles and trailers moving out of the city as a caravan of "uncovered wagons that bumped out to Greendale" taking the first families to the new town.[3] The *Cincinnati Post* compared the first residents moving into Greenhills with the city's founding fathers "trudging wearily into old Cincinnati."[4] The first issue of the *Greenbelt*

Cooperator carried an editorial entitled "We Pioneers."[5] The first issue of the *Greenhills News-Bulletin* included an editorial by Edwin B. Cunningham which read:

> We, the residents of Greenhills, are pioneers in the fullest sense of the word. . . . While we are not engaged in the conquest of a physical frontier, nevertheless, on our shoulders rests the solution of a problem most vital in our day . . . the art of getting along with each other. . . . It is as pioneers in this field that we can blaze paths of greater happiness.[6]

Greenbelt's residents were particularly self-conscious under the watchful observation of a generally hostile press. Residents wrote many letters to their own newspaper and to the city papers complaining about the unfair stories and the "ugly rumors" about the town.[7] One man urged his fellow citizens to do their complaining within the community rather than in the local papers which "under pressure of strong real estate interests . . . are endeavoring to ridicule our town. Our complaints . . . are excellent fodder for their slander."[8]

The following month, commenting on an article in the *Washington Star*, the *Cooperator* wrote that most residents were learning to "take with a grain of salt all 'news' of the newspapers when they hear warped reports of their community."[9] One Greenbelt resident was stopped in his government office by his supervisor and asked, "What do you really think of Greenbelt wives not being permitted to have babies unless the Administration gives its official okay?" An article was produced as the source of the absurd allegation.[10] So numerous were the reports of regimentation and sinister activities at Greenbelt that George F. Carnes, an early columnist for the *Cooperator*, wrote in the following vein:

> Something should be done for the sightseers who come out Greenbelt way over the weekends. It makes me feel bad to see the hurt look on their faces after they have spent the

whole afternoon vainly searching for signs of regimentation, liberty-throttling rules and restrictions and barefoot women who use their frigidaires for china closets.

. . . .

Why not a little entertainment for them? Say for instance some of us could put on the oldest, ragged clothes we have, pull a rickety chair out on the lawn facing the street and prop our bare feet up in the sunshine. That would give the visitors a chance to see how the underprivileged spends his Sundays, and then too, maybe some newspaper man would happen along and we would get our picture in the paper under a caption something like this: BAREFOOT GREENBELTER CAN'T TELL FRONT FROM BACKYARD.

Portable signs, something light which we could remove after the rubbernecks had gone back home, with large illustrations indicating the dire punishment which would befall anyone who was caught stepping on the grass, hanging out wash after four o'clock, or buying groceries outside of Greenbelt, would serve the purpose of convincing the trekkers that the trip wasn't in vain; that they had so much to be thankful for in the personal liberty and exercise of free will granted them by their own city government.

Then last, but not least, we could erect a small booth in which we could place a uniformed guard with instructions to salute any and everyone as they left our city limits.[11]

At the close of 1938, George A. Warner, town councilor and later mayor of Greenbelt, reminded his neighbors more seriously of "The Challenge of Nineteen Thirty-nine":

We in Greenbelt . . . have a contribution to make to history. . . . It is for us to prove that more can be accomplished cooperatively than selfishly. . . . Let us make our town a model of good fellowship, neighborliness, tolerance, and practical democracy.[12]

While Greenbelt attracted the most national publicity, the other two towns came in for a fair share of uncomfortable observation. At times the eyes of the world seemed to be, quite literally, on the residents. During the early weeks at Green-hills and Greendale, residents were often startled to see a group of visitors standing on their porches watching them eat dinner. For a time the F.S.A. was forced to limit tourists in the towns to weekends only.[13] On these occasions the entire town popula-tion became Sunday afternoon tour guides. The first "Guest Day" at Greendale attracted over 4,000 people.[14] In addition there were continual visits by professional groups, who were guided by young men employed by the National Youth Ad-ministration. A delegation from the Soviet Union preceded by a few months a group of Americans from a convention of the National Association of Real Estate Boards. The *Greendale Review* proudly told its readers that both the Communists and the real estate people were surprised and impressed by the community.[15] Visitors from hostile newspapers were regarded with suspicion and treated coldly. The *Greendale Review* cas-tigated the press for "hitting below the belt" by publishing er-roneous information about Greendale—particularly the allega-tion that its homes cost $16,400 each.[16]

The residents exercised strict discipline over any tendency to dependency on the F.S.A. An editorial in the *Greenbelt Co-operator* criticized those who would turn to the government for funds and equipment as supportive of criticism that people would only demand more if anything was given to them. "After all, this is not a slum clearance project, and we surely do not want either relief or charity. Let's stand on our own feet."[17] In August, 1938, when the possibility of building a recreation cen-ter was being discussed, the *Cooperator* asked that citizens either pay for it themselves or forget the idea and certainly not ask, "Won't the F.S.A. dish out another helping?"[18] The Green-dale Citizens' Association, discussing a proposal to build a com-munity center separate from the school, likewise decided not to seek government money. The majority of residents believed the F.S.A. had done enough for them and that they should fi-nance their own building. Even during the local recession in

1939, while Greendale residents eagerly sought federal aid for unemployment relief, they established their own Labor Relations Committee to find jobs for Greendale's unemployed and set up an Exchange of Skills Office where a register of available jobs and a list of those with particular skills were kept. The citizens complained bitterly about W.P.A. labor from Milwaukee completing the groundwork at Greendale when Greendale men were jobless. So serious was the unemployment that a special fund was established by the Citizens' Association in early 1940 to help the needy of Greendale.[19] Greenbelt citizens also sought government help to relieve unemployment there but to no avail. The situation continued through 1939 until May, 1940, during which time the wage earners of more than forty Greenbelt families were out of work.[20]

There is no question that the towns relied on federal officials—particularly the community / town manager—for initial direction and continuing advice. But the local societies and institutions grew primarily through the enthusiastic efforts of almost every citizen. During the first year at Greenbelt approximately thirty-five organizations were founded in addition to a large number of temporary committees. Meeting rooms had to be booked weeks in advance.[21] Almost every adult belonged to at least one organization or committee. The rivalry for positions was intense.[22] A political scientist from the University of Maryland studied Greenbelt in the winter of 1938–39 and concluded that the citizens were "over-stimulated" and organized more groups and activities than the community could possibly have time or money for.[23] The Greenbelt movie theater was losing money because people were too busy with meetings to attend films.[24] In December, 1938, the people decided to call an end to all meetings or other functions during the week between Christmas and New Year's Day. The *Washington Star* considered the move evidence of a revolt against "experiments in regimentation" and concluded that even in the federal showcase of Greenbelt residents "prefer staying at home . . . minding their own business to organizing details of their own and their neigh-

bor's lives."[25] Walter Volckhausen answered the *Star* that, aside
from providing a respite during the holidays, the residents realized they were moving too quickly in too many directions. In
attempting to do everything necessary to start a new community, the average citizen had been moving "at top speed . . .
not because he has been 'regimented,' but because he has been
set free."[26] He concluded by saying,

> If Washington newspapers would endeavor to see the sig-
> nificance of this town, and not use it as a political football,
> they would find that they have been scoring a development
> which holds more for the future of democracy than all the
> impassioned utterances that will ever decorate their paper.
>
> Democracy will grow not from your saying things, but from
> people doing things.[27]

One explanation for the frenetic activity of the townspeople
derives from their backgrounds. They were selected, in part,
for their interest in community affairs. Because of the experimental nature of the towns, a commitment to their success was
keenly felt. One writer posited that Greenbelt's residents sensed
"the first real chance they ever had to express themselves, and
overdid it a bit."[28] Most came from poor sections of Washington where they had had few opportunities for social organization and no city government to which they could contribute—
as one might expect they were culturally and politically starved.
Their general educational backgrounds were unusually high. In
1940 the median school year completed by Greenbelt residents
over twenty-five years of age was 12.5. Approximately sixty-
five percent had completed high school, thirty-four percent had
some college education, and only three percent had less than
an eighth grade education.[29] The national median educational
level in 1940 for whites over twenty-five was 8.75 years of
school.[30] In 1960, to compare, the national median was still only
10.6 years.[31] The high educational level of Greenbelt may be
explained by the fact that 72.6 percent of these original residents

were white-collar workers—almost all employed by the government.[32] Greendale and Greenhills included many more residents from blue-collar factory employees. Forty-two percent of Greendale students were high school graduates and fourteen percent had some college education. Nevertheless, Greendale's median educational level was eleven years—considerably above the national average. Another contrast between Greenbelt and the other two towns was the age of the residents.[33] If young people can be characterized as idealists, Greenbelt must have been a most idealistic town in 1938. The median age of its adults in that year was twenty-nine while in the other two towns it was thirty-three—hardly a middle-aged group either.[34]

Another contributing factor to the process of rapid community acclimation was the small number of homes initially occupied. It took almost a full year for the 885 homes in Greenbelt to be completed and occupied. Only fourteen people—ten adults and four children—moved into Greenbelt on opening day. In two weeks forty-five families had arrived. The Greenbelt Citizens' Association, the first and most important organization established in the early months, was founded on November 8, 1937, with approximately 100 families in residence. The first town council was elected on November 23, 1937, with less than 150 families in the town. By April, 1938, the town had 483 families and by September, 1938, all 885 units were filled.[35] The 100 to 150 families who started organizing during October and November, 1937, naturally obtained leadership and maintained an esprit de corps based on close contact during the early weeks. By the end of November organizations, in addition to the Citizens' Association and the town council, were the *Greenbelt Cooperator*, Greenbelt Woman's Club, Greenbelt American Legion, the community church, the Roman Catholic church, the Boy Scouts, Girl Scouts, Greenbelt Federal Credit Union, the Greenbelt P.T.A., and the Greenbelt Players Theater Club. Temporary committees were formed to solve the transportation problem and establish institutions such as kindergarten, the Greenbelt Consumer Services, and the Greenbelt

Health Association. Town newcomers in December and January complained that the "early settlers" of the town "have taken over all the authority where it is possible to do so . . . and are running the town to suit themselves."[36] Fortunately, such accusations soon disappeared from the pages of the *Cooperator*, and the high level of participation in all town organizations throughout 1938 indicates they were baseless.

If attendance at meetings of the Greenbelt Citizens' Association is any guage of activity, 1939 reflected a turning point from hyperactivity to what Philip Brown called a "second and somewhat more efficient stage—one of struggling with routine management problems and spreading responsibility."[37] Weekly meetings of the association in the beginning of 1939 were rarely attended by less than two hundred people, but by October the *Cooperator* lamented the decrease in attendance implying the association was "on its last legs."[38] A similar trend appeared in the other two towns. Most of the temporary committees in Greenhills had achieved the specific goals for which they were created—to select a dentist, investigate methods of municipal incorporation, or devise a policy towards door-to-door salesmen. Other committees, such as the Transportation Committee, the committee to establish church services, and the committee to print a newspaper, became permanent but required fewer meetings.[39] Greendale had acquired over fifty organizations in the first two years—"For everything you could think of," said one resident.[40] During the first year there were so many meetings that a number of people resigned in the new year to spend more time at home.[41] Regular attendance at meetings of most groups decreased to about thirty-five percent of the memberships.[42] The Greendale Citizens' Association, founded in January, 1939, with large turnouts of residents, floundered after two years.[43] Despite the natural lessening of interest in active participation, the process of creating community institutions, ranging from car pools to complex consumer cooperatives, was most significant to the cooperative and democratic nature of the communities. This phenomenon is not unique with the greenbelt towns. It has been marked by observers of newly born communities in the United States as early as De Tocqueville and as recently as the 1950s by sociologist Robert K. Merton. The process of community formations has led two American historians to isolate it as the most significant factor in Frederick Jackson Turner's frontier democracy.[44]

A brief analysis of Greenbelt's major institutions reflects the growth and subsequent disintegration of cooperation in the town. The two major political institutions were the town council and the citizens' association. The council was established in the town charter as the official representative body of the citizens. On November 23, 1937, five councilors were elected from a field of twelve after a short nonpartisan campaign. Almost every voter went to the polls.[45] Neither of the two conservative candidates was elected.[46] The councilors selected Louis Bessemer as chairman—thus he became the first mayor. Bessemer was an employee of the U.S. Public Health Service and a long-time member of the District of Columbia Cooperative League. The council also elected Roy Braden to the post of town manager. Braden worked closely and amicably with the council—never becoming involved in local political disputes.[47] Local politics remained nonpartisan; but interest in national parties was high. A Greenbelt Democratic Club was founded in the summer of 1939, and the Democratic Party was the overwhelming preference of Greenbelt's voters.[48]

The alter ego of the town council was the Greenbelt Citizens' Association founded two weeks before the first council was elected. The association immediately leaped into action—its many committees investigating literally hundreds of problems and establishing dozens of new organizantions. During periods of controversy the Citizens' Association operated as a town meeting and provided an instant channel of communication between the residents and the town council or the federal government.

The day following the election of the town council, Greenbelt's residents saw the first edition of the *Greenbelt Co-*

operator. Founded by the new Journalism Club, the paper remains to this day a nonprofit enterprise staffed by unpaid volunteers. This is the only one of the three greenbelt town papers which has survived as an independent local newspaper. It is an invaluable record of Greenbelt's development. The first issue advised readers that "We Pioneers" had a responsibility to create a self-governing democratic community and "develop a Greenbelt philosophy of life."[49] An article "In the Public Eye" urged citizens to "help make the facts clear" when writers and photographers came to Greenbelt.[50] The fame of the paper was itself the subject of controversy. One person thought it sounded too "preachy" and had a "tendency to associate Greenbelt with regimentation and paternalism." He suggested the name *Greenbelt Town Crier.*[51] Another citizen retorted that town crier conjured up images of "powdered wigs and knee britches—outmoded symbols of an outmoded age. Greenbelt has been pronounced the town of the future."[52] The *Cooperator* espoused a liberal view, selecting such books for review as Eleanor Roosevelt's *This Is My Story,* Upton Sinclair's *Co-op,* and G. J. Holyoak's *History of the Rochdale Pioneers,* a history of an early cooperative movement.[53] The paper attacked the "horrors" of Japan's army in China in January, 1938. In March, it discussed the fall of Austria and Roosevelt's rearmament proposals, scoring "misguided and deluded pacificists" who believe that "gangsterism can be stopped by protests."[54] However, it defended the right of pacifists and Jehovah's Witnesses to dissent, warning against "Super-patriots" such as members of the D.A.R. and the Dies Committee.[55] The consumer cooperative movement was supported against the charge by J. B. Matthews, research director for the House Un-American Activities Committee (Dies Committee), that "communists were working through consumer organizations to destroy the American profit system."[56] The *Cooperator* pointed out that Matthews, previous to his job with the H.U.A.C., had been vice president of Consumers Research, a private group opposed to the consumer cooperative movement.[57] The paper endorsed President Roosevelt in 1940.

In those years the *Greenbelt Cooperator* was the rarest of suburban newspapers—interested in national and international affairs and their relation to the local community. It was the defender and conscience of Greenbelt—attacking the community's critics, praising, scolding, and preaching to the pioneers.

The Greenbelt Consumer Cooperative founded in January, 1940, was the keystone in Greenbelt's structure of mutual aid. It survived the sale of the town and through careful management, has expanded into Baltimore, Washington, and northern Virginia.[58] A consumer co-op to operate the retail establishments at the three towns had long been planned by the Resettlement Administration. The R.A. hoped to loan the residents funds repayable through the sale of stock and the proceeds of sales. No action was taken, however, and the R.A. was merged with the Department of Agriculture. The solicitor of the department noted that no loans could be made to the town co-ops because all funds allocated to the R.A. and transferred to the F.S.A. were for "rural rehabilitation." He regarded the retail co-ops as contributing to the rural rehabilitation of the residents "only by a very tenuous line of argument."[59] The F.S.A. then turned to the Consumer Distribution Corporation financed by the Boston merchant, Edward A. Filene. Filene's organization agreed to establish a subsidiary called Greenbelt Consumer Services, which received the exclusive right to operate all commercial facilities in Greenbelt. These included a supermarket, valet shop, barber shop, beauty parlor, motion picture theater, and a gasoline station. Rent for the buildings was based on a percentage of the sales and was comparable to the ratio for privately rented stores.[60] The G.C.S. was a nonprofit, self-liquidating subsidiary. It would return all profits to the consumers and turn over ownership to Greenbelt residents by December 31, 1940.[61]

On October 3, 1937, the grocery store opened in temporary quarters and sold $11.45 worth of food to twenty-four customers. By 1939, after the opening of the permanent supermarket and the other establishments, G.C.S. was doing an average daily business of almost $1,000.00.[62] During 1938 and 1939, Walter Volckhausen and a large number of Greenbelt residents organized a Greenbelt Consumer Co-op, selling $5,000 worth of stock at $10.00 per share to over 400 residents.[63] On January 2, 1940, Greenbelt Consumer Services was sold to the resident stockholders for $40,000 of which $5,000 was paid in cash and the balance, in the form of a Consumer Distribution Corporation loan at four percent interest, was paid off over the following six years. Volckhausen, a mathematics instructor at the University of Maryland, was selected as the first president.[64]

A survey of the Greenbelt Co-op by the University of Maryland in 1940, revealed that sixty-seven percent of the residents had purchased stock. Generally, it was in a strong financial position. The beauty parlor, however, was losing money because few Greenbelt women patronized it regularly and almost one-third of them had never patronized one. The supermarket accounted for half the co-op's revenue. Average food prices were nine percent lower than District of Columbia chain stores and 9.3 percent lower than independent food stores.[65] It could have changed even lower prices had it not been for Maryland's retail price maintenance law.[66] All members (stockholders) of the co-op, of course, received dividends on their purchases—in 1940 these amounted to 3.85 percent.[67] The strength of the co-op's financial position was due, not only to lower prices and the desire to succeed on the part of the residents, but to a monopoly position in Greenbelt. The nearest private competitors were in Beltsville, three miles away.

In 1943, after the completion of 1000 defense homes in Greenbelt, the co-op stores expanded, and a second food store opened adjacent to the new homes.[68] The government also depended on G.C.S for new services such as operation of a swimming pool opened in 1939 and a local bus service in Greenbelt from 1945 to 1951. A large turnover of residents, and thus of shareholders, weakened the institution. By May, 1944, membership had dropped from sixty-seven percent of the population in 1940 to approximately fifty percent, and attendance at shareholder's meetings was far below quorum.[69] The addition of the defense home residents, however, increased membership in absolute numbers, and, in November, 1944, the co-op had the good fortune to obtain the services of Samuel F. Ashelman as general manager. Under his imaginative and careful administration the Greenbelt Consumer Services launched an expansion program that helped it survive the sale of the town and the opening of competitive private retail stores.

The Greenbelt Federal Credit Union also survived the sale of the town and vigorous private competition. Founded in part to fill the need for banking facilities, it was granted a charter on December 13, 1937, by the Farm Credit Administration. Beginning with twenty-four members, it grew in one year to a membership of 334 with total assets of $6,175. By 1945 assets rose to $54,800 and in 1964 to $66,752. It has continued to grow in spite of competition from the Twin Pines Savings and Loan bank, established in 1957, and a branch bank of the Suburban Trust Company. Part of the reason for its success has been the excellent administration by a number of Greenbelt's leading citizens. Its current president, Benjamin Rosenzweig, was an original resident, a leader in the community for thirty years, and a charter member of the credit union.[70]

The Greenbelt Health Association, like the Credit Union, was established to serve immediate needs. There was no doctor in Greenbelt and no hospital in Prince George's County. The Health Association was patterned after a consumer-owned clinic in Washington, founded in 1937 by federal employees. It began with seventy-five families each contributing a $5.00 entry fee and a monthly payment of $1.50 for a single person to $2.25 for a family of six. By December, 1938, 212 families had joined.[71] On April 1, 1938, the Greenbelt Health Association opened a clinic and employed a doctor whose salary was paid to treat members, although he could treat nonmembers on a fee-for-service basis.[72] This arrangement was not satisfactory to the doctor, and he resigned. Two more were hired in his place, one of whom, Dr. Joseph Still, was an enthusiastic supporter

of cooperative health associations. Through his efforts Greenbelt was able to open a small twelve-bed hospital in May, 1939.[73]
Unfortunately disagreements arose regularly between the doctors and the association board. One resigned but Dr. Still
remained—fighting the board to the point of being fired. Membership pressure on his behalf was exerted resulting in the resignation of the board and the rehiring of Dr. Still. He was apparently the only doctor committed enough to Greenbelt and the
association to persevere. His loss to the Army Medical Corps
in 1941 was a great one.[74] A husband and wife team was hired
and resigned in November, 1941, having worked less than a
year.[75] In January, 1942, the F.S.A. dealt the association a severe,
probably mortal, blow, by refusing to pay $23,000 to cover the
hospital expenses for fiscal 1942. The town council held a referendum to determine if the residents wanted to pay the cost
themselves. Two plans were presented, one calling for annual
payments of $12.00 and one calling for annual payments of
$6.00. The $12.00 plan lost 347 to 175 and the $6.00 plan lost
285 to 260. One reason given for rejection of both plans was
that the county was constructing a hospital in nearby Riverdale.
Despite protests to the F.S.A. and an appeal to Mrs. Roosevelt,
the hospital closed its doors on January 31, 1942, and its only
doctor left two months later.[76] The health problems of Greenbelt became even more serious after the construction of the defense homes; and the G.H.A., even with its declining membership, succeeded in hiring two more doctors. Again there was
feuding. Both doctors resigned as did the board members. In
March, 1944, after the sudden resignation of one of two remaining doctors and membership had dropped to 300 from the 1940
peak of 377, the Federal Public Housing Administration ruled
that private doctors could open offices in Greenbelt. Soon
thereafter the last G.H.A. doctor resigned and opened a private
office in the town. Several more doctors came and went and the
membership, which rose to 350 in November, 1944, declined
after the war until the last 180 members dissolved the organization in June, 1950.[77]

The women of Greenbelt, noting that public schools provided nothing for preschool children, organized a cooperative nursery school, which, like the kindergarten, was the first in Prince George's County. They also organized a Better Buyers' Club which studied products, labeling, and consumer legislation. The elementary school children even organized a co-op for selling candy, pencils, and other small items—it was reportedly dubbed the "Gum Drop Co-op" by the local press.

The residents also organized a wide range of clubs and special interest organizations. One of the earliest was the American Legion Post No. 136, which was to play an important role in the negotiations over the sale of the town. Cultural interests flourished in three groups—the Greenbelt Community Band, the Greenbelt Players, and the Bi-Weekly Book Club. The community band became familiar to many Washington area residents. Under the direction of Paul Garrett, a striking man with a goatee, the band performed concerts throughout the area and played sacred music for churches and popular music for parades and other events. There was also a Choral Society and Chamber Music Society, the latter composed of members of the Navy Band and the National Symphony. The theater group presented classic and contemporary plays such as Clifford Odets's "Awake and Sing." The book club reviewed such books as Hemingway's *For Whom the Bell Tolls*, Hans Zinsser's *As I Remember Him*, and John F. Kennedy's *While England Slept*. There were, of course, Boy Scouts, Cub Scouts, Girl Scouts, and many special interest clubs to serve athletes, camera bugs, bridge players, riflemen, radio operators, and gardeners. The garden club was the largest of these. Almost half the families joined during the summer of 1938 and received portions of a plot on the edge of town.[78]

The spirit of cooperation in the early years was strong enough to exercise unusual influences. In November, 1939, the Citizens' Association and the town council firmly rejected the suggestion of a group of residents that Negroes be excluded from the supermarket lunch counter. This is more remarkable in light of the rigid segregation in Prince George's County and the rest of Maryland. Also surprising for the time was the decision of the co-op board of directors not to show the racist film "Birth of a Nation" at the Greenbelt Theater.[79] There was, on the other hand, no record that residents ever considered the possibility of opening the town to Negroes.[80]

Another example of the influence of cooperative effort was in religion. Roman Catholic, Protestant, Jewish, and Mormon services began shortly after the town opened. In May, 1939, the heads of these four denominations formed a Permanent Conference on Religious Life in Greenbelt, the purpose of which was to "foster a clearer understanding of religious principles among various groups . . . serve as a clearing house for interdenominational differences and curb religious prejudices and to participate jointly in efforts to achieve social justice and to aid in community improvements."[81] Reverend Kincheloe, the Protestant minister, began a movement to build a single structure for all denominations.[82] This ecumenism was short-lived. In January, 1940, the Catholics, who were part of the Berwyn, Maryland, parish, voted unanimously to seek F.S.A. approval for the construction of their own church. The *Cooperator* said the move caused keen disappointment among a number of citizens who thought that "in these days of intolerance and persecution . . . and segregation . . . we had hoped for cooperation here, at least in the field of religion."[83] In a reply to the article Reverend Leo J. Fealy, the Berwyn-Greenbelt parish priest, wrote:

> Speaking of cooperation, we Catholics would like to find some spirit of cooperation on the part of the *Cooperator*— yes, and on the part of some others in Greenbelt. . . . The Catholics of Greenbelt are going ahead with plans for a church building. Whether it be a separate building or a part of a combined building depends on future developments and on the decision of His Excellency, the Archbishop of Baltimore.[84]

During the spring of 1940, Reverend Kincheloe negotiated with the archbishop on the question and led a group which drew up blueprints for a religious center to serve all the denominations. The war crisis stopped all plans for the construction of churches or other facilities at Greenbelt. Reverend Kincheloe left Greenbelt in June, 1941, to become an army chaplain and never returned. Greenbelt's churches all built separate houses of worship, and the Catholic church built its own primary school in 1949.[85]

The Greenbelt schools provided a more lasting source of community participation for people of all ages. The community centered school, as Cedric Larson called it, offered education for the children during the day, and served as an adult education and community center at night. The elementary school was the focus of this activity since it was located adjacent to the commercial center and also contained the library.[86] The kindergarten was promoted by a committee of eight Greenbelt women who convinced the F.S.A. to hire a teacher in the fall of 1938.[87] The elementary students, it will be remembered, instituted a co-op in the fall of 1939. Shares were sold for ten cents, and the first profits were distributed by the end of the first half of the year.[88] The curriculum was labeled progressive, and the teaching staff was of a high quality.[89]

Considering the size of Greenbelt, adult educational opportunities were great. Art instruction was given both to the children and the adults by graduates of the Maryland Institute of Art under an instructional grant from the Federal Arts Project. Also, the F.S.A. employed a man and a woman as full-time directors of recreation. They taught physical education in the day schools and directed athletic activities for the adults in the evening. The best educational asset was the Greenbelt extension of the University of Maryland which opened in 1939. Two courses were offered the first year—accounting and contemporary American political problems. The latter was described in a brochure as dealing with "a select list of problems . . . the conflict between government and business, housing, social security, freedom of the press, labor relations, etc."[90]

The $142,000 regional high school at the west end of Greenbelt served the town and the surrounding rural area. In 1939,

forty percent of the students came from outside Greenbelt.
Vocational training, a general course, and a college preparatory
program were provided. School officials expected ten to fifteen
percent to attend college.[91] Since the entire Greenbelt public
school system was administrated by the Prince George's County
Board of Education, there were continual disagreements—usually about money for the high school. The elementary school
was supported entirely by the F.S.A. through payments-in-lieu-
of-taxes to the county; but the high school budget was jointly
supported. In 1937 the F.S.A. paid three-fourths of the $36,000
and was anxious to have the county pay a slightly larger share
in 1938.[92] The two parties could not agree on which would pay
the telephone bill so the school operated the first few months of
the 1938–39 year without a telephone. The same delay occurred
in bus service for the Greenbelt students. The county refused
to offer bussing until it received equitable compensation.[93] The
county and the F.S.A. had just begun to cooperate more easily
when the war and the addition of 1000 new families upset all
the educational programs.

The cooperative spirit flourished in the other two towns but
failed to maintain its initial momentum to the degree seen at
Greenbelt. The Greendale Cooperative Association was
launched by the residents in the summer of 1938 at the suggestion of Sherwood Reeder.[94] A cooperative committee was
formed in July which decided to follow Greenbelt's example
and establish a consumer cooperative to operate Greendale's
commercial facilities. The Co-op was incorporated on August
22, 1938, with a loan from the Consumer Distribution Corporation (the same organization that financed the Greenbelt co-op)
and staff members borrowed from the Midland Cooperative
Wholesale Corporation. The Greendale Cooperative Association leased the commercial center from the F.S.A. A food store
and a variety store opened on September 17, 1938. A drug store,
movie theater, shoe repair and valet shop, barber shop, beauty
parlor, tavern-restaurant, and a gasoline station were all subsequently opened by the G.C.A.[95]

At its third annual meeting in March, 1941, the Greendale Cooperative Association, which had remained a subsidiary of the Midland Cooperative Association, became independent. At that time all its enterprises were earning a net profit. The Co-op had angered some residents in the early years by refusing to give credit, but it remained a vital and popular institution throughout the war.[96] After the war the Public Housing Administration leased several of the stores to private proprietors because the Co-op no longer wished to operate them. In 1948 the P.H.A. refused to renew the leases on remaining Co-op businesses and opened them to competitive bidding. The Co-op lost the food store, the variety store, and the barber shop—retaining only the tavern-restaurant and the gasoline station. The Co-op disbanded in December, 1948.[97]

Co-op directors blamed the P.H.A.'s action for its failures, but this is not entirely fair. Greendale was the smallest of the greenbelt towns and was located closer to private stores than any of the other towns. While the Co-op stores sold to a few people outside Greendale, the town residents traded in much larger numbers with outside competitors.[98]

Greendale also attempted to establish a cooperative medical organization. Two groups were established in 1938. The Greendale Medical Union failed after several months of trial operation. The Greendale Health Association, founded with the aid of the Milwaukee Medical Center, operated successfully until after the war when, hampered by pressure on its doctors from Milwaukee hospitals, other area doctors, and P.H.A. sanctioned competition from private physicians in Greendale, it merged with the Milwaukee Medical Center.[99]

The Greenhills Consumer Services survives today, but on a much smaller scale than of the Greenbelt co-op. As in the other two towns, a consumer cooperative was established, this time, with the aid of the Co-Operative League of Cincinnati and a loan from Filene's Consumer Distribution Corporation. In April, 1938, when there were only one hundred families in the town, a meeting was held at which, at the suggestion of

Community Manager Carlton Sharpe, a committee presented the co-op plan. It was immediately adopted by a unanimous vote. In 1939, the Co-op signed a ten-year lease with the F.S.A. for the commercial center and opened a food store, service station, barber shop, valet shop, beauty shop, drug store, and general merchandise store. By 1940, approximately four hundred residents were members of the Co-op. Not all were pleased with the Co-op, however, and a number perferred private chain stores. During the war the Co-op ran into financial trouble and divested itself of all businesses except the food and drug stores. In 1954 the food store built a new and larger structure and in 1960 opened a second store in the neighboring community of Mt. Healthy. By 1962 its total sales had risen from $200,000 in 1940 to $2,200,000.[100] This is, of course, small compared with the Greenbelt co-op sales which in 1962 were over $20,000,000.

Why did cooperative enterprise disintegrate at Greendale, decline at Greenhills, and expand at Greenbelt? One reason was the smaller size of the latter two towns compared to Greenbelt, which made it much harder to support the variety of business operated by the co-ops. Had Greendale's co-op consolidated its efforts in the food and drug stores during the war as did the Greenhills co-op, it might have survived. Also, the Greenbelt co-op met its competition by the expansion of its own facilities, through a stock sale to the residents in 1945 to 1947 resulting in the construction of a larger and more modern supermarket in 1948. In 1951 it opened another supermarket in nearby Takoma Park. During the years 1954–56, when Greenbelt was adjusting to its sale, the co-op made some basic decisions which have since guided its policies. All its Greenbelt business except the food, drug, and general merchandise stores which were consolidated in the supermarket through a $200,000 extension of the building, were ended. The small service station in the commercial center was also abandoned, but in its place the Co-op opened a $100,000 automobile service plaza. Thus while divesting itself of less profitable businesses, the total operation of the Co-op expanded, as did its membership.

Finally, the Co-op absorbed the Westminister Cooperative in neighboring Carroll County in 1956 and in 1959 merged with the Rochdale Cooperative in Prince George's County, which brought not only more members, but two more supermarkets. By 1967, Greenbelt Consumer Services had become a major business enterprise with 17,000 members and fourteen retail stores in the Baltimore–Washington area.[101]

The Greenbelt Co-op appears to have attracted far wider support from the residents than did the other two ventures, particularly during the years following the war. In 1945–46, there was an attempt to discredit G.C.S. by a small group of local citizens. In 1947, the group was aided by a Subcommittee of the House Small Business Committee in its August hearings. The subcommittee, composed of two Republicans (Walter Ploeser of Missouri and R. Walter Riehlman of New York) and one Democrat (Wright Patman of Texas), heard a number of witnesses condemn the exclusive control of G.C.S. at Greenbelt. In a two to one party line vote the committee's report stated that the lease between the P.H.A. and G.C.S. was "monopolistic" and recommended that it be revoked.[102] The G.C.S. held a special meeting and voted 400 to 0 to adopt a resolution charging the subcommittee with bias against cooperatives, inaccurate and prejudiced press releases, and use of witnesses who were all opposed to G.C.S.[103] The Greenbelt town elections on September 23, 1947, reflected the struggle between the antico-op group, organized as the Greenbelt Improvement Association under Mayor George Bauer, and the proco-op group called the Committee for Better Government. The latter group controlled the editorial board of the *Greenbelt Cooperator* and charged that the Improvement Association was in collusion with Congressman Ploeser and other outsiders to sell Greenbelt to private real estate interests. The Improvement Association waged a defensive campaign claiming that it was not really against the co-op, but merely wanted private business in Greenbelt also.[104] The group was embarrassed by its association with James Flynn, whose accusations of disloyalty and of being a communist against one of the town's most respected citizens, Walter Volckhausen, plus his physical assault on another citizen at a town meeting in 1945, won him the disfavor of all groups including the American Legion.[105] Also, it appears that the townspeople reacted as they had in 1937–40 to attacks from the outside and closed ranks in defense of their institutions. The entire slate of Co-op candidates won.[106] The opposition group started publication of a newspaper called the *Greenbelt Independent* dedicated to "further the principal of the American way of life here in Greenbelt. In order to achieve this end, the town must be opened to private enterprise. Competition is the essence of our country's success. It is the American way."[107] The editorial stated that the recommendation of the Small Business Subcommittee should be supported and the G.C.S. monopoly broken. The newspaper soon died and G.C.S. remained the sole commercial outlet in the town for another five years until it independently gave up control. There seems little doubt that G.C.S. was strengthened by the attacks against it as a majority of residents rallied to its support. In Greendale only the *Greendale Review* supported the Co-op, and there were no mass meetings in its defense. In the postwar years, therefore, only Greenbelt evidenced a continuing interest in the democratic cooperatives founded in 1937–38. But even Greenbelt, it will be recalled, opened its doors to private businesses after the war— business which soon outdistanced the growth of the Greenbelt co-op.

It appears that cooperative democracy atrophied as a result of special circumstances in each community, but there were also common underlying causes. Basically, the residents were unwilling, perhaps unable, to devote the time and energy necessary to establish and to maintain the highly participatory democracy required by the political, economic, and social institutions; and they lacked the money to hire enough agents to handle the administration. The cooperative businesses particulary required continuous citizen support. Participatory democracy and economic cooperation thrived in the early years, one suspects, because it was new and exhilarating for those who had never experienced such things before; but it soon became institution-alized and therefore less emotionally satisfying. What was a joy to plan and build became a dull burden to administrate. The structure was also weakened by families moving in and out of the towns faster than they could be assimilated into the unique and demanding community institutions. Permanence of residency was made difficult by the F.S.A., as has been stated; but the coming of the Second World War made it impossible. If local democracy and economic cooperation require a rela-tively stable population, this factor alone would explain the devolution of the greenbelt towns into more traditional sub-urban communities.

1. *Washington Post*, September 30, 1937.

2. *Greenbelt Cooperator*, November 24, 1937.

3. *Milwaukee News-Sentinel*, May 1, 1938.

4. *Cincinnati Post*, March 31, 1938.

5. *Greenbelt Cooperator*, November 24, 1937.

6. *Greenhills News–Bulletin*, May 21, 1938.

7. *Greenbelt Cooperator*, November 24, 1937.

8. Ibid., April 13, 1938.

9. Ibid., May 18, 1938.

10. Ibid., December 15, 1938.

11. Ibid., November 23, 1938.

12. Ibid., December 29, 1938. After leaving Greenbelt, Warner wrote a memoir and historical sketch of the community during its first four years. See George A. Warner, *Greenbelt: The Cooperative Community*.

13. *Greenhills–Forest Park Journal*, Anniversary Edition, April 23, 1963; and interview with Mrs. Bgent Sandstrom, Greendale, Wisconsin, February 4, 1965.

14. *Greendale Review*, October 6, 1938.

15. Ibid., August 24, 1938, November 17, 1938.

16. Ibid.

17. This derogatory view of slum clearance public housing projects

expressed in the *Cooperator* on January 26, 1938, indicates that there may have been some degree of snobbery among the Greenbelt residents and an effort to dissociate themselves from any comparison with the P.W.A. or U.S.H.A. inner city project. Greendale's residents entertained a large group of people from the Julia Lathrop Housing Project in Chicago, who had come to Milwaukee to visit Greendale and Parklawn, the P.W.A. slum clearance project. The Greendale residents were invited to return the visit, but there is no record they ever did so, nor did they carry on any programs with Parklawn (*Greendale Review*, August 24, 1938).

18. *Greenbelt Cooperator*, August 31, 1938.

19. *Greendale Review*, December 15, 1938, March 25, 1939, and February 7, 1940.

20. *Greenbelt Cooperator*, July 27, 1938, April 11, 1940, April 18, 1940, and May 2, 1940.

21. Brown, "What Has Happened at Greenbelt?" *The New Republic* 105 (August 11, 1941): 184.

22. William H. Form, "Status Stratification in a Planned Community," *American Sociological Review* 10 (October, 1945): 607.

23. Bone, "Greenbelt Faces 1939," *The American City* 54 (February, 1939): 61.

24. O. Kline Fulmer, *Greenbelt*, p. 26.

25. *Washington Star*, n.d. in *Greenbelt Cooperator*, December 15, 1938.

26. *Greenbelt Cooperator*, December 15, 1938.

27. Ibid.

28. Brown, "What Has Happened at Greenbelt?" p. 184.

29. Form, "The Sociology of a White Collar Suburb," p. 67.

30. U.S., Department of Commerce, Bureau of the Census, *Historical Statistics of the United States, Colonial Times to 1957*, p. 214.

31. Department of Commerce, Bureau of the Census, *Historical Statistics of the United States, Colonial Times to 1957: Continuations to 1962 and Revisions*, p. 33.

32. Form, "Status Stratification in a Planned Community," p. 612.

33. Douglas G. Marshall, "Greendale," pp. 40–43.

34. U.S., Farm Security Administration, *Annual Report: 1938*, p. 20.

35. *City of Greenbelt, 25th Anniversary*, p. 3; *Greenbelt Cooperator*, December 22, 1937, April 6, 1938; and Form, "The Sociology of a White

Collar Suburb, p. 241; and Hall, "Appraised Report and Valuation Analysis," p. 4.

36. *Greenbelt Cooperator,* January 26, 1938. Similar complaints were made in the Greendale Review. The first residents who lived in one section of town close to the center were charged with "dominating town offices." One editorial suggested that this situation could be corrected by allowing only one office to each resident. This was the last mention of any problem of that nature. See *Greendale Review,* April 8, 1939, and May 4, 1939.

37. Brown, "What Has Happened at Greenbelt," p. 184.

38. Bone, "Greenbelt Faces 1939," p. 59; and *Greenbelt Cooperator,* November 2, 1939.

39. *Greenhills News-Bulletin,* May 21, 1938; Sharpe, "Greenhills Progress Report," Lansill Papers, official files, p. 3.

40. *Milwaukee Journal,* February 17, 1946.

41. *Greendale Review,* December 15, 1938.

42. Marshall, "Greendale," pp. 36, 40–43.

43. *Greendale Review,* March, 6, 1940.

44. Stanley Elkins and Eric McKitrick, "A Meaning for Turner's Frontier," *Political Science Quarterly* 69 (September, 1954): 325–26.

45. Roy S. Braden, "A Plan for Community Living: Greenbelt, Maryland," *Public Management* 20 (January, 1938): 13. The percentage of eligible voters casting ballots in subsequent council elections decreased. See George A. Warner, *Greenbelt,* pp. 127–28.

46. *Greenbelt Cooperator,* November 24, 1937.

47. Ibid., August 27, 1943.

48. Ibid., July 27, 1939, November 6, 1942, November 10, 1944.

49. Ibid., November 24, 1936.

50. Ibid.

51. Ibid., December 22, 1937.

52. Ibid., December 29, 1937.

53. Ibid., November 24, 1937, December 8, 1937, December 29, 1937.

54. Ibid., January 5, 1938, March 16, 1938.

55. Ibid., January 22, 1940, September 12, 1940, December 28, 1939.

56. Ibid., December 14, 1939.

57. Ibid., December 21, 1939. Matthews later served on Senator Joseph McCarthy's staff until he was pressured out in 1953 for stating that the nation's Protestant clergymen were the largest procommunist group in America; see Earl Latham, *The Communist Controversy in Washington* (Cambridge: Harvard University Press, 1966), p. 401.

58. Greenbelt Consumer Services, *Co-Op Newsletter* 11, no. 8 (May 19, 1965): 1.

59. Memo to Mastin G. White from Monroe Oppenheimer, May 27, 1937, R.O.A., H.H.F.A., Drawer 527.

60. *New York Times*, January 28, 1940.

61. Victor W. Bennett, "Consumers and the Greenbelt Cooperative," *Journal of Marketing* 6 (July 1941): 4.

62. *New York Times*, January 28, 1940; and *City of Greenbelt, 25th Anniversary*, p. 32.

63. Bennett, "Consumers and the Greenbelt Cooperative," p. 4.

64. *Greenbelt Cooperator*, January 4, 1940; Warner, *Greenbelt*, pp. 59–60, 91–92.

65. Bennett, "Consumers and the Greenbelt Cooperative," p. 9.

66. "Coop Stores Grow in Greenbelt," *Business Week*, May 14, 1938.

67. Bennett, "Consumers and the Greenbelt Cooperative," p. 10.

68. *City of Greenbelt, 25th Anniversary*, p. 6.

69. *Greenbelt Cooperator*, May 26, 1944.

70. *City of Greenbelt, 25th Anniversary*, p. 34; Greenbelt Federal Credit Union, *Newsletter*, January, 1965; Greenbelt Federal Credit Union, *Your Greenbelt Federal Credit Union*, 1965 (pamphlet).

71. Walker, "Life in a Greenbelt Community," p. 17; and Warner, *Greenbelt*, p. 44.

72. Warner, *Greenbelt*, p. 45–48.

73. Ibid., pp. 82–84.

74. Ibid.; and *Greenbelt Cooperator*, May 30, 1941.

75. *Greenbelt Cooperator*, August 13, 1943, March 10, 1943, April 7, 1943, July 28, 1944, September 8, 1944, November 3, 1944.

76. Ibid., January 2, 1942, January 23, 1942, April 24, 1942. The appeal to Mrs. Roosevelt, her letter to the U.S.D.A., and the reply of the acting secretary of agriculture on February 6, 1942, are found in the National Archives, R.G. 16.

77. *City of Greenbelt, 25th Anniversary*, p. 5; and *Greenbelt Cooperator*, September 12, 1941, November 28, 1941.

78. *City of Greenbelt, 25th Anniversary*, p. 5, 18, 28, 34, 37; and

Greenbelt Cooperator, November 16, 1939, May 23, 1940, March 7, 1941; and Walker, "Life in a Greenbelt Community," p. 17; Bone, "Greenbelt Faces 1939," p. 60; and Fulmer, *Greenbelt,* pp. 26–28.

79. *Greenbelt Cooperator,* November 16, 1939, November 30, 1939, August 8, 1940.

80. On September 11, 1967, the Greenbelt City Council voted unanimously to ask all owners and managers of apartments to adopt nonsegregated rental practices. See *Greenbelt News Review,* September 14, 1967.

81. *Greenbelt Cooperator,* June 1, 1939.

82. Warner, *Greenbelt,* p. 35; and *Greenbelt Cooperator,* June 1, 1941.

83. *Greenbelt Cooperator,* January 18, 1940, January 25, 1940, February 8, 1940.

84. Ibid., February 8, 1940.

85. Ibid., February 8, 1940, April 11, 1940, June 1, 1941; and *City of Greenbelt, 25th Anniversary,* pp. 28–29.

86. Larson, "Educational Activities," pp. 59–60.

87. *Greenbelt Cooperator,* July 6, 1938.

88. Bone, "Greenbelt Faces 1939," p. 61.

89. Larson, "Educational Activities," pp. 62–70.

90. Ibid., p. 105.

91. Ibid., pp. 83, 87; and *City of Greenbelt, 25th Anniversary,* p. 27.

92. *Greenbelt Cooperator,* September 21, 1938.

93. Ibid., October 27, 1938, November 10, 1938.

94. Interviews with Mrs. Ethel Shweer and Mr. and Mrs. Bgent Sandstrom, Greendale, Wisconsin, February 4, 1965.

95. "The Story of Greendale: A Government Demonstration in Community Planning and Public Housing," rev., April, 1944, mimeographed brochure found in R.O.A., H.H.F.A. Copies in possession of author. *Greendale Review,* August 24, 1938, September 10, 1938, September 6, 1940.

96. *Greendale Review,* April 2, 1941, March 11, 1939; Marshall, "Greendale," p. 61; "The Story of Greendale," rev., 1944, pp. 5–6.

97. "The Story of Greendale," rev., May, 1948, p. 6; and *Greendale Review,* May 14, 1948, November 12, 1948, December 10, 1948.

98. *Milwaukee Journal,* February 17, 1942; and interviews with several Greendale residents agree with this assessment.

99. "The Story of Greendale," rev., 1944, p. 6–7; and interview with Mrs. Ethel Shweer.

100. *Greenhills-Forest Park Journal,* Anniversary Edition, p. 4;

"Greenhills, Second Anniversary, 1940," pamphlet prepared by the Greenhills News–Bulletin Association, 1940, p. 16; and letter to the author from Carlton Sharpe.

101. *City of Greenbelt, 25th Anniversary,* pp. 31–32; Greenbelt Consumer Services, *Co-Op Newsletter* 11, no. 8 (May 19, 1965), p. 1.

102. *Greenbelt Cooperator,* August 29, 1947.

103. Ibid. The original copy of the resolution is in P.H.A., R.G. 196, Box 2.

104. *Greenbelt Cooperator,* September 12, September 19, and September 26, 1947; Community Manager Charles Cormack to Joseph C. Gray, P.H.A., F.G. 196, Box 2.

105. *Greenbelt Cooperator,* September 14, 1945. In November, 1945, Flynn, on behalf of the Greenbelt Improvement Association, had introduced a resolution to G.C.S. that the Co-op withdraw from the Eastern Cooperative Wholesale Association. The resolution was defeated 528–10 (*Greenbelt Cooperator,* November 30, 1945).

106. *Greenbelt Cooperator,* September 26, 1947. Memo from Cormack to Gray, September 25, 1947, P.H.A., R.G. 196, Box 2.

107. *Greenbelt Independent,* December 11, 1947 (copy in P.H.A., R.G. 196, Box 2).

11

🍁 NEW FRONTIER

OR FEDERAL MENACE

Favorable public reaction to the greenbelt towns was the crucial goal of the entire program. Unless public pressure could be generated, Congress would not expand the program and private builders would continue to construct disjointed little housing developments. The R.A. failed to achieve this essential goal. It is obvious that the majority of those who wrote and spoke about the towns reacted negatively.

Opponents of an expanded greenbelt town program based their objections on three arguments. First, it put the federal government in unnecessary competition with private enterprise; second, it was part of a broad trend towards socialistic regimentation disguised as cooperative planning; and third, there was the refusal to accept the fact that one-third of the nation was ill housed. Herbert Hoover said flatly that it was "statistically false."[1] Many local officials, when presented with a New

Deal housing plan, declared they had no need of help since all their citizens were adequately sheltered. Such was the case with the city council of Winston-Salem, North Carolina, where the P.W.A. wanted to build a project.[2] Similar views were expressed by some citizens in Bound Brook, New Jersey. The *Cincinnati Enquirer*, referring to Greenhills, implied that the Suburban Division would have to make a real effort to rent the homes.[3]

Many who believed that a large number of Americans were inadequately housed felt that private industry could and should do the job. This was the position of the National Association of Real Estate Boards and the Building and Loan League which opposed all public housing programs until 1937. A writer in the U.S. Chamber of Commerce magazine stated that ill-housed citizens deserved their fate in most cases.

> Some are satisfied with their condition. They are doing nothing to improve it. Others do not have sufficient means to live as well as they would like. Initiative spurs them to better their condition. Others are engaged in wishful waiting.[4]

Hugo Parth, one of the leading directors of the Milwaukee Real Estate Board, objected to Greendale and Parklawn (the P.W.A. project) on the grounds that the low rents would impede a recovery of the private home building industry. This recovery could only happen when "renters get squeezed hard."[5] Parth further argued that Greendale did not serve the really low income groups, which, amazingly, he admitted did exist and did need publicly subsidized housing. Greenbelt, too, was accused of being "merely a smoke screen to conceal a reckless venture in a field of construction that should be left to private industry."[6] The R.A. was even reproached for competing unfairly with private industry for the profits to be made from the $800–$1,440 income group.[7]

The United States Building and Loan League did back a plan to build planned communities—a plan that depended on private industry. It was a proposal made by the Committee for

Economic Recovery (a business group) to form forty housing companies, each to raise at least $1,000,000 through public stock sales, which would build several planned communities at moderate cost. Unfortunately, no group ever got far enough to sell stock and the proposal was abandoned.[8]

Herbert U. Nelson, chief spokesman for the N.A.R.E.B., represented the view that the towns were impractical and of little value. Testifying before a Senate committee in 1936, Nelson said, "We have had a number of demonstration projects erected and are somewhat at a loss to know what has been demonstrated."[9] After returning from Europe in the fall of 1937, Nelson declared, "Our subdivisions with their wide streets, generous lots and complete municipal improvements are far in advance of anything that is known in these countries."[10] Admitting that Europe "has its garden cities here and there, as, for example, Letchworth and Welwyn" which were built as a single unit "in a roomy fashion," Nelson concluded that "the idea of planning houses by neighborhoods, as well as community planning on a large scale, is stronger in the United States than is the case in any other country."[11]

A more revealing comment on the thinking of the N.A.R.E.B. is seen in its response to the regional planning reports of the National Resources Committee. The N.A.R.E.B. *Confidential Weekly Letter* reflects the extent to which planning was advocated.

> The real unit of community life is the neighborhood. Until we learn how to plan the neighborhood, the planning that might be undertaken for cities, regions, states and the nation would appear to have a weak foundation. The average good citizen can comprehend the logic and purpose of neighborhood plans, because they come within the scope of his daily experience. They are concrete, not abstract.[12]

The N.A.R.E.B. was, of course, the servant of its thousands of members, most of whom dealt only with single houses or very small developments and could not easily move very far in advance of them. The days of the Levitts, Rouses, and other large scale private builders lay ahead. It was only at their 1930 convention that the N.A.R.E.B. supported, for the first time, a policy of planning entire neighborhoods, or "subdivisions," as they were called. *Business Week* labeled this a "Drastic Change in Residential Development."[13]

The greenbelt town program appeared too utopian for serious consideration—if, indeed, it was understood at all by those who wrote or commented on it. Even in 1960 the architect Carl Feiss wrote that the phrase "new towns" is "meaningless to most of us, or it is considered part of Cloud Nine, or it is simply misunderstood."[14] Felix Bruner's series of articles in the *Washington Post* on the Resettlement Administration was entitled "Utopia Unlimited."[15] Gordon Ames Brown, in a similar series, used the word "utopian" to describe the towns, and T. A. Huntley, in another article, compared Tugwell to Bellamy, Howard, Moore, and Plato, who all "dreamed of a better order, of a world made over."[16] The architects and planners were ridiculed along with Tugwell. *Nation's Business* reported sarcastically that to plan the towns "Men of Vision were called in—Social Engineers, Planners, Builders, outriders of the March of Progress."[17] The N.A.R.E.B. said Greenbelt cost $10,000 per unit because "dream boys" were building "a little Utopia of their own."[18]

The cost of the greenbelt towns—no aspect of the suburban town program caused more confusion or was more consistently misinterpreted. As was mentioned earlier, the cost cannot be satisfactorily computed. The first official figures released by the government on the final cost of any of the towns were those for Greenbelt, Maryland, given in June, 1937, by the General Accounting Office in response to a request by Senator Byrd. The cost was slightly over $14,000,000 which meant, by the senator's count, $16,182 per unit. On the fourth of July, Byrd said resettlement spending was approaching a national scandal for its "sinful and absurd waste. . . . Every Congressman and Senator in Washington should visit Tugwelltown and see where more than $14,000,000 of public money has been spent."[19] The final report of project costs at Greenbelt was published August 30, 1937, and set the total cost of $14,016,270.61. There was, of course, no deduction for relief labor, excess land and facilities, farm improvements on the greenbelt, or furniture sold to the residents.[20] *Newsweek* interpreted the total figure as the cost of housing Greenbelt's families.[21] *Time*, calling Greenbelt the "most spectacular" of all the R.A.'s "grandiose ventures," said it was also a fitting monument to the R.A. because it cost $14,227,000, although, later in the article, the cost of relief labor was deducted and the cost of the towns was reduced to $8,500,000.[22]

The most complete breakdown of costs was given by *Nation's Business* which stated that the R.A. deducted $4,902,000 for inefficient relief labor, $643,000 for excess land, and $284,000 for leftover materials, which brought the unit cost down from $16,000 to $9,600. When the cost of the community center, school, streets, and lake and recreational areas was deducted the unit cost fell to $5,423. The article, however, was titled "$16,000 Homes for $2,000 Incomes: Greenbelt, Maryland."[23] Thus, the national news magazines, while noting the relief nature of the project, generally judged the cost of Greenbelt as though it had been built by a private developer. Even some architects of low-cost housing criticized the cost of the towns. Corwin Wilson, writing in the progressive journal *Shelter* in 1938, called Greenbelt's cost an "extravagance" which was "slyly shunted onto the backs of Montana and Texas farmers by ambidextrous accountants in order to prettify the stage set for a few hundred families."[24]

While some of the Suburban Division planners believed the towns could be financed as self-liquidating projects, Tugwell was never so sanguine. As far back as February, 1936, he said,

> Let me frankly admit there may be some element of subsidy if we are to maintain building and maintenance standards and keep rents down. . . . Of course, subsidies for workers' home are no new thing in our American economy, though

we have generally preferred not to recognize them as such. Housing for low income groups is not paying its way in America today. . . . The lowest-cost housing areas in large cities pay in taxation scarcely one-fourth the cost of essential services which their inhabitants receive from the municipalities. This is a form of hidden subsidy of which we do not avail ourselves in Resettlement communities.

It may be that there will turn out to be an element of subsidy in our charges. But it will be an open one, not a hidden one; and I, for myself, shall not pretend to like it in any instance. . . . I do not believe in throwing the poor a basket of groceries; I do not believe in keeping them in subsidized poorhouses. I am, however a realist . . . for now either wages are too low or monopolized materials and processes are held at too high a price.[25]

The degree of subsidy was not apparent then, but few people outside the R.A. were prepared to defend the cost figures. One year later, Tugwell wrote that until there was mass production of houses with prefabricated sections there would never be any really low cost housing in America.[26] Walter H. Blucher, director of the American Society of Planning Officials, rejoined that criticism of the cost of the towns was foolish because anything built with relief labor was expensive.[27] Likewise, Edith Elmer Wood concluded that the high cost "proves only that relief labor is expensive."[28]

Along with allegations that the towns were unnecessary, impractical, and expensive, the argument was made that they were part of a sinister plan to impose foreign, socialist, or communist ways of life on the American people or at least that they forced unwanted regimentation by being planned.[29] Albert Mayer understated the case when he said that "the impression has gotten around that they are in some vague way radical."[30] In this respect, the towns suffered heavily from their association with the New Deal and Rexford Tugwell, and were often tagged "Tugwelltowns" in the press and in Congress.[31]

Tugwell's popularity with the public and with Congress

was, as several historians have noted, less than cordial.[32] During the 1936 campaign, he was often labeled a communist mastermind who, like Lenin, would soon dispose of his Kerensky (Roosevelt).[33] While few credited Senator Davis's accusation that Tugwell was really a communist, many congressmen complained about the R.A.'s supposed plans for "shifting people around from where they are to where Dr. Tugwell thinks they ought to be."[34] Some newspapers added to these fears by entitling articles such as "First Communist Town in U.S. Nears Completion" and "Tugwell Abolishes Private Property."[35] One landlord, contacted by the Suburban Division for a reference on a prospective Greenbelt resident, refused to give out any information saying he would not participate in projects which were "un-American and tend to Communism."[36]

The fact that the towns had drawn on intellectual theories and European designs made them suspect. Bruner warned that the R.A.'s housing program was "like all things Tugwellian . . . far different from accepted ideas—at least far from those accepted in America."[37] The New York *Sun* found the architectural style of Greenbelt un-American and wondered why the Cape Cod or Nantucket style cottage was not used. "But the Tugwell outfit wanted nothing in the American Tradition. They found their inspiration in Europe and the Near East and the result was a collection of houses that look like hideous barracks."[38] Bruner deprecated the towns, writing that Greenbelt houses would surround a "campus" and that "there is always something collegiate about Tugwell schemes."[39] An article called "The Sweetheart of the Regimenters: Dr. Tugwell Makes America Over," traced the "fantastic" ideas behind the Tugwell programs to the fact that "the Sweetheart of the Regimenters was seventeen years a pedagogue."[40]

Fear of regimentation and coercion on the part of the government was easily exploited. *Nation's Business* was convinced that tenants would be treated like inmates in a poorhouse. "Much emphasis is placed on the 'spirit of cooperation'. The assistant manager, like Professor Tugwell, went to Russia to observe the Great Experiment and learn new ways of dealing with individualists and dissenters."[41] An interview with Greenbelt's town manager, Roy Braden, allegedly revealed that the government would "hold a whip hand over society," and that the R.A. would "invite" (the paper put the word in quotation marks) residents to form a citizen's association in an attempt to "socialize" (also in quotation marks) them.[42] When the R.A. announced that residents of the towns would not be permitted to have dogs, there was a storm of protest. The *New York Times* sympathized editorially with prospective residents who would be forced to give up their pets and suggested that "before it plans any more Utopias, perhaps the government would do well to draft a bit of human nature into the blueprints."[43] Every new rule in the towns was reported, often in headlines; "Greenbelt Bans Display of Wash After 4 P.M. And On Sundays—Private Mutterings of 'Regimentation' Are Heard As New Rules Go Into Effect—Tricycles Regulated."[44] This type of press coverage exemplified what Nathan Straus, first administrator of Public Housing, called a double standard of judging public and private housing. Editorials seldom rise to the support of tenants forced to give up pets to move into private housing; few articles condemn landlords who regiment their tenants through more detailed and arbitrary regulations than were imposed on the Greenbelt residents.[45]

Another ominous possibility raised by the greenbelt town program was the prospect of the government resettling Negroes in the suburbs. This was, of course, speculation since the announced policy of the R.A. was to exclude them from the towns; but there seems little doubt that it was on the minds of a number of people. Alva Johnston, a conservative critic of Tugwell and the New Deal, wrote,

> Among the largest Tugwell towns is the Greenhills project near Cincinnati and the Berwyn project near Washington, D. C. There is a large Negro population in both cities. There is a constitutional question whether the government, no mat-

ter what incorporation tricks it employs, can exclude Negroes from these communities.[46]

The N.A.R.E.B. never publicly expressed concern over the greenbelt town program opening suburban areas to Negroes, but its members were continually informed of the attempts of Negroes to move into white suburban areas. In the highly publicized attempt of Joshua Cockburn, a West Indian Negro, to move into a $20,000 home purchased in Westchester County, New York, in an area restricted to whites, the N.A.R.E.B. stated that if the court decided in favor of Cockburn, "the results would be serious to many protected neighborhoods."[47] The resistance of suburban communities and fringe areas of cities to the outward movement of Negroes hardly needs documentation. Nathan Straus, in the early 1950s, stated that fear of Negro migration had set white suburbanites against any dispersion of public housing from the old slum districts.[48] Martin Meyerson and Edward C. Banfield have detailed the continual policy of the Chicago Housing Authority program to keep public housing with its Negro residents out of all middle-class white areas of the city.[49]

The Resettlement Administration carefully followed press accounts of the projects, attempting to counter the hostile ones with a stream of press releases and illustrated pamphlets.[50] A Legal Division report warned that most newspaper coverage would be unfavorable and therefore the government literature would "serve to combat any unfounded attacks."[51] Nevertheless, most Americans learned about the towns through confusing newspaper and magazine reports. There was an inability, for instance, to recognize that the towns were complete communities as distinguished from ordinary housing developments. On June 11, 1936, eight months after the Greenbelt, Maryland, plans had been announced, the *Washington Post* used "Greenbelt, Maryland" as the dateline for an article, and Lansill noted beside it—"This is the first recognition given in the dateline of Greenbelt as a town."[52] The *Evening Star*, in September of the same year, was still referring to Greenbelt as the "Berwyn Housing Project"—Berwyn being the closest town to Greenbelt.[53]

Some who were enthusiastic while studying the plans of the towns were disillusioned at their first sight of the actual construction area. At Greendale, reporters found "streets that go nowhere, front yards in the back, back yards in the front, little space between the houses . . . hilly land left ungraded and a hundred and one other things never before seen."[54] The editors of the *Cincinnati Times-Star* toured Greenhills in October, 1937. What they had thought was a "nice idea" dismayed them. "For instead of the comely, rustic little village we had thought of, we saw the once beautiful countryside desecrated, and on its tortured surface a confused jumble of box-like shacks, looking for all the world like an ill-designed army barracks."[55]

Newspapers favorable to the New Deal public housing programs found it difficult to separate the greenbelt program from the subsistence homesteads program. The *St. Louis Star-Times* inaccurately described the towns as "garden homesteads on the fringes of industrial communities where workers can have decent low-cost housing with an acre or two of land on which to raise their own food."[56] The *Milwaukee Journal* breaking, for the first time, the news of a resettlement project of the Milwaukee area, said that Milwaukee's "Tugwelltown" would follow the pattern of the subsistence homesteads—providing land for each family to raise food "and keep a goat or cow or pig."[57]

It is ironic that the greenbelt towns should have suffered from a confusion with the subsistence homesteads, for the advocates of the towns were some of the severest critics of the subsistence homesteads. Beginning with Ebenezer Howard the garden city movement was urban centered; aimed at fostering a better *urban* environment including within it the open spaces and vegetation of the countryside. The essential factor in the agricultural belt or greenbelt was not that it preserve farms and fields, but that it remain open land. In the United States, Josiah Strong, one of the earliest supporters of the garden city movement, had been a most outspoken opponent of the back-to-the-land movement.[58]

Albert Mayer, one of the architects of Greenbrook, thought the subsistence homesteads program was utterly foolish, being based on a "misapplication of the real meaning of decentralization with overtones of sentimentalism and nostalgia."[59] Catherine Bauer, whose 1934 study, *Modern Housing*, was a standard reference for public housing administrators, said that subsistence homesteads were certainly *not* modern housing. She feared that these defeatist "schemes" would create "a new American peasantry with a standard of living and an outlook for the future probably about equal to that obtainable in the Balkan rural regions."[60]

Rexford Tugwell was certainly the most widely quoted spokesman for the Resettlement Administration. He based the suburban resettlement program on studies of population movements in the United States which indicated that both the countryside and central city were losing population to suburban areas. Suburban resettlement "accepted a trend instead of trying to reverse it."[61] Building entire suburban communities according to a fixed plan could prevent overcrowding within the towns and encroachments from without.[62] Slum clearance could not begin to provide adequate space for homes and recreation. While Tugwell admitted that the towns would not be less expensive than slum housing, he believed that slum dwellers would strain to meet the slightly higher rents and would find, under improved conditions, the incentive to work harder for what they had.[63] The cities, Tugwell argued, would fight to retain the residents by opposing the suburban towns, but the Resettlement Administration had shown how well the federal government could do the job. "There ought to be 3,000 such projects rather than three," he concluded.[64]

Several new ideas inherent in the program interested professional planners. Unfortunately, this interest was generally limited to discussion in professional journals with specialized circulations. The *Architectural Record* stated that the comprehensive nature of the town plans "are commencing a new chapter in American town planning and community architecture."[65] The article hoped one result of the program would be knowledge of exact initial costs and maintenance expenses for a whole town, since a typical American community could not be so measured, and the information could be of tremendous value to planners.[66] Walter Blucher agreed with critics that some aspects of the plans could be improved, but they nevertheless "show to Americans for the first time how communities providing for adequate living can be constructed according to a plan."[67] Blucher optimistically wrote, "We laugh at the early models of the Ford, but I believe it is fair to say that the first attempts in a new form of city building in America are much more advanced than was the first Ford."[68]

The towns also attracted attention in professional planning journals outside the United States.[69] Richard L. Reiss, vice-chairman of Welwyn Garden City, stated that the greenbelt towns were a valuable contribution to rational urban decentralization and called particular attention to the significance of the federal role in the construction of the towns in a nation "where the prejudice against any form of public enterprise which appears to conflict with ordinary business, is still very strong."[70] He was surprised that "these projects should have been started at all."[71] From a British point of view he saw the program as a first step towards publicly directed regional planning. Not all American planners and housing experts agreed with this assessment, but the program did provide a concrete example for those advocating a radically new type of decentralized public housing.

The most vivid and beautiful presentation of the greenbelt towns is Pare Lorentz's film "The City," which was shown at the New York World's Fair in 1939 and later throughout the nation. Lorentz, who had directed "The Plough that Broke the Plains" for the federal government, engaged Aaron Copland to write the musical background and Lewis Mumford to write the script. The film was financed by a $50,000 grant from the Carnegie Foundation through the American Institute of Planners.[72] It portrays the city's dirt, smoke, noise, confusion, and demoralizing slums. Only a temporary escape can be found in the drab monotony of jerry-built residential neighborhoods because creeping blight soon reduces them to slums. Greenbelt, Maryland, is shown in all its grassy splendor as the decentralized city of the future. "The City" was universally praised in the press, but *Time* magazine alleged the film lost impact by using Greenbelt as an example of the future city since the town was financially impractical.[73]

The most extensive discussion of decentralized public housing occurred during a symposium at the Annual Meeting of the American Institute of Planners in January, 1939. Harland Bartholomew, one of the nation's leading authorities on urban planning, presented the case for downtown locations contending that "American cities are not congested."[74] He believed that extension of public services to fringe and suburban developments would, in the long run, prove more expensive than building in the central city even with its higher land costs. Also, downtown residents do not expend their time and money commuting. He concluded that the decentralized city was "a beautiful idea, but like all such theories is largely if not wholly impractical and unsound."[75]

Clarence Stein spoke for the new town advocates. He asserted that construction of adequate housing projects in existing cities was almost impossible due to archaic street patterns, high land costs, and obsolete municipal laws. Adequate housing could only be provided in "complete new neighborhoods knit together by a new pattern of streets and open spaces."[76] He presented statistics to show that raw land could be improved with all utilities as was done at the greenbelt towns for less money than it cost to build a number of the housing projects in New York City. He closed saying that new towns could not be built in the old cities primarily because of the "high but false value placed on land by unrealized hopes for expansion."[77] The only hope for new towns within cities would be for these values to fall to their "use value" and "either the real estate owners or the entire community will have to pay for it."[78] Bartholomew answered that while he agreed on the need to develop neighborhood patterns, he still believed that decentralizing cities "into isolated sectors is a theoretical ideal but a practical impossibility" and that such an occurrence would be both foolish and expensive for urban America.[79] In the general discussion that followed, it was apparent that most of the speakers doubted the usefulness of new towns. Even Roland Wank, one of the architects of Greenhills, said he hoped suburban towns would not wipe urban agglomerations off the map because it takes a certain size city to support many functions of civilization. Frederick L. Ackerman agreed with Bartholomew that suburban new towns were a form of "escapism" from the problems of the central city. Arthur Comey feared that building entire towns would result in their becoming obsolete in a few years and thus very expensive to remold to new conditions.[80]

While a number of planners and housing experts did agree that some form of decentralization was needed, few saw the greenbelt program solving that need. Mabel L. Walker, whose *Urban Blight and Slums* was published in 1938, devoted a chapter to the subject "Siphoning Off Slum Population," but gave only passing comment to the greenbelt towns and did not foresee them as a solution.[81] The Committee on Urbanism of the National Resources Committee endorsed the greenbelt idea without ever mentioning the towns by name, but it was not a major focus of their report.[82] Frederic Delano, chairman of the National Resources Planning Board's Central Housing Committee, recommended privately a program of federally financed purchases of large tracts for the purpose of "planning communities or large scale neighborhoods."[83] However, when he restated his view in *The American City* in January, 1937, he said:

> The municipality, usually through a Housing Authority, might properly purchase entire neighborhoods in blighted areas or perhaps in suburban or undeveloped territory. . . . Sometimes slum conditions can be made tolerable by draining off part of the population through . . . the purchase of convenient outlying land. . . . The orderly development of

residential neighborhoods, of adequate size to guarantee
their stability, would thus be possible on cheap land.[84]

Apparently Delano chose to discuss only neighborhood developments rather than *community* developments with internal
governments and institutions. This difference is crucial to the
whole garden city and greenbelt town concept. Richard Fernbach explained it in regard to Greendale:

> The vision of the Greendale planners extended far beyond
> the mere physical plan of the town. It recognized govern-
> ment housing as more than the provision of shelter—it is the
> creation of communities in which democratic processes of
> living can best be developed.[85]

The only other aspect of the greenbelt town program that
interested professional planners and administrators was the
purchase of excess land around the site of each town. The acquisition of such large amounts of vacant land was, it will be
remembered, somewhat of an accident when the Suburban Division discovered after the land purchases were made, that
money was not available to build towns as large as originally
contemplated. However, the opportunity was presented to experiment with the holding of what was called "urban land reserves." The cities of Europe had been purchasing undeveloped land for future expansion since the start of the 20th
century. Raymond Unwin had suggested a similar policy to
Americans as early as 1914 and it had been recommended in
1935 by the Committee on Research in Urban Land Policies of
the National Conference on Planning.[86] Jacob Crane was a
member of this committee; and when he became one of the
chief planners of Greendale, he was able to present a concrete
example of urban land reserves using Greendale's tract for detailed analysis.[87] The resulting report urging the purchase of
urban land reserves was met with little comment and no
action.[88]

The American Society of Planning Officials numbered only ninety-one members in 1938. They were not united in support of the new towns, and their influence was circumscribed by public indifference or suspicion towards their profession. The National Association of Real Estate Boards maintained that twenty years of city planning had had no beneficial effect on cities and further,

> until city planners have shown more wisdom and foresight than they have to date, any demands on their part, whether voiced through the National Resources Board or through their associations, for a further extension of city planning functions and powers should be received with considerable caution and scepticism.[89]

America's city councilmen agreed with the N.A.R.E.B. by refusing city planners money or authority. A 1936 survey found that, of 933 city and county planning commissions, only sixty-four had annual budgets over $1,500. The other 869 could not employ full-time planners, much less give them projects to plan.[90] Planning commissions were run by part-time amateurs who were not taken seriously by municipal officials.[91]

Another deterrent to public enthusiasm for the greenbelt towns was lack of interest on the part of public housing groups such as the National Association of Housing Officials, the National Public Housing Conference, and the Labor Housing Conference. Members of these groups together with leading figures in the public housing movement met in Baltimore in October, 1935, and issued a report called "A Housing Program for the United States," which became the basis of the Wagner Housing Act of 1937.[92] That act prohibited the establishment of housing projects with their own legal governments and police powers. Judging by the difficulties incurred in passing the act at all, the inclusion of powers to construct new towns might very well have blocked the entire piece of legislation. Senator Byrd, a leading opponent to the bill, attacked it for opening yet another door to federal construction of costly housing projects.

> What assurance has the Senator Wagner that the same extravagances which existed under the Resettlement Administration at Tugwelltown, when that unit was built as a low cost housing unit, will not continue? At Tugwelltown the unit cost was $16,000 per unit. What guaranty can the Senator give that the same extravagances will not appear in connection with the program under his bill?[93]

Intimation of this kind of attitude was noted in the Baltimore report which stated that the building of complete new towns "involves much more than housing" and could not be initiated by the federal government in the immediate future. Further it stated that while the concept was a good one, "the provision of adequate housing cannot wait until the satellite type of development is generally adopted."[94]

Organized labor supported the greenbelt town program both locally and nationally. The building trades councils and other A.F. of L. affiliated unions in the town locations passed resolutions supporting the projects both as work relief and housing programs.[95] The *Trade Unionist* published an enthusiastic article on the greenbelt towns emphasizing that moderate-income families could purchase low-cost homes because of the savings resulting from "bulk purchase and large scale cooperation."[96] However, the A.F. of L. devoted its primary efforts to the housing program as suggested in the Wagner Act and merely endorsed a resolution supporting the greenbelt town program.[97] Labor's view was that, while understanding the advantages of garden cities, a slum clearance program presented fewer problems.[98]

President Roosevelt championed the towns as a demonstration of what American communities should be doing but did not suggest that the government would build any more such projects.[99] Will Alexander remembers Roosevelt's visit to Greenbelt vividly.

F.D.R.'s first trip away from the White House after his election in '36 was to Greenbelt. He was very excited about it and had wanted to go earlier but was too busy with the campaign, but soon after he called the office and said he wanted to see it. There was a crowd of 6,000–7,000 around the White House gate and people lined the streets all the way to Greenbelt. F.D.R. asked, "What are all these people doing here?" Tugwell told him it had probably been in the papers that he was going out. He had the time of his life with that crowd that afternoon. Oh, he was happy. He just glowed under the response of the people.[100]

The president toured Greenbelt for two hours, stopping six times to look at various projects. He was accompanied by all the top officials of the Resettlement Administration and the Suburban Division, along with Maryland's Senator Radcliff, Representative Gambrill, State Delegate Kent Mullikin, and many other officials. F.D.R. said that no effort should be spared to give people easy access to the town because it was "too good an exhibit of what can be done in planning not to make it easy for visitors to come and go and for residents to get to their work without danger and delay."[101] He asked how the local bodies had cooperated with the project and was told they had cooperated very well. At his request he was shown areas set aside for Boy Scouts, Girl Scouts, and 4-H Clubs. He wanted the streets, water system, electrical system, and playgrounds explained. Roosevelt was impressed with the savings resulting from overall planning of streets and utilities and noted that application of the same principles in other towns would reduce municipal debts.[102] While touring the school and community building, the president asked architect Douglas Ellinton about the materials and construction, remarking, "Very nice, very nice indeed."[103] As he left one of the apartments he told reporters,

I have seen the blueprints of this project and have been greatly interested, but the actual sight itself exceeds anything I dreamed of. This is a real achievement and I wish

everyone in the country could see it. . . . The homes being
built here are to serve primarily the low income group of
citizens. It is an experiment that ought to be copied by every
community in the United States.[104]

While there appears to be no direct connection between
the president's visit to Greenbelt and Tugwell's resignation
four days later, the R.A. administrator may have wanted Roosevelt to see what he, Tugwell, considered the single most significant R.A. project. This possibility is suggested by Tugwell's
concurrent effort to convince Roosevelt and Wallace to transfer
the R.A. to the Department of Agriculture.[105] The transfer was
effected on December 31, 1936, the same day that Tugwell left
the government. The R.A. was placed under the administration
of Will Alexander.[106] One of his first actions was to fire the entire
publicity staff, saying that he didn't want any more publicity.
Nor did he and the Suburban Division staff consider building
any more towns. "They had been terribly criticized," said Alexander. "We all believed in them but we felt that three was as
many as we could get away with."[107]

The most plausible reason for the unpopularity of the greenbelt towns is that the leaders of the building industry, real
estate, finance, mass media, and many others were wedded
to individualistic private enterprise in housing and community planning. They were almost all critical of the state of the
American metropolitan areas, but believed that planning by
thousands of individual land owners and builders—the free market—was preferable to the regimentation involved in public
planning. Sir Raymond Unwin, lecturing at Columbia University in 1937, said that "rugged individualism" was instinctive in
Americans and was the most serious obstacle to "planning for
the common good of all."[108] An editor of *Plan Age* noted that
Americans seemed to prefer the "disguised coercion" of an individualistic system and shuddered at the suggestion of a small
degree of regimentation through government planning.[109] After
his experience with the greenbelt towns and subsequently with

the Regional Plan Association of New York, Tugwell decided that Americans refuse to support government planning primarily out of "fear of regimentation."[110] Marquis W. Childs said that after listening to Tugwell and the other planners explain the programs of the Resettlement Administration,

> I remembered being exhilarated and at the same time disturbed after a dinner or a lunch with the pioneers of the brave new world. I felt that somehow they didn't know the Middle West that I knew and the people in the Middle West. The whole process seemed far removed from the deeper currents of American life. . . . In many respects it was typical of the effort to superimpose from Washington a ready-made Utopia . . . without some political nourishment. As Doctor Tugwell found out, it is impossible to lay down a blueprint for even a small section of society in this vast, powerful well-nigh ungovernable country.[111]

Lawrence Hewes, more charitably, believed that many Americans supported the R.A. program; but, after listening to Congressional committees attack the R.A., he realized that "our support consisted of the President and a great number of unvocal, unimpressive, unimportant non-voters."[112] Edward McKernon, publicity advisor in 1937 to the New York Regional Plan Association as well as the state planning boards of New York, New Jersey, and Pennsylvania, avowed that planning could only be "sold" to the nation as a profitable business program which will appeal to the selfish interest of powerful individuals. While recognizing that most planners are great humanitarians, planning could never appeal in that manner because "society as a whole is not interested in society as a whole."[113]

1.   Herbert Hoover, *The Memoirs of Herbert Hoover*, 3: 412.
2.   Michael Straus and Talbot Wegg, *Housing Comes of Age*, p. 61.
3.   *Cincinnati Enquirer*, January 12, 1936.
4.   George Morris, "$16,000 Homes for $2,000 Incomes! Greenbelt,

Maryland," *Nation's Business* 26 (January, 1938): 21. Earlier, however, a Special Committee on Housing of the National Chamber of Commerce recognized the necessity of subsidizing the shelter of the lowest income group, but suggested it be done through rent subsidies paid by local relief agencies rather than through the construction of public housing. See the *New York Times*, February 1, 1936. Nor did the N.A.R.E.B. oppose all types of government aid to the housing industry. It helped draft legislation creating the Federal Housing Administration in 1933–34 and endorsed a program of federal information collection and dissemination. See the *New York Times*, June 14, 1936. The direct construction and management of public housing was opposed by several groups in addition to the chamber of commerce and N.A.R.E.B. See Robert M. Fisher, *Twenty Years of Public Housing*, p. 21; Timothy McDonnell, *The Wagner Housing Act*; Ray W. Bronez, "Interest Groups and Public Housing," pp. 191–98, 267–75.

5. *Milwaukee Journal*, March 1, 1936.

6. *Washington Post*, October 23, 1935.

7. Ibid.

8. *New York Times*, January 14, 1936.

9. U.S., Congress, Senate, Committee on Education and Labor, *Hearings on S. 4424, United States Housing Act of 1936*, 74th Cong., 2d sess., 1936, p. 316.

10. N.A.R.E.B., *Confidential Weekly Letter*, September 21, 1936.

11. *New York Times*, September 27, 1936.

12. N.A.R.E.B., *Confidential Weekly Letter*, May 2, 1938.

13. "Realtor Want Drastic Change in Residential Development," *Business Week*, May 28, 1930, p. 21.

14. Carl Feiss, "New Towns for America," *Journal of the American Institute of Architects* 33 (January, 1960): 85.

15. *Washington Post*, February 10, 1936.

16. *Washington Star*, September 13, 1936; and *Washington News*, January 23, 1937.

17. "Fever Chart of a Tugwell Town," *Nation's Business* 26 (November, 1938): 13.

18. N.A.R.E.B., *Confidential Weekly Letter*, September 7, 1937.

19. *New York Times*, July 5, 1937.

20. U.S., Farm Security Administration, "Final Report of Project Costs," p. 10.

21. "Co-Op: R.A.'s First Community Becomes a New Deal Guinea Pig," *Newsweek*, September 13, 1937, p. 10.

22. "Greenbelt," *Time*, September 13, 1937, p. 10.

212 THE NEW DEAL IN THE SUBURBS

23. *Nation's Business* 26 (January, 1938): 21–22.

24. Corwin Wilson, "Mr. Mumford's Castle," *Shelter* 3, no. 4 (November, 1938): 23.

25. Tugwell, Address to the Regional Planning Commission of Hamilton County, Ohio, pp. 12–14.

26. Tugwell, "Meaning of the Greenbelt Towns," *The New Republic* 90 (February 17, 1937): 42.

27. Tracy B. Augur and Walter H. Blucher, "The Significance of the Greenbelt Towns," *Housing Yearbook: 1938*, p. 224.

28. Edith Elmer Wood, "Housing: United States," *Britannica Book of the Year, 1938* (Chicago: Encyclopedia Britannica, Inc., 1938), p. 324.

29. Using quotation marks around the word "planning" was the most common way writers in the 1930s indicated the sinister portent of government planning. See, for example, Warren Bishop, "A Yardstick for Housing," *Nation's Business* 24 (April, 1936): 29.

30. Mayer, *New York Times Magazine*, February 2, 1936, p. 8.

31. Duncan Aikman, "Tugwelltown: The Story of Greenbelt the Government's New Socialized Community," *Current History* 44 (August, 1936); 96–101; *Nation's Business* 26 (November, 1938), p. 13; and "Plan Federal 'Tugwelltown' on Tract at Hale's Corners," *Milwaukee Journal*, December 4, 1935. Tugwell did not like his name used to identify the towns and asked the Suburban Division to give them proper names. The staff found the name Greenbelt expressive of the town's most unique feature, but it sounded somewhat artificial. A search was made by Wallace Richards for local names, but no suitable one could be found; and therefore Greenbelt was decided upon (interview with Wallace Richards in *Washington Star*, March 18, 1936). After another search of all towns in the United States beginning with "green," the other three towns were given this same prefix. (The list of towns with the prefix "green" is found in Lansill Papers, personal files.) The names first appear in the R.A.'s "Weekly Progress Report No. 40," March 28, 1936.

32. Bernard Sternsher, *Rexford G. Tugwell and the New Deal*, pp. 279–84, 321, 347–53; Paul K. Conkin, *Tomorrow a New World*, pp. 175–76; Lawrence Hewes, *Boxcar in the Sand*, pp. 175–76; and Will W. Alexander, *Oral History Memoir*, pp. 471–72, 638.

33. The most complete discussion of the literature naming Tugwell a communist mastermind is found in Sternsher, *Rexford G. Tugwell*, pp. 348–55.

34. Davis's comment was made in an address to a Republican rally (*New York Times*, October 4, 1936). Representative Woodruff's comment is from the U.S., *Congressional Record*, 74th Cong., 2d sess., 1936, 80, pt. 6: 6111.

35. "First Communist Towns in America Near Completion," *Chicago American*, October 28, 1936; "Tugwell Abolishes Private Property," *New York American*, October 29, 1936.

36. Fulmer, *Greenbelt*, p. 19.

37. *Washington Post*, February 11, 1936.

38. *New York Sun*, July 11, 1936.

39. *Washington Post*, February 11, 1936.

40. Blair Bolles, "The Sweetheart of the Regimenters: Dr. Tugwell Makes America Over," *American Mercury* 39 (September, 1936): 78.

41. Fred Thornhill and Fred DeArmond, "Another Social Experiment Goes Sour," *Nation's Business* 28 (October, 1940): 109. Mr. Thornhill was a former resident of Greenbelt who was reported to have been overwhelmingly defeated for the town council in an election and was refused another important position in the town cooperative. See *Greenbelt Cooperator*, October 17, 1940.

42. *Washington Star*, September 14, 1936.

43. *New York Times*, November 15, 1937.

44. *Washington Star*, March 30, 1938.

45. Nathan Straus, *Two-Thirds of a Nation: A Housing Program*, p. 119.

46. Alva Johnston, "Tugwell, the President's Idea Man," *Saturday Evening Post* 209 (August 1, 1936): 73.

47. N.A.R.E.B., *Confidential Weekly Letter*, February 23, 1937.

48. Straus, *Two-Thirds of a Nation*, pp. 141–42.

49. Martin Meyerson and Edward C. Banfield, *Politics, Planning and the Public Interest: The Case of Public Housing in Chicago*.

50. Newspaper clippings were passed around to the R.A. officials and then kept in a large notebook, two of which are retained at the National Archives, Record Group 96. For a brief description of the information activites of the R.A., see U.S., Resettlement Administration, *First Annual Report*, pp. 97–98.

51. Report from James E. Reid (Legal Division) to Franklin S. Pollack (chief, Legal Division), August 27, 1935, R.O.A., H.H.F.A., Drawer 527.

52. Lansill Papers, personal files.

53. *Washington Star*, September 13, 1936.

54. *Milwaukee Journal*, August 16, 1936.

55. *Cincinnati Star-Times*, October 4, 1937.

56. *St. Louis Star-Times*, May 14, 1936.

57. *Milwaukee Journal*, December 4, 1935.

58. Josiah Strong, *The Challenge of the City*, pp. 30–33.

59. Albert Mayer, "Why Not Housing?" *The New Republic* 84 (September 4, 1935): 97.

60. Catherine Bauer, *Modern Housing*, p. 251. One effect of this criticism was that the R.A. Management Division changed the names of these projects from subsistence homesteads to "part-time farming homesteads." U.S., Resettlement Administration, *First Annual Report*, p. 66.

61. Tugwell, "Meaning of the Greenbelt Towns," p. 42.

62. This idea was expressed in Tugwell's first public statement on the towns in his NBC Radio Address, December 2, 1935, Roosevelt Papers, O.F. 1568.

63. Tugwell, Address to the Regional Planning Commission of Hamilton County, Ohio, p. 11.

64. Tugwell, "Meaning of the Greenbelt Towns," p. 42.

65. "Greenbelt Towns," *Architectural Record* 80 (September, 1936): 215.

66. Ibid., p. 218.

67. American Society of Planning Officials, *Newsletter* 3 (October, 1937): 81.

68. National Association of Housing Officials, *Housing Yearbook: 1938*, p. 224.

69. J. M. de Casseres, "Amerikaansche reiservaringen op stedebouwkundig gebied," *Tijdschrift Voor Volkshuisvesting en Stedebouw* 20 (February, 1939): 41–51; Giorgio Rigotti, "I Borghi dalle 'Siedlungen' alle 'Greenbelt Towns,'" *Urbanistica* 6 (January–February, 1937): 1; R. Kantorowich, "A Report on the Greenbelt Towns in the United States of America," *Architectural Record* (South Africa), 27 (December, 1942): 385–92; and "Los Pueblos Greenbelt en Estados Unidos," *El Arquitecto Peruano* 8 (May, 1944): 4–6.

70. Richard L. Reiss, "American Greenbelt Towns," *Town and Country Planning* 6 (January, 1938): 18.

71. Ibid.

72. "The City," *The Planners' Journal* 5 (July–September, 1939): 70–71.

73. "The City," *Time* 33 (June 5, 1939): 66–67. For a more critical view of the film's central theme, see Scott, *American City Planning*, pp. 362–63.

74. The entire discussion was published under the title, "Planning Considerations in the Location of Housing Projects," *The Planners' Journal* 5 (March–June, 1939): 33.

75. Ibid., p. 34.

76. Ibid., p. 39.

77. Ibid., p. 41.

78. Ibid.

79. Ibid., p. 42.

80. Ibid., pp. 43–44.

81. Mabel L. Walker, *Urban Blight and Slums*, Harvard City Planning Studies, Vol. 12 (Cambridge, Mass.: Harvard University Press, 1938), pp. 125–30.

82. Committee on Urbanism of the National Resources Committee, *Our Cities: Their Role in the National Economy* (Washington: U.S. Government Printing Office, 1937), pp. 48, 76.

83. Confidential memo from Frederic Delano to members of the Central Housing Committee, September 16, 1936, Lansill Papers, personal files (photostatic copy in posession of author).

84. Frederic Delano, "To Meet the Housing Needs of the Lower Income Groups," *The American City* 52 (January, 1937): 45–48.

85. Richard Fernbach, "Greendale," *The Planners' Journal* 3 (November–December, 1937): 161.

86. Raymond Unwin, "Land Values and Town Planning," *The Annals of the American Academy of Political and Social Science* 51 (January, 1914): 23; "National Conference on Planning," *Planning and Civic Comment* 1 (April–June, 1935): 32.

87. John S. Lansill and Jacob Crane, "Metropolitan Land Reserves as Illustrated by Greendale, Wisconsin," *The American City* 52 (July, 1937): 55–58.

88. Committee on Urbanism, *Our Cities*, p. 76.

89. N.A.R.E.B., *Confidential Weekly Letter*, June 21, 1937.

90. Robert A. Walker, "Is the City Planning Commission Meeting Today's Problems?" *The American City* 55 (December, 1940): 68.

91. Ibid., p. 69.

92. McDonnell, *The Wagner Housing Act*, pp. 72–80, 88–89. See also the Wagner Housing Act or U.S., Congress, *The United States Housing Act of 1937*, Public Law 412, 75th Cong., 1st sess., 1937.

93. U.S., Congressional Record, 75th Cong., 1st sess., 1937, 81, pt. 7: 7982.

94. National Association of Housing Officials, *A Housing Program for the United States*, Public Administration Service Publication, no. 84 (Chicago: Public Administration Service, 1935), pp. 15–16.

95.　A complete list of these resolutions is found in the Summary Information Reports for Greenbelt, Greenbrook, Greendale, and Greenhills, Lansill Papers, personal files. A partial list, including selected quotations from endorsement letters, is found in U.S., Resettlement Administration, *Resettlement Administration Program: In Response to Senate Resolution No. 295,* p. 21. Local newspapers did not always print news of labor unions which passed resolutions supporting the projects, but some that did include the *New Brunswick Daily Home News,* December 11, 1935, and the *Cincinnati Enquirer,* January 24, 1936 (which placed the endorsement of Greenhills by the Cincinnati Building Trades Council on page five while the condemnations of the project by the Cincinnati Chamber of Commerce appeared the same day on page one). Support by the Milwaukee Federated Trades Council and the Milwaukee Building and Loan Council was read into the U.S., *Congressional Record,* 74th Cong., 2d sess., 1936, 80, pt. 6: 8090, by Senator LaFollette.

96.　The American Federation of Labor, *The Trade Unionist,* June 6, 1936.

97.　The American Federation of Labor, *Report of the Proceedings of the Fifty-sixth Annual Convention of the American Federation of Labor* (Washington, D.C.: Judd and Detweiler, 1936), pp. 177, 280.

98.　McDonnell, *The Wagner Housing Act,* p. 69 n.

99.　A few newspapers believed Roosevelt's visit to Greenbelt and his remarks there at least raised the possibility of more funds flowing into the suburban town program. See the *Washington Herald,* November 13, 1936, the *Washington Daily News,* November 14, 1936, and the *New York Times,* November 18, 1936.

100.　Alexander, *Oral History Memoir,* p. 563.

101.　*The Prince Georgian* (Mt. Rainer, Maryland), November 25, 1936. This is the most complete and detailed account of the president's visit to Greenbelt to be found in any newspaper.

102.　Ibid.

103.　*New York Herald-Tribune,* November 14, 1936.

104.　*The Prince Georgian,* November 25, 1936, but see also the *Washington Post,* November 14, 1936, and the *New York Times,* November 14, 1936.

105.　Sternsher, *Rexford G. Tugwell,* p. 324.

106.　See Executive Order No. 7530, December 31, 1936, in Rosenman, *Papers and Addresses,* 4: 624.

107.　Alexander, *Oral History Memoir,* pp. 549, 638.

108.　Sir Raymond Unwin, *Housing and Town Planning Lectures 1936–1937,* p. 9.

109. Lewis L. Lorwin, "Planning in a Democracy," *Plan Age* 1 (February, 1935): 4–5.

110. Rexford G. Tugwell, "The Fourth Power," *Planning and Civic Comment* 5, part 2 (April–June, 1939): 14.

111. Marquis Childs, *I Write from Washington*, pp. 13–14. By 1950 Tugwell himself came close to the same view. See his "Foreword" in Edward C. Banfield, *Government Project*, p. 11.

112. Hewes, *Boxcar in the Sand*, p. 83.

113. Edward McKernon, "Selling the Planning Idea," *The Planners' Journal* 3 (July–August, 1937): 85.

12

※ THE WAR YEARS

The strains of the Second World War fell unevenly on the three greenbelt towns. Greenhills and Greendale felt the loss of their young men who went to the armed forces, but the wives, children, and parents remained in the two communities. The original residents of Greenbelt, most of them federal employees, were scattered throughout the nation, and one thousand families were added to the town when a defense housing project was constructed there in 1942. Thus the town with the most vigorous cooperative democracy was the most severely disrupted.

Citizens of Greenbelt were overwhelmingly opposed to the Fascists. The editors of the *Cooperator* gave increasing attention to the international scene in 1938–39, lamenting the Munich Agreement and condemning the neutrality legislation prohibiting aid to the "people of Spain in their struggle against foreign fascist agression."[1] On December 5, 1938, the citizens' association agreed not to purchase any goods produced by agressor nations.[2] The "peace politicians" and "peace societies" were scored for their failure to see that the only way to keep oppression out of the Western Hemisphere was to increase our military strength. The *Cooperator* was opposed, however, to sending U.S. troops to defend European nations.[3] A strong military defense program at home and aid to the allies short of troops was the position taken by eighteen out of the twenty leading citizens polled by the *Cooperator*. Isolationist citizens had their views presented in early June, 1940, when Senator Gerald P. Nye visited Greenbelt to debate a professor from the University of Maryland. A crowd of over 300 heard Nye state that we should have nothing to do with the war in Europe, a comment which "brought a stirring round of applause from the audience."[4] However, a resolution to that effect which was to be sent to the president was discussed briefly by the 100 people who remained after the debate and the final vote to send it was only 59–26.[5] The debate continued at Greenbelt until December 7, 1941.

Greendale was much more clearly opposed to American entry into the war. The *Greendale Review*, commenting on the Munich crisis, believed the answer to world peace lay in the development of "cooperative principles applied to world affairs."[6] The development of an international cooperative economy would eliminate the primary cause of international hostilities.[7] The current European conflicts were mainly economic and the paper suggested that the United States stay out of that war and spend its money on public housing instead of battleships. Armistice Day was celebrated in Greendale in 1938, with a world peace pageant by Greendale Junior High School, highlighted by the crowning of a goddess of peace. In June, 1940, while the Germans invaded France, the citizens of Greendale sent a resolution to Congress and the president, stating that while they would defend their nation if it was attacked, they urged the government to "exert every effort to keep the United

States from armed participation in the war."[8] The attack on
Pearl Harbor and the declaration of war by Germany on the
United States ended further debate at Greendale. A large number of its men fought in the war—five of them lost their lives in
battle.[9]

Greenbelt was the only one of the three towns to be significantly altered by the Second World War. Long before Pearl
Harbor the community began to feel the effect of the war. Important residents who had built the close cooperative society
that characterized Greenbelt left the town. In October, 1940,
567 Greenbelt men registered for the selective service, and fifteen days later nine of them were drafted.[10] Mayor Henry
Maurer resigned his post when his government agency transferred him in January, 1940. George A. Warner was elected to
replace him, but was also transferred in February, 1941. The
same happened to the next replacement, Arthur Gawthorp, who
served only seven months. An even larger number of councilmen were likewise forced to resign. The high turnover in local
government officials was not as damaging as it might have been
without the excellent guidance of Roy Braden and his staff—but,
of course, that changed too. O. Kline Fulmer, the assistant manager, was transferred to work on defense housing in February,
1941. Vincent Holochworst, the recreation director since 1938,
left for the Navy in June, 1942. In 1943 Braden himself resigned.
Fortunately his replacement, James T. Gobbel, proved to be another efficient and well-liked manager.[11] The turnover in other
institutions was even greater. The *Cooperator* had nine different editors between May, 1940, and July, 1945. Three of the
five directors of the Greenbelt Consumer Services elected in
August, 1941, had to resign by October. Francis Fosnight, noting in his editorial on June 6, 1941, that the latest announce-
ments of people included an unusually large number of past and
current community leaders, asked sadly, "Who will replace
these men? We can only hope that we will be able to find others
who can at least carry on the fine tradition each of these men
has established in his own sphere."[12] Fifteen months later,

September, 1942, editor Fosnight and 661 of the other original residents of Greenbelt were gone.[13] Those who remained awaited the arrival of the families which would move into the nearly completed one thousand unit defense homes project, which would more than double the size of the town.

As the government expanded its facilities to accommodate the administration of a gigantic defense program in 1940, residents of Greenbelt, many of them government employees, discussed rumors concerning the future use of the townsite. In July, 1940, when the F.S.A. switched from an annual lease to a monthly one, the rumor spread that the residents would all be evicted and the town "converted into a barracks."[14] In October, 1940, Congress passed the Lanham Defense Housing Act, which permitted the construction and management of housing for defense workers by the federal government. The following month the Greenbelt town engineer let slip that the government planned to build defense housing at Greenbelt, and the citizens again pressed the F.S.A. for confirmation—without success. When the 1000 unit project was finally announced in February, 1941, it elicited a mixed response. On the one hand, Mayor Warner said it would be a great asset by reducing service costs and providing more potential membership for Greenbelt organizations and more business for its cooperative stores. On the other hand, Dayton Hull, president of the citizens' association, questioned whether the new housing units would be "of the present Greenbelt quality." Both men were correct.

The project, officially called MD-1811, was built under the direction of the Federal Works Agency at a total cost of $4,481,023. The net construction cost of the dwellings was $3,900 per unit.[15] Ground was broken in May, 1941, and the first families moved in eight months later.[16] The defense homes were only for employees of the War and Navy Departments, but were managed by the Farm Security Administration until the towns were all transferred to the Federal Public Housing Authority.[17] They were of inferior quality compared to the original Greenbelt homes. A government appraiser in 1948 re-

ported that the defense housing was built with inferior materials, but was better than most other war housing classified as
"permanent."[18] It was said that the insulation was so thin between apartments that "you can hear your neighbors break an
egg."[19] Street and utility systems had been installed during the
original construction, but landscaping was put off until the complaints of the residents produced some small effort in that direction. In 1947 the residents were still petitioning for shrubs,
hedges, and trees, but nothing was done until after the sale of
the town.[20] Also inferior to the original parts of town was the
site planning by the architects and engineers of the Federal
Works Administration. While the street plan dictated placement of the row houses fronting on interior parks, the system
of internal parks and sidewalks with underpasses was abandoned. This resulted in numerous traffic hazards unknown in
the original town. The first child in Greenbelt to be killed was
run over by a truck as she played in a defense home parking lot.
Maintenance costs on the defense housing units became a significant problem in the years following the war.[21]

The prediction that the town institutions would benefit
from the presence of the new families was fulfilled. The Co-op
business flourished with the influx of new customers. On the
other hand, Greenbelt's schools were almost drowned in a
tidal wave of new students. When school opened in the fall of
1941, the classes were overcrowded. The number of first-grad-
ers jumped from forty-three to eighty-seven, and classrooms
built to hold thirty-six students contained up to forty-nine.[22]
The relative youth, and therefore the larger number of children, of the original residents had been underestimated in the
beginning, so when even more children moved in the facilities
proved totally inadequate.[23] In June, 1942, the town council
threatened to seek an injunction to prevent more families from
moving into the defense homes until the government provided
more classrooms. Jointly with a reluctant Prince George's
County Board of Education, the government financed conver-
sion of a row house into a temporary school for two hundred

kindergarten and elementary school children, but it was not ready until the autumn of 1943. In 1942 schools had to open on a double shift. In the fall of 1943 the high school had to use the cafeteria for classrooms and due to lack of an instructor there was no physical education program. The elementary school was overflowing with seven hundred students, two hundred fifty more than in 1941. It operated on a double shift for all grades except kindergarten, which had a triple shift for its one hundred seventy-five children. There were no qualified teachers for the seventh and eighth grades.[24]

In March, 1944, General Philip Flemming of the Federal Works Administration announced that $282,000 had been appropriated for the construction of a twelve-classroom elementary school and an addition of five classrooms to the high school. The new facilities, scheduled to be ready by the autumn of 1944, were finally completed in May, 1945.[25]

An important factor in the maintenance of stability and continuity in Greenbelt was the nucleus of three hundred original families who remained during the war years.[26] After three mayors in a row were called away from Greenbelt in 1940–41, the office went to Allen D. Morrison, a member of the first town council in 1937. He served from September, 1941, to September, 1945. Francis Lastner, another original resident, with substantial experience in municipal administration, served as a council member from 1941–45 and from 1947–55.[27] Some initial resentment towards the defense home families was gradually dispelled. When Dayton Hull, an original resident, resigned as president of the citizens' association to serve in the Army in April, 1944, he was replaced by Wells Harrington, who had moved into the defense homes only eighteen months earlier.[28]

With the influx of new people, there were obvious changes in interests and emphasis. The Greenbelt Chamber Music Society and the Greenbelt Players folded during the war, and the annual Greenbelt Town Fair was abandoned in 1940.[29] A noticeable difference in the editorial policies of the *Cooperator* occurred. Articles on the cooperative spirit disappeared along with those on public housing. National and international issues were no longer presented, and no comment was made on the 1944 presidential election. The paper still presented wide coverage of local news, but it no longer expressed the crusading zeal of the prewar years. The need for town identification seemed past.

On the other hand, a new cooperative service was founded during the war to satisfy new needs. The child daycare center for 150 to 250 mothers who took full-time jobs in Washington began with a grant from the government and continued on a cooperative basis when the funds were withdrawn after the war.[30] Also, the Greenbelt town council appropriated funds for a youth center in 1944 after several incidents of vandalism temporarily closed the soda fountain at the drug store. The Greenbelt Woman's Club also contributed to the center.[31]

A sociological study of Greenbelt conducted during the war indicated that enthusiasm for the cooperative idea had declined. Thirty percent of the men in 1943 belonged to no organization at all, and only forty-five percent belonged to two or more. Interviews with a sample group of residents revealed that thirty-one percent endorsed the cooperative idea without reservation, forty-eight percent had some reservations, nine percent thought both co-op and private business should be allowed, and thirty-nine percent preferred private business over co-op business. Few residents considered Greenbelt their home. The personal columns of the *Cooperator* were filled with articles about families who "go home" for vacations and to be married. Only six of the sixty people who died in Greenbelt between 1937 and 1944 were buried in the town cemetery. Finally Greenbelt had developed a complex status system similar to that of an average suburban community. Seven "status groups" were identified ranging from the federal administrators and residents with professional occupations to the maintenance laborers and Negro janitors. Those who comprised the leadership of Greenbelt's institutions were found to be individuals whose occupations had more prestige, whose family background was white collar and middle class, and whose tenure in the community was longer. It was noted, however, that members of lower status groups (not the maintenance or janitorial groups) could achieve more status through active participation in local affairs than in the typical American town.[32]

The war years were also marked by change in the administration of Greenbelt. While there were no precise policy changes, there was an increased tendency on the part of the new administrators—including the new community/town manager, to regard Greenbelt "more as a housing project than a social experiment."[33] In April, 1943, the Federal Public Housing Administration announced that after June 1, 1943, rents would be raised from the old scale of $18.00–$42.00 per month to $24.00–$65.00, and the income requirements would be raised to a scale of $1,400–$4,000. In practice, the F.P.H.A. allowed all residents to stay throughout the war, regardless of how high their incomes went. The citizens' association, which had only twelve people in attendance at the March, 1943, meeting, called a special meeting in May to discuss the rent increase and over five hundred attended. Roy Braden, the community/town manager, explained that while the average rent was increasing from $31.50 to $44.00, the percentage of incomes spent on rent would actually be lower than it had been in 1939. The $31.50 in 1939 comprised twenty-four percent of the average resident's income of $2,962. After an emotional discussion, the justice of the increase was acknowledged by the majority. A second meeting, several days later, intended to arouse further protest, drew only two hundred people. A Rent Protest Committee was formed, but dissolved after four months. In December, 1943, the F.P.H.A. made a concession to residents in the original town by agreeing to allow wives of those serving in the armed forces, whose incomes were naturally reduced, to pay rent either on the old scale or at a rate of twenty percent of their gross income, whichever was higher.[34] The new administrators showed good sense and liberalism in small matters too. James Gobbel became extremely popular when, having replaced Braden, in October, 1943, he lifted the "clothes line curfew" on hanging up wash after 4 P.M. and on Sundays.[35]

V-J Day saw town residents, after a heated campaign, vote

four to one to reject a proposal permitting a liquor store in the town. Greenbelt, its 8,000 residents comprising the largest community in Prince George's County, looked forward to the reopening of the Town Fair on August 30th—the first since 1940. Overcrowding due to wartime expansion was finally alleviated with the completion of the new school facilities. Greenbelt Consumer Services planned major expansion. The only cloud on the horizon was a rumor which had appeared in the Washington papers that Greenbelt was going to be put up for sale. It was denied by all government officials.[36] But the announcement of the F.P.H.A.'s decision to sell the town finally came in September, 1945, plunging the town into another period of major change.

1. *Greenbelt Cooperator*, October 13, 1938.

2. George A. Warner, *Greenbelt*, p. 96.

3. *Greenbelt Cooperator*, March 9, 1939.

4. Ibid., June 6, 1904.

5. Ibid., June 13, 1940, May 23, 1940, and June 20, 1940.

6. *Greendale Review*, November 3, 1938.

7. Ibid.

8. Ibid., November 11, 1938, April 22, 1939, October 7, 1939, June 12, 1940, and June 26, 1940.

9. Ibid., April 26, 1945.

10. Warner, *Greenbelt*, p. 173.

11. *Greenbelt Cooperator*, January 18, 1940, December 12, 1940, February 21, 1941, June 12, 1942, and October 1, 1943; and *City of Greenbelt, 25th Anniversary*, pp. 7, 9.

12. *Greenbelt Cooperator*, June 6, 1941.

13. *City of Greenbelt, 25th Anniversary*, p. 33; and *Greenbelt Cooperator*, October 17, 1941, and October 2, 1942.

14. *Greenbelt Cooperator*, July 11, 1940.

15. U.S., Farm Security Administration, *Annual Report, 1942*, Project Report, MD-1811, P.H.A., R.G. 196, Box 6, pp. 25–26.

16. *Greenbelt Cooperator*, May 30, 1941, December 26, 1941.

17. Baird Snyder, acting administrator, F.W.A., to the secretary of agriculture, February 10, 1942, National Archives, R.G. 16.

18. Survey Preliminary to the Appraisal of Greenbelt, Maryland, P.H.A., R.G. 196, Box 1.

19. Frederick A. Gutheim, "Greenbelt Revisited," *Magazine of Art* 40 (January, 1947): 18.

20. *Greenbelt Cooperator*, June 3, 1942. The original copy of the petition is found in P.H.A., R.G. 196, Box 6.

21. Clarence S. Stein, *Towards New Towns for America*, pp. 137–45; Albert Mayer, "Greenbelt Towns Revisited," *Journal of Housing* 24, no. 2 (February–March, 1967): 82; and interview with James K. Giese, Greenbelt city manager, May 18, 1965.

22. *Greenbelt Cooperator*, September 26, 1941.

23. Some observers believe that Greenbelt's high birth rate, four times the national average, was due to the town's healthy environment. In reality the rise was due to the large number of young couples at the peak childbearing age. When Greenbelt's birth rate was adjusted for this age group, it fell below the national average and was insufficient to maintain the town's population. See Greenbelt reports in "A Planned Community Appraised: Greenbelt, Maryland," *The Architectural Record* 22 (January, 1940): 62, and the *New York Times*, June 25, 1939. For the statistical analysis, see Elbridge Sibley, "Fertility in a Greenbelt Community," *Social Forces* 20 (May, 1942): 476–77.

24. *Greenbelt Cooperator*, June 12, 1942, June 26, 1942, September 3, 1943, and January 8, 1943.

25. Ibid., March 31, 1944, June 16, 1944, July 21, 1944, and May 18, 1945.

26. The *Cooperator* reported on October 6, 1944, that 313 of the original families still resided in Greenbelt. Only sixty original families remained by 1962. A complete list of town council members from 1937–62 is found in *City of Greenbelt, 25th Anniversary*, p. 7.

27. *City of Greenbelt, 25th Anniversary*, p. 7.

28. *Greenbelt Cooperator*, April 7, 1944.

29. Ibid., April 23, 1943; *City of Greenbelt, 25th Anniversary*, p. 5.

30. Gutheim, "Greenbelt Revisited," p. 19; *Greenbelt Cooperator*, January 9, 1941.

31. *Greenbelt Cooperator*, November 10, 1944, November 24, 1944, December 29, 1944; *City of Greenbelt, 25th Anniversary*, pp. 21, 38.

32. William H. Form, "Status Stratification in a Planned Community," *American Sociological Review* 10 (October, 1945): 610–11; William

Form, "The Sociology of a White Collar Suburb, Greenbelt, Maryland," p. 86, 425.

33. Form, "The Sociology of a White Collar Suburb," p. 33 n.

34. *Greenbelt Cooperator*, April 9, 1943, May 21, 1943, May 28, 1943, July 16, 1943, September 17, 1943, December 24, 1943; Form, "The Sociology of a White Collar Suburb," p. 58 n.

35. *Greenbelt Cooperator*, October 22, 1943.

36. Ibid., August 3, 1945, August 17, 1945, August 31, 1945.

13

⁂ GREENBELT TOWNS

FOR SALE, 1945–1954

For more than ten years the Federal Public Housing Authority, which managed the Greenbelt towns, attempted to dispose of them in a manner satisfactory to Congress, the residents, and the original planners. The F.P.H.A., created primarily as a war housing authority under the National Housing Agency, received control of the towns in June, 1942, as part of a general consolidation of federal housing agencies ordered by President Roosevelt in February of that year.[1] F.P.H.A. officials have been charged with treating the greenbelt towns as housing projects rather than social experiments.[2] Such does not appear to be the case regarding the sale. A number of F.P.H.A. officials —Oliver C. Winston in particular—attempted to expand the towns to the size contemplated by the original planners and/or sell them to institutions which would do the same. It was hoped the enlarged towns would adequately support their municipal services and commercial facilities, thus making their entire property more attractive for potential purchasers. Winston believed the completed towns "should be maintained as at least three outstanding examples of good community planning . . . which could do much to influence future developments by private enterprise throughout the country."[3]

The F.P.H.A. believed it had a clear obligation to sell the greenbelt towns. Congressional Appropriations Committees from 1939 to 1942 had construed Title IV, Section 43 of the Bankhead-Jones Act as providing for the liquidation of the entire F.S.A. community program—including the greenbelt towns.[4] The commissioner of the F.S.A., Oliver Winston, director of the F.P.H.A. General Field Office, gave the job of expanding and then liquidating the towns.[5] During 1944 and 1945 he discussed the question confidentially with Greenbelt's town councilmen.[6] He decided, however, to use Greendale as the pilot project in his disposition program. In the summer of 1944 initial plans were made for the expansion of the town.[7] F.P.H.A. officials met with Greendale Manager Walter Kroening, Warren Vinton, and a Greendale Tenants Advisory Committee.[8] Also consulted were Elbert Peets, planners from the F.P.H.A. who reviewed literature on the English garden cities, and the research director of the British Association for Planning and Regional Reconstruction who happened to be in Washington. Alexander Bing, the builder of Radburn, discussed the plans and asked to be informed when the time came to seek a developer. The proposal resulting from these studies recommended the sale of the town, together with the entire tract, to a single corporation or syndicate. The village of Greendale should retain ownership of all public property plus the commercial center, industrial sites, and the area set aside for the greenbelt—the last three could then be leased to private developers as the village saw fit.[9] The preliminary development plan drawn up by Peets in January, 1945, contemplated four new villages approximately the same size as the original one. In addition there were to be an expanded commercial area and an industrial park, but over half of the undeveloped tract was to remain either as parks or farmland.[10]

When the plans were first unveiled, the Greendale Tenants Advisory Committee was pleased with them. The committee's recommendation that the town be sold to a tenant cooperative received little support from the residents, who preferred to purchase their present dwelling individually or to build in one of the four new proposed villages.[11] Winston's office made contact with possible buyers, several of whom showed interest. During the summer and fall of 1945, however, construction costs in the Milwaukee area rose so rapidly that prospective buyers became unwilling to make the required investment.[12] Winston, therefore, gave up immediate plans to sell the town.

During 1945 and 1946 both Congress and residents pressed F.P.H.A. to dispose of the towns. Greenbelt townspeople, angry that their town councilmen had kept plans to sell the property secret, unanimously voted to form a mutual homeowner's corporation to buy Greenbelt. In January, 1946, Councilman Allan Morrison, one of the organizers of the American Legion in Greenbelt, suggested the town be turned over to returning veterans and renamed Veteran, Maryland.[13] There were no suggestions, however, as to how the residents or the returning veterans could purchase the town which was valued by the government in 1945 at almost $19,000,000.[14] The congressional appropriations committee, from which the F.P.H.A. received its funds, was perplexed when the towns were not sold at once. Committee member Ben F. Johnson thought the towns had been abandoned.[15] Representative Albert Gore wondered why the F.P.H.A. "procrastinated" when the project could be sold "overnight" at a price which would almost recover the initial investment. F.P.H.A. Commissioner Philip Klutznick replied that the projects presented many complex disposition problems and that to determine the real value of the property and the best method to dispose of them would cost time and money.[16] The F.P.H.A. received $99,500 (derived from management receipts of the three towns) to facilitate further study of the problem, but only $60,000 of it was used during fiscal 1947.[17] The funds were used to plan for the expansion of the other towns in a fashion similar to the plan for Greendale.[18] In January, 1947, Hale Walker presented the Greenbelt version of expansion to the residents. Accompanied by Winston, Walker painted a glowing picture of the future with two thousand additional homes surrounded by extensive parks and open lands.[19] "The only fly in the ointment," commented the *Greenbelt Cooperator*, "is the question of who is to do this and how it is to be done."[20]

All plans were altered by President Truman's announcement in May, 1947, to seek congressional reorganization of all federal housing agencies under a single Housing and Home Finance Administration.[21] Under this reorganization plan the General Field Office of the F.P.H.A. was to be abolished. Winston decided to leave government service to become executive director of the Baltimore City Housing Authority.[22] Before leaving, however, he tried to find a private foundation willing to purchase the towns and develop them as model communities. He contacted the Rockefeller Foundation and the Russell Sage Foundation, neither of whom was interested.[23] His attempt to have the Social Science Research Council undertake a study of the greenbelt towns also failed to stir any action.[24]

A week after the General Field Office was abolished, Raymond Foley, the new administrator of the Housing and Home Finance Administration, issued Public Regulation No. 1, which declared that in order to encourage home ownership by small investors, all properties being sold by the agency "should be subdivided into the smallest feasible units of sale consistent with a practical plan for their disposition."[25] Preference was to be given to veterans occupying the homes, then to veterans intending to occupy a home for sale, and finally to nonveterans occupying a unit to be sold. Within each of the preference groups, sales were to be made for cash to the highest bidder after public advertising—the method long established by Congress.[26] Fortunately, John Taylor Egan, commissioner of the Public Housing Administration, was committed to the sale of the towns as a unit to "safeguard the educational and demonstrational value of these examples of community planning."[27] Egan prevailed on Foley to exclude the towns from sale under the Public Regulation No. 1, thus allowing the Public Housing Administration to sell them for cash on a competitive bid basis, with restrictions to protect the character of the existing communities.[28]

For tenants hoping to purchase the towns, the chief problem was inability to obtain financing. In order to aid them, Congress enacted legislation authorizing F.H.A. insured loans on greenbelt town mortgages. Charles P. Taft, brother of Senator Robert A. Taft, drafted the bill. Veterans and other tenants at Greenbelt, who had formed a purchasing group in 1946, were imitated by similar groups in Greendale and Greenhills. Early in 1948 the Greenhills Homeowners Corporation, composed of two-thirds of the town residents, many of whom were veterans, employed Charles Taft to negotiate purchase of the property.[29] Taft's bill authorized the F.H.A. to insure mortgages on the towns at four percent interest and to cover up to ninety percent of the mortgage with a maturity of twenty-five years. Taft discussed the measure with Philip Glick, general counsel for the H.H.F.A., who sent it on to Administrator Foley. After minor revisions, Foley sent the bill to Congressman Jesse Wolcott, who introduced it in the House.[30] The Eighty-first Congress passed it as Public Law 901, on August 10, 1948.[31]

The requirement that the towns be sold for cash to the highest bidder impeded purchase efforts of the resident and veteran groups. Not only would the process take a long time, but there was no assurance that mortgage loans could be obtained even with F.H.A. insurance. To obviate these problems, the Greendale group, called the American Legion Community Development Corporation, sought legislation to allow sale on terms through direct negotiations with the Public Housing Commissioner.[32] Senator Joseph McCarthy of Wisconsin introduced a bill providing for the sale of the three towns through negotiation rather than competitive bidding. A similar bill was intro-

duced in the House by Representative Monroney, a member of
the Committee on Banking and Currency, which was to hold
hearings on the resolution.

When hearings began on February 22, 1949, only the Greendale group had contacted the Public Housing Administration
in regard to the proposed legislation, but subsequent hearings
were attended by veterans groups in Greenbelt and Greenhills.[33] The Greendale American Legion Community Development Corporation appeared to be the most thoroughly prepared—presenting elaborate plans for the development of the
entire tract.[34] The most serious problem, the committee was
told, was raising the capital because banks were reluctant to
make even F.H.A. insured loans to veterans' groups for fear of
bad publicity in the event the loan had to be foreclosed.[35] Commissioner Egan testified that the House and Senate bills were
slightly different, but he was satisfied with the general provisions.[36] Senator Paul Douglas was concerned that the development groups protect the undeveloped lands from haphazard
growth and was assured by a member of the Greenhills Home
Owners' Corporation that no such thing would be allowed.[37]
Douglas was the only congressman showing interest in the preservation of the towns' heritage of imaginative planning. In the
House hearings Representative Wright Patman and Representative Lansdale Sasscer wanted assurances that the veterans'
groups would not immediately evict the present residents after
the sale; and Senator McCarthy, appearing on behalf of the
Milwaukee group, agreed heartily.[38] The bill was reported out
of the House committee on April 6, 1949. It was amended first to
allow purchasers to pay ten percent down, the balance to be
amortized over a period of not more than twenty-five years—
essentially the same terms insured by the F.H.A. Also, a provision was added allowing present occupants of the towns to retain their homes by joining the veteran development groups.[39]

H.R. 2440 was brought to the House floor on April 13, 1949,
by Representative Brent Spence of Kentucky, chairman of the
House Committee on Banking and Currency, and author of

House Report No. 402. He told the House he was pleased to see the towns sold to veterans' groups and noted that Charles P. Taft was interested in Greenhills as the representative of a group that was anxious to buy the town immediately. Representative Smith of Wisconsin agreed that the sale of the towns to veterans "is a fine way for the government to get out of the real estate business."[40] The bill passed unanimously and was sent to the Senate where Senator Douglas amended it in his committee report to allow the Public Housing Commissioner to transfer streets, public buildings, playgrounds, parks, and open land surrounding or adjacent to the towns to nonfederal government agencies under terms he considered to be in the public interest.[41] The Senate bill, containing both the House amendments and the Senate committee amendments passed unanimously on May 6, 1949. The House accepted the Senate version passing it on May 10. President Truman signed it on May 19, 1949.[42]

Public Law 65 was intended to transfer the towns to private ownership, aid veterans in finding homes, protect occupants in the homes, and allow the P.H.A. commissioner to retain some of the green open spaces from which the towns derived their names. In Greendale only the first goal was achieved. The potential purchasers, American Legion Community Development Corporation, failed to purchase any portion of Greendale. After initiating the legislation and presenting its formal application to qualify as a negotiator for the sale of Greendale, the group ran into serious problems.[43] The corporation expected financial support from the city of Milwaukee, but was never able to reach a lasting agreement.[44] Also, the group was overwhelmingly distrusted by other Greendale residents, who formed a rival housing group called the Greendale Cooperative Veterans Homes Association, which was supported in a special referendum on August 23, 1949, by 621 residents, as against ninety-eight for the corporation. The most serious blow to the corporation was the sudden death of its organizer, Arthur Marcus, who had originally interested Senator McCarthy in the project.[45] As a result of the divisions between the two rival veterans' groups, each blamed the other of bad faith and scared off local mortgage bankers. As a result neither group was able to purchase the town, and the P.H.A. prepared to break up the property and sell it in any size parcels which would bring the most money. Even the village hall was to be sold off for private use.[46] The residents were allowed to make offers to the P.H.A. on their own houses. During 1952 ninety-seven percent of the residents purchased their own homes for a total price of $4,666,825.[47] The 2,280 acres of undeveloped land and all the commercial facilities including the town hall were advertised for sale to the highest bidder in 1952, but the bids received were so low that the P.H.A. rejected all of them. Shortly thereafter, the Milwaukee Community Development Corporation, one of the bidders, entered into negotiations with the P.H.A. and purchased the entire property for $825,727.[48]

The Greenhills Home Owners Corporation told the Senate committee, in 1949, that it was prepared to purchase the entire 4,000 acre tract.[49] Unfortunately, the corporation was only able to purchase the town site. In 1950, the P.H.A. transferred title to all the houses, the commercial center, the town hall, and 601 acres of land at a price of $3,511,300. Approximately four hundred acres of land along Mill Creek were transferred to the Hamilton County Park Commission and the remaining 3,378 acres of undeveloped land was sold to Cincinnati Community Development Corporation for $1,200,000.[50]

The Greenbelt Mutual Home Owners Corporation, which had been formed in 1947, represented a majority of the residents and their hopes to continue the original concept of cooperative ownership and careful planning.[51] Their attitude toward the sale of the community is clear. R. J. Wadsworth, who had helped plan Greenbelt in the 1930s and was now aiding in its disposition, made the following observation:

There is deeply rooted in the thinking of most tenants the original conception upon which the planning of the commu-

nity was based, namely, that it would be held in one ownership, preferably a local public agency, to which the Federal
Government would transfer title . . . but there is a great
lack of understanding on the part of the tenants as to what
disposition may mean to them.[52]

The Greenbelt Mutual Home Owners Corporation was organized by several hundred tenants to carry out the community's
intentions. While the organization occasionally pressured reluctant residents to join, it had no rivals and enrolled the great
majority of families by the spring of 1949.[53] It employed Colonel
Lawrence Westbrook, the former director of the R.A. Rural
Rehabilitation Division, to negotiate the sale and direct planning for furture community expansion using Hale Walker's
master plan of 1946. Westbrook told the House committee that
the corporation intended to purchase the entire Greenbelt property, but did not think it could finance it with less than a forty
year mortgage.[54]

   To meet the requirements of Public Law 65, the G.M.H.O.C.
was reorganized as the Greenbelt Veteran Housing Corporation. At the time of the congressional hearings in 1949, half the
members of the corporation were veterans.[55] By 1952, the number grew to fifty-five percent, of which one-fourth were not
residents of Greenbelt.[56] The corporation entered into negotiations with the P.H.A. in 1950. The government decided to transfer to the town of Greenbelt, the community building, Greenbelt Lake, and the swimming pool, the roads, sewers, and
other government properties. The entire southeast quarter of
the tract (1,362 acres) was transferred to the National Park
Service. Offerred for sale was the original town, the war housing,
the commercial center, and approximately 2,000 acres of undeveloped land. The total price was $8,886,700.[57] Negotiations
were halted in June, 1950, by the Korean War and did not resume until 1952. By then, the G.V.H.C. decided to purchase
only the row houses and 800 acres of undeveloped land.[58] A
canvass of residents showed little interest in cooperative owner-

ship of the apartment units or of the commercial center. The balance of the undeveloped land was not purchased because the corporation was unsure it could develop it. Its financial backing was almost entirely drawn from nonresident sources —the residents provided only one-fourth of the down payment. The mortgage was financed by a subsidiary of the Nationwide Insurance Company.[59] The 1,580 housing units and 708 acres of land were purchased in December, 1952, for a total price of $6,995,669.[60]

The twelve apartment buildings in the original town containing 306 units were sold at public auction to the highest bidder. Six individual purchasers bought them in April, 1953, for a total price of $914,342.[61] The last undeveloped land was sold to private real estate developers in June, 1954. The commercial area was sold in October to the highest bidder—the Gilbert Realty Company of Philadelphia.[62] With the transfer of the commercial center on January 1, 1955, the federal government severed its last connection with the New Deal experiment begun twenty years before by Rexford Tugwell. The dismemberment of Greenbelt under the auctioneer's hammer was a fitting end for a project which cut so deeply against the American grain.

1. See Executive Order 9070, February 24, 1942.

2. William Form, "The Sociology of a White Collar Suburb, Greenbelt, Maryland," p. 33 n.

3. Oliver C. Winston to commissioner of F.P.H.A., October 28, 1946, P.H.A., R.G. 196, Box 1.

4. U.S., Congress, House, Subcommittee of the Committee on Appropriations, *Hearings on Agriculture Department Appropriation Bill for 1940*, 76th Cong., 1st sess., 1939, pp. 1187–88; U.S., Congress, House, Subcommittee of the Committee on Appropriations, *Hearings on the Agriculture Department Appropriation Bill for 1943*, 77th Cong., 2d sess., 1942, pt. 2: 236, 239, 261. Section 43 of Title IV of the Bankhead-Jones Act of July 22, 1937 (50 Stat. 522, 530), provided "the Secretary of Agriculture is authorized to continue to perform such of the functions vested in him

pursuant to . . . the Bankhead-Black Act as shall be necessary only for the completion and administration of those resettlement projects."

5. Philip Glick, general counsel, Public Housing Administration, General Counsel's Opinion No. 28, General Considerations Underlying Disposition of the Greentown Projects, March 24, 1948, p. 11 n.

6. *Greenbelt Cooperator*, September 14, 1945.

7. *Greendale Review*, August 16, 1944, and September 28, 1944.

8. "Greendale, Wisconsin: Report on Studies, Disposition and Development Plan," June 13, 1945, R.O.A., H.H.F.A., Drawer 537; and *Greendale Review*, April 26, 1945.

9. "Greendale, Wisconsin: Report on Studies, Disposition and Development Plan," June 13, 1945, R.O.A., H.H.F.A., Drawer 537.

10. Preliminary Development Plan of Greater Greendale by Elbert Peets, January 31, 1946, R.O.A., H.H.F.A., Drawer 537.

11. *Greendale Review*, February 15, 1945, April 26, 1945, and November 15, 1945.

12. Winston to commissioner of F.P.H.A., October 28, 1946, P.H.A., R.G. 196, Box 1.

13. *Greenbelt Cooperator*, September 14, 1945, November 9, 1945, and January 18, 1946.

14. U.S., Congress, House, Subcommittee of the Committee on Appropriations, *Hearings on the Government Corporations, Appropriation Bill for 1947*, 79th Cong., 2d sess., 1946, p. 1383.

15. Ibid., p. 1380.

16. Ibid., pp. 1380–82. See also U.S., Federal Public Housing Authority, *Fifth Annual Report, 1946*, pp. 256–57.

17. U.S., Congress, House, Subcommittee of the Committee on Appropriations, *Hearings on the Government Corporations, Appropriation Bill for 1948*, 80th Cong., 1st sess., 1947, pt. 2: 96.

18. Oliver C. Winston to Charles S. Lawrence, director, Region III, July 22, 1946, P.H.A., R.G. 196, Box 2.

19. *Greenbelt Cooperator*, January 13, 1947. The plans had been drawn with the aid of Henry Churchill and Elbert Peets. Memo from Oliver C. Winston, July 1, 1946, P.H.A., R.G. 196, Box 2.

20. *Greenbelt Cooperator*, January 17, 1947.

21. For a brief discussion of the history of this action, see Richard O. Davies, *Housing Reform in the Truman Administration*, pp. 62–63.

22. Oliver C. Winston correspondence, P.H.A., R.G. 196, Box 2.

23. Nelson A. Rockefeller to Oliver C. Winston, June 13, 1947, and

Oliver C. Winston to Shelby M. Harrison, Russell Sage Foundation, May 15, 1947, P.H.A., R.G. 196, Box 2.

24.   Professor Richard U. Ratcliff to Oliver C. Winston, July 2, 1947, P.H.A., R.G. 196, Box 2.

25.   U.S., Public Housing Administration, *First Annual Report of the Public Housing Administration, 1947*, p. 17.

26.   Ibid., p. 18. U.S., *Revised Statutes of the United States*, 2d ed., 43d Cong., 1st Sess., 1873–74, Title 42, Sec. 3709 (March 2, 1861) as amended by the Surplus Property Act of 1944 (50 U.S.C., App. 1638) and by amendments to R.S., Sec. 3709, August 2, 1946 (60 Stat. 809).

27.   J. T. Egan, assistant commissioner, to Orville R. Olmsted, director, Region III, November 10, 1947, P.H.A., R.G. 196, Box 6.

28.   Memo from J. T. Egan to R. M. Foley, March 17, 1948, R.O.A., H.H.F.A., Drawer 538. See also U.S., Public Housing Administration, *Third Annual Report of the Public Housing Administration, 1949* p. 30.

29.   U.S., Congress, House, Committee on Banking and Currency, *Hearings on H.R. 2440*, 81st Cong., 1st sess., 1949, p. 49.

30.   Memo from Philip Glick to J. T. Egan, March 15, 1948, R.O.A., H.H.F.A., Drawer 538; and R. M. Foley to Representative Jesse Wolcott, March 18, 1948, P.H.A., R.G. 196, Box 6.

31.   U.S., Public Housing Administration, *Second Annual Report of the Public Housing Administration, 1948*, p. 29.

32.   Village of Greendale, Wisconsin: Disposition, June 24, 1949, R.O.A., H.H.F.A., Drawer 537.

33.   U.S., Congress, Senate, Subcommittee on Housing and Rents of the Committee on Banking and Currency, *Hearings on S. 351, A Bill to Authorize the Sale of Greenbelt, Greendale, and Greenhills Suburban Resettlement Projects*, 81st Cong., 1st sess., 1949, pp. 3, 27–30, 67–75; and U.S., Congress, House, Committee on Banking and Currency, *Hearings on H.R. 2440*, 81st Cong., 1st sess., 1949, pp. 13, 30–36.

34.   U.S., Congress, Senate, Subcommittee on Rents and Housing of the Committee on Banking and Currency, *Hearings on S. 351*, 81st Cong., 1st sess., 1949, pp. 17–21.

35.   Ibid., p. 11.

36.   Ibid., p. 7.

37.   Ibid., p. 30.

38.   U.S., Congress, House, Committee on Banking and Currency, *Hearings on H.R. 2440*, pp. 6, 31–32.

39.   U.S., Congress, House, Committee on Banking and Currency, *Report on Disposition of Greentown Projects*, Report No. 402, April 6, 1949, 81st Congs., 1st sess., 1949, pp. 1–2.

40. U.S., *Congressional Record*, 81st Cong., 1st sess., 1949, 95, pt. 4: 4493.

41. U.S., Congress, Senate, Committee on Banking and Currency, *Report on Disposition of Greentown Projects*, Report No. 312, April 29, 1949, 81st Cong., 1st sess., 1949, p. 5.

42. U.S., *Congressional Record*, 81st Cong., 1st sess., 1949, 95, pt. 5: 5833–34, 5980, and pt. 6: 7254.

43. The corporation application dated April 18, 1949, is found in the Papers of Harry S. Truman, Harry S. Truman Library, Independence, Missouri, Official File (hereafter cited as Truman Papers, Official File).

44. Village of Greendale: Disposition, June 24, 1948, R.O.A., H.H.F.A., Drawer 537.

45. *Greendale Review*, March 4, 1949, July 22, 1949, August 5, 1949, and September 2, 1949.

46. Ibid., June 8, 1951.

47. U.S., Public Housing Administration, *Fifth Annual Report of the Public Housing Administration, 1951*, p. 31; and U.S., Public Housing Administration, *Sixth Annual Report to the Public Housing Administration, 1952.*

48. U.S., Public Housing Administration, *Sixth Annual Report*, p. 30; and "Businessmen Make a New Deal Idea Work," *Business Week*, March 10, 1962, pp. 92–94.

49. U.S., Congress, Senate, Subcommittee on Housing and Rents of the Committee on Banking and Currency, *Hearings on S. 351*, 81st Cong., 1st Sess., 1949, p. 28.

50. U.S., Public Housing Administration, *Sixth Annual Report*, p. 30.

51. U.S., Congress, Senate, Subcommittee on Housing and Rents of the Committee on Banking and Currency, *Hearings on S. 351*, 81st Cong., 1st sess., 1949, p. 66.

52. R. J. Wadsworth to C. R. Cravens, October 4, 1949, R.O.A., H.H.F.A., Drawer 538.

53. R. J. Wadsworth to M. R. Bailey, March 16, 1948, R.O.A., H.H.F.A., Drawer 538; and J. T. Egan to Edmund Freitan, March 26, 1948, P.H.A., R.G. 196, Box 2; and U.S., Congress, Senate, Subcommittee on Housing and Rents of the Committee on Banking and Currency, *Hearings on S. 351*, 81st Cong., 1st sess., 1949, p. 70.

54. U.S., Congress, House, Committee on Banking and Currency, Hearings on H.R. 2440, 81st Cong., 1st Sess., 1949, pp. 43, 70; and U.S., Congress, Senate, Subcommittee on Housing and Rents of the Committee on Banking and Currency, Hearings on S. 351, 81st Cong., 1st Sess., 1949, p. 70.

55. U.S., Congress, Senate, Subcommittee on Housing and Rents of the Committee on Banking and Currency, *Hearings on S. 351*, 81st Cong., 1st sess., 1949, p. 66.

56. Michael Salzman, president, G.V.H.C., to John T. Egan, commissioner, P.H.A., R.G. 196, Box 1.

57. Sale of Greenbelt, Maryland, to Veteran Group, May 1, 1950, P.H.A., R.G. 196, Box 1. Also excluded from the sale was a large tract of land later transferred to Bureau of Public Roads for the Baltimore-Washington Parkway, which, to the dismay of Greenbelt's residents, was built within four hundred feet of the closest residences. See the *Greenbelt Cooperator*, May 24, 1946, June 7, 1946, and July 26, 1946.

58. U.S., Public Housing Administration, *Fourth Annual Report of the Public Housing Administration, 1950*, p. 31; and Salzman to Egan, June 30, 1952, P.H.A., R.G. 196, Box 1.

59. *City of Greenbelt, 25th Anniversary*, pp. 8–9, 36.

60. The housing units sold for $6,285,450; the purchase price covered by a ten percent down payment and the balance secured by a twenty-five year mortgage at four percent interest. The 708 acres of land sold for $670,219 on the same terms except for a ten-year, rather than a twenty-five year mortgage. U.S., Public Housing Administration, *Sixth Annual Report of the Public Housing Administration*, p. 31.

61. U.S., Public Housing Administration, *Seventh Annual Report of the Public Housing Administration, 1953*, p. 34.

62. "Value of Property Sold at Greenbelt, Maryland, 1954," P.H.A., R.G. 196, Box 1. The *Eighth Annual Report of the Public Housing Administration* does not mention these transactions, noting only that during the year the greenbelt town program had been completely liquidated (U.S., Public Housing Administration, *Eighth Annual Report of the Public Housing Administration, 1954*, p. 26).

CONCLUSION

The history of the greenbelt towns is the story of a road not taken. The most important fact in this history is that the suburban town program was rejected by Congress and ignored by the real estate and construction industries. The failure of the greenbelt towns to impress either government officials or industrial leaders is rather easily traceable to the program's radical challenge to fundamental patterns of urban growth and real estate practice. That the program was sponsored by the New Deal and thus became a partisan political issue only sealed its doom.

In assessing the greenbelt program it is important to separate the physical planning from the socioeconomic planning. In terms of the physical plan the three towns have little to offer community builders of the 1970s. Their overall design, site planning, and architectural innovations are now antique. They

certainly contribute to the realization that comprehensive preplanning does indeed result in long term savings, although the
point is more usefully made by larger and more balanced new
towns. Even the opponents of the program agreed that the
greenbelt towns produced a residential and commercial environment superior to most suburban "developments," but were
financially infeasible for all save the affluent. Nevertheless, in
their comprehensive planning and large scale construction, the
greenbelt towns were at least moving with the tide of the private housing and construction industries. Since the end of the
Second World War, increasing numbers of very large, compre-
hensively planned suburban communities have been built,
many of them of a size that dwarf the greenbelt towns.

On the other hand, when the history of community building
is examined for socioeconomic experimentation, the greenbelt
towns still stand disturbingly close to the urban frontier. It is
clearly the Suburban Division's social, economic, and political
experimentation that stirred the greatest suspicion and opposition in the 1930s. It is also the only part of the greenbelt program which, regardless of its sponsorship by the government or
a private builder, directly countered long developing urban
patterns. First, the towns aimed at reversing the trend towards
increasing economic and social segregation of metropolitan
areas. By raising the spector of suburban areas containing poor
as well as affluent families, the program threatened one of the
most fundamental attractions of suburban areas. Though the
Suburban Division itself failed to resettle a full spectrum of
socioeconomic families in their towns, the program was basically oriented in this direction. In addition, the creation of an
interrelated system of cooperative institutions to operate stores,
care for preschool children, deliver medical services, provide
transportation, and arrange a host of educational and social
activities is without parallel in twentieth-century American
cities. Finally, the establishment of a new community in which
the residents were given a municipal charter allowing them a

degree of legal control over their government-owned community was a bold experiment which no other public housing agency has seen fit to imitate even in modified form.

Fifty or a hundred little greenbelt towns scattered around the suburban fringes of our metropolitan areas, no matter how modest the housing and landscaping, would have cost no more than our typical monolithic public housing projects in the central cities. Certainly not all public housing should have been built in the suburbs, but enough could have been to give the less affluent something of the choice open to the average citizen. The greenbelt experiment giving public housing residents a local government as a counterweight to the housing authority might have saved our current authorities from their habits of insensitive and oppressive administration. Community organization among the tenants of public housing projects is next to impossible if "the project" is not recognized as a physical or legal community.

But even these solutions are ultimately unsatisfactory. Poor house islands in the central city or the suburbs—even when they are as attractive as the greenbelt towns—are inherently demoralizing for the residents. They remain separated from the larger community and stigmatized by it. Such a program merely perpetuates the unhealthy segregation which lies at the root of many of our urban problems. If the nation's cities are ever going to reverse this pattern of economic and racial segregation, it will have to be carried out on a metropolitan-wide scale. Planting patches of segregated low-income housing in suburban areas is politically impossible and inevitably results in the deterioration of the surrounding neighborhood. Permanent integration can occur only when low-income housing is scattered in very small numbers throughout the entire community—a community with the will and the power to prevent any tipping of the economic balance in any single neighborhood. New towns offer the best opportunity to produce this stable economic mixture. They can initiate a land use pattern that provides housing priced for every income group without threatening any one of them with the uncertainty of who the majority of their neighbors will be.

The three greenbelt towns have by accident developed into small examples of economic integration since the original modest housing units have been infiltrated and surrounded by newer, larger, and more expensive homes. It is fitting that just a few miles from Greenbelt, Maryland, the unique new town of Columbia is making the first large scale experiment with racial and economic integration. Developed by the Rouse Corporation, a private mortgage and land development firm, Columbia is composed of an interlocking network of small neighborhoods called villages, each containing a wide spectrum of housing prices. The town has living accommodations ranging from subsidized, low-income row houses to $70,000 estates and a proportion of Negro residents approximately equal to that of the nation as a whole. If Columbia points the way for future suburban developments, the poor and the nonwhite may finally gain access to the trees, grass, and jobs which grow in the suburbs. The affluent may be freed to live in the central city without fear of being surrounded by slums. If this is the road we are now traveling, the greenbelt towns of the 1930s were the first faltering step.

BIBLIOGRAPHY

Manuscript Sources

Brant, Irving R. "Policies of Local Housing Authorities," for the Third Conference on Slum Clearance and Low Rent Housing. Washington, D.C., 1936. (Mimeographed copy in the Library of Congress.)

Bronez, Ray W. "Interest Groups and Public Housing." Ph.D. dissertation, University of Chicago, 1938.

Dudley, Tilford E. "Report of Land Section, Suburban Division, Resettlement Administration." (Manuscript copy in Wesleyan University Library, Middletown, Connecticut.)

Form, William. "The Sociology of a White Collar Suburb, Greenbelt, Maryland." Ph.D. dissertation, University of Maryland, 1944.

Greenbrook Project Book. Copy in possession of Albert Mayer, New York.

Hyde Park, N.Y. Franklin D. Roosevelt Library. Franklin D. Roosevelt Papers.

Independence, Missouri. Harry S. Truman Library. Papers of Harry S. Truman (official files).

Kroening, Walter. "The Story of Greendale." April, 1944. (Mimeographed copy in possession of the author.)

Larson, Cedric A. "Educational Activities of the Federally Planned Community of Greenbelt, Maryland." Master's thesis, George Washington University, 1939.

Lexington, Kentucky. John S. Lansill Papers. Personal files. (This collection includes Land Acquisition reports, 1935–36; Land Utilization and Suburban Division correspondence, 1935–38; "Notes on Greenbelt Town Program," by Lansill; Suburban Division reports, 1935–37; "Summary Information Reports: Greenbelt, Greenbrook, Greenhills and Greendale, 1936.")

Lexington, Kentucky. University of Kentucky Library. John S. Lansill Papers (official files). (This collection includes "Address before the Regional Planning Commission of Hamilton County, Ohio, February 3, 1936," by Lansill; "Final Report on Greenbelt Town Program," by Lansill; "General Historical Analysis: Greenhills Project"; Greenbelt Project Book; Greendale Project Book; photographs of Suburban Division offices and construction of greenbelt towns; Project Plan Approval Sheets, 3 vols.; Research Division correspondence, 1935–36; Resettlement Administration, Project Description Book; Suburban Division correspondence, 1935–38; "Summarized History of Bound Brook"; "Summarized History of Greenbelt Project"; "Summary Chronological History of Greenhills Project"; "Summary Description of Greenbelt, Prince George's County, Maryland.")

Marshall, Douglas G. "Greendale: A Study of a Resettlement Community." Ph.D. dissertation, University of Wisconsin, 1943.

New Haven, Connecticut. Yale University Library. Press releases, 1935–36. U.S. Resettlement Administration.

Tugwell, Rexford G. "Address to the Regional Planning Association of Hamilton County, Ohio, February 3, 1936." Bound copy in the Library of Congress.

Washington, D.C. General Services Administration, Region III, Records Center 62A–65I. Housing and Home Finance Administration. (Records here relate to management and disposition of the greenbelt towns, 1944–54.)

Washington, D.C. National Archives. Record Groups 16 and 96. (Record Group 16 contains records of the office of the secretary of agriculture, 1935–38. Record Group 96 contains records of the Farmers' Home Administration in which the few surviving documents of the Resettlement Administration Suburban Division and other R.A. documents relating to the Suburban Division Program are located.)

Washington, D.C. Public Housing Administration Library. Reports and Recommendations, Greendale, Wisconsin. Greendale Planning Staff.

Washington, D.C. Records of the Office of the Administrator. Housing and Home Finance Administration. (These records contain some of the working papers of members of the Suburban Resettlement Division, the legal Division of the R.A., and the Management Division of the Federal Public Housing Authority and the Public Housing Administration. They were located in a warehouse in Washington, D.C., but have been removed to the National Archives where they are awaiting cataloging.)

Personal Interviews

Eugene Agger, special assistant to Resettlement Administrator Rexford G. Tugwell. New Brunswick, New Jersey, October 9, 1964.

Tracy Augur. Washington, D.C., January 12, 1965.

C. B. Baldwin. Greenwich, Connecticut, August 17, 1967.

Tilford E. Dudley, former chief of Land Acquisition Section, Suburban Resettlement Division. Washington, D.C., March 15, 1965.

James K. Giese, Greenbelt city manager. Greenbelt, Maryland, May 18, 1965.

John M. Kuglitsch, village manager. Greendale, Wisconsin, February 4, 1965.

John S. Lansill, former chief of Suburban Resettlement Division. Lexington, Kentucky, February 8, 1965.

Albert Mayer. New York, October 5, 1964.

Mrs. John W. Mettler. Bound Brook, New Jersey, October 9, 1964.

Mrs. Ethel Shweer. Greendale, Wisconsin, February 4, 1965.

Warren J. Vinton. Washington, D.C., November 25, 1964.

Public Documents

Maryland General Assembly, Senate. *Journal of Proceedings.* January, 1937, Session. Baltimore, 1937.

Unwin, Sir Raymond. *Housing and Town Planning Lectures, 1936–1937.* U.S. Department of Interior, Central Housing Committee. Washington: U.S. Government Printing Office, 1937.

U.S. *Congressional Record.* Vols. 79, 80, 81, and 95.

U.S. Court of Appeals for the District of Columbia. *Franklin Township* v. *Tugwell,* 85 F (App., D.C.) 208 (1936).

U.S. Court of Appeals for the District of Columbia. Transcript of Record No. 6619, *Township of Franklin et al.* v. *Rexford G. Tugwell et al.,* October Term, 1935.

U.S. Department of Commerce, Bureau of the Census. *Historical Statistics of the United States, Colonial Times to 1957.* Washington: U.S. Government Printing Office, 1960.

U.S. Department of Commerce, Bureau of the Census. *Histori-cal Statistics of the United States, Colonial Times to 1957: Continuations to 1962 and Revisions.* Washington: U.S. Government Printing Office, 1965.

U.S. Farm Security Administration. *Greenbelt Communities.* Washington, D.C. Pamphlet in files of the Public Housing Administration Library. Washington, D.C., January 25, 1940.

U.S. Federal Public Housing Authority. *Fifth Annual Report, 1946.* Washington: U.S. Government Printing Office, 1946.

U.S. Federal Public Housing Authority. "Greenbelt Communities," November, 1945, Washington, D.C. (Mimeographed).

U.S. House of Representatives, Committee on Banking and Currency. *Hearings on H.R. 2440, A Bill to Authorize the Public Housing Commissioner to Sell the Suburban Resettlement Projects Known as Greenbelt, Md.; Greendale, Wis.; and Greenhills, Ohio, without Regard to Provisions of Law Requiring Competitive Bidding or Public Advertising.* 81st Cong., 1st sess., 1949.

U.S. House, Committee on Banking and Currency. *Report on Disposition of Greentown Projects.* Report No. 402, April 6, 1949, 81st Cong., 1st sess., 1949.

U.S. House of Representatives, Select Committee on Agriculture. *Hearings to Investigate the Activities of the Farm Security Administration.* 78th Cong., 1st sess., 1942–43.

U.S. House of Representatives, Subcommittee of the Committee on Appropriations. *Hearings on Agriculture Department Appropriation Bill for 1940.* 76th Cong., 1st sess., 1939.

U.S. House of Representatives, Subcommittee of the Committee on Appropriations. *Hearings on the Agriculture Department Bill for 1942.* 77th Cong., 1st sess., 1941.

U.S. House of Representatives, Subcommittee of the Committee on Appropriations. *Hearings on the Agriculture Department Appropriation Bill for 1943.* 77th Cong., 2d sess., 1942.

U.S. House of Representatives, Subcommittee of the Committee on Appropriations. *Hearings on the Government Corporations, Appropriation Bill for 1947.* 79th Cong., 2d sess., 1946.

U.S. House of Representatives, Subcommittee of the Committee on Appropriations. *Hearings on the Government Corporations, Appropriation Bill for 1948.* 80th Cong., 1st sess., 1947.

U.S. House of Representatives, Subcommittee of the Committee on Ways and Means. *Hearings on H.R. 12876, Payments in Lieu of Taxes on Resettlement Projects.* 74th Cong., 2d sess., 1936.

U.S. National Resources Committee, Committee on Urbanism. *Our Cities: Their Role in the National Economy.* Washington: U.S. Government Printing Office, 1937.

U.S. National Resources Planning Board. *Housing: The Continuing Problem.* Washington: U.S. Government Printing Office, 1940.

U.S. Public Housing Administration. *Annual Report of the Public Housing Administration, 1st-8th.* Washington: U.S. Government Printing Office, 1947–54.

U.S. Senate, Committee on Education and Labor. *Hearings on S. 4424, United States Housing Act of 1936.* 74th Cong., 2d Sess., 1936.

U.S. Senate. *Resettlement Administration Program, In Response to Senate Resolution No. 295: A Report on the Activities, Accomplishments and Effects of the Resettlement Program.* Senate Doc. 213, 74th Cong., 2d Sess., 1936.

U.S. Senate, Committee on Banking and Currency. *Report on Disposition of Greentown Projects.* Report No. 312, April 29, 1949, 81st Cong., 1st Sess., 1949.

U.S. Senate, Subcommittee on Housing and Rents of the Committee on Banking and Currency. *Hearings on S. 351, A Bill to Authorize the Sale of Greenbelt, Greendale, and Greenhills Suburban Resettlement Projects.* 81st Cong., 1st Sess., 1949.

U.S. Resettlement Administration. *First Annual Report.* Washington: U.S. Government Printing Office, 1936.

U.S. Resettlement Administration. *Greenbelt Towns*. Washington, D.C., September, 1936. Pamphlet in Library of the Public Housing Administration.

U.S. Resettlement Administration. *Information for Greenbelt Applicants*. Washington: U.S. Government Printing Office, 1936. Pamphlet located in the Vertical Files of the Public Housing Administration Library, Washington, D.C.

U.S. Resettlement Administration. *Interim Report of the Resettlement Administration*. Washington: U.S. Government Printing Office, 1936.

U.S. Resettlement Administration. *What the Resettlement Administration Has Done*. Washington: U.S. Government Printing Office, 1936. Pamphlet.

U.S. *Statutes at Large*. Vols. 11 and 49.

Wood, Edith Elmer. *Slums and Blighted Areas in the United States*. Washington: U.S. Government Printing Office, 1935.

Pamphlets

City of Greenbelt, 25th Anniversary, 1937–1962. Brochure prepared under the auspices of the Silver Anniversary Committee, from material provided by the *Greenbelt News Review*, with the assistance of local organizations.

Fulmer, O. Kline. *Greenbelt*. Washington: American Council on Public Affairs, 1941.

Greenbelt Federal Credit Union. *Your Greenbelt Federal Credit Union*. Greenbelt Federal Credit Union, 1965.

Greendale Woman's Club. *Greendale . . . thru . . . 25 years . . . 1938–1963*. Prepared by the Greendale Woman's Club for Greendale's 25th Anniversary.

Mayer, Albert. "Site Planning." *Four Papers on Housing Design*. Chicago: National Association of Housing Officials, 1942.

National Association of Housing Officials. *A Housing Program for the United States.* Public Administration Service Publication No. 48. Chicago: Public Administration Service, 1935.

This is Greendale. Brochure privately printed, 1948.

Newspapers and Newsletters

American Federation of Labor. The Trade *Unionist.* June 6, 1936.

American Society of Planning Officials. *Newsletter.*

Chicago's American.

Cincinnati Enquirer.

Cincinnati Post.

Daily Home News, The. (New Brunswick, New Jersey).

Evening Press (Albany, New York).

Greenbelt Consumer Services, *Co-Op Newsletter* 9, no. 8 (May, 1965).

Greenbelt Cooperator.

Greenbelt Federal Credit Union. *Newsletter.* January, 1965.

Greendale Review.

Greenhills-Forest Park Journal.

Milwaukee Journal.

Milwaukee Sentinel.

National Association of Real Estate Boards. *Confidential Weekly Letter.*

New York American.

New York Herald Tribune.

New York Times.

Plainfield Courier News (Plainfield, New Jersey).

Record, The (Kingston, New Jersey).

St. Louis Globe Democrat.

St. Louis Star-Times.

Somerset Messenger Gazette (Somerset, New Jersey).

Sun, The (New York).

Sunday Times, The (Sunday edition of the *Daily Home News,* New Brunswick, New Jersey).

Trenton Evening Times.

Trenton Times (Sunday edition of *Trenton Evening Times*).

Washington Post.

Washington Star.

Books

Adams, Thomas. *Outline of Town and City Planning.* New York: Russell Sage Foundation, 1935.

———. *The Design of Residential Areas.* Cambridge: Harvard University Press, 1934.

Alexander, Will W. *Oral History Memoir.* New York: Columbia Oral History Project of Columbia University.

Aronovici, Carol, and Elizabeth McCalmont. *Catching Up With Housing.* Newark, New Jersey: Beneficial Management Corporation, 1936.

Banfield, Edward C. *Government Project.* Glencoe, Illinois: The Free Press, 1951.

Bauer, Catherine. *Modern Housing.* Boston: Houghton-Mifflin Company, 1934.

Blum, John Morton. *From the Morgenthau Diaries, Years of Crises 1928-1938.* Boston: Houghton-Mifflin Company, 1959.

Brown, Josephine C. *Public Relief 1929–1939.* New York: Henry Holt and Company, 1940.

Burchard, John, and Albert Bush-Brown. *The Architecture of America, A Social and Culture History.* Boston: Little, Brown and Company, 1961.

Chambless, Edgar. *Roadtown.* New York: Roadtown Press, 1910.

Childs, Marquis. *I Write From Washington.* New York: Harper and Brothers, 1942.

Conkin, Paul K. *Tomorrow a New World, The New Deal Community Program.* Ithaca, New York: Cornell University Press, 1959.

Davies, Richard O. *Housing Reform in the Truman Administration.* Columbia, Missouri: University of Missouri Press, 1966.

Dykeman, Wilma, and James Stokely. *Seeds of Southern Change: The Life of Will Alexander.* Chicago: University of Chicago Press, 1962.

Fisher, Robert M. *Twenty Years of Public Housing.* New York: Harper and Brothers, 1958.

Fusfeld, Daniel R. *The Economic Thought of Franklin D. Roosevelt and the Origins of the New Deal.* New York: Columbia University Press, 1956.

Gowans, Alan. *Images of American Living: Four Centuries of Architecture and Furniture as Cultural Expression.* Philadelphia: J. B. Lippincott Company, 1964.

Greer, Thomas H. *What Roosevelt Thought: The Social and Political Ideas of Franklin D. Roosevelt.* East Lansing: The University of Michigan Press, 1958.

Hegemann, Werner. *City Planning Housing.* 2 vols. New York: Architectural Book Publishing Co., Inc., 1937.

Hegemann, Werner, and Elbert Peets. *The American Vitruvius: An Architect's Handbook of Civic Art.* New York: The Architectural Book Publishing Company, 1922.

Hewes, Lawrence I. *Boxcar in the Sand.* New York: Alfred A. Knopf, 1957.

Hoover, Herbert. *The Memoirs of Herbert Hoover.* New York: Macmillan Company, 1952.

Howard, Donald S. *The W.P.A. and Federal Relief Policy.* New York: Russell Sage Foundation, 1943.

Howard, Ebenezer. *Garden Cities of Tomorrow.* London: Faber and Faber, Ltd., 1946.

Ickes, Harold L. *The Secret Diary of Harold L. Ickes.* 3 vols. New York: Simon and Schuster, 1953.

Lanciani, Senatore R. *Ancient and Modern Rome.* Boston: Marshall Jones Company, 1925.

Leuchtenburg, William E. *Franklin D. Roosevelt and the New Deal.* New York: Harper and Row Publishers, Harper Torchbooks, 1963.

Lord, Russell. *The Wallaces of Iowa.* Boston: Houghton-Mifflin, 1947.

McDonnell, Timothy. *The Wagner Housing Act: A Case Study of the Legislative Process.* Chicago: Loyola University Press, 1957.

Meyerson, Martin, and Edward C. Banfield. *Politics, Planning and the Public Interest: The Case of Public Housing in Chicago.* Glencoe, Illinois: The Free Press, 1955.

Mitchell, Broadus. *Depression Decade 1929–1941.* New York: Holt, Rinehart and Winston, 1947.

Mumford, Lewis. *The City in History: Its Origins, Its Transformations, and Its Prospects.* New York: Harcourt, Brace and World, Inc., 1961.

Porter, Kirk H., and Donald B. Johnson. *National Party Platforms: 1840-1960.* Urbana, Illinois: The University of Illinois Press, 1961.

Rogers, Cleveland. *Robert Moses: Builder for Democracy.* New York: Henry Holt and Company, 1952.

Rosenman, Samuel I., ed. *Papers and Addresses of Franklin D. Roosevelt.* 13 vols. New York: Random House, 1938-1950.

Schevill, Ferdinand. *Medieval and Renaissance Florence.* 2 vols. New York: Harper and Row, Publishers, Harper Torchbooks, 1961.

Schlesinger, Arthur M., Jr. *The Coming of the New Deal.* Boston: Houghton, Mifflin Company, 1959.

Searle, Charles F. *Minister of Relief: Harry Hopkins and the Depression.* Syracuse, New York: Syracuse University Press, 1963.

Sherwood, Robert E. *Roosevelt and Hopkins: An Intimate History.* New York: Harper and Brothers, 1948.

Stein, Clarence S. *Towards New Towns for America.* Cambridge, Mass.: The M.I.T. Press, 1966.

Sternsher, Bernard. *Rexford G. Tugwell and the New Deal.* Rutgers, New Jersey: Rutgers University Press, 1964.

Stolberg, Benjamin, and Warren J. Vinton. *The Economic Consequences of the New Deal.* New York: Harcourt, Brace and Company, 1935.

Straus, Michael W., and Talbot Wegg. *Housing Comes of Age.* New York: Oxford University Press, 1938.

Straus, Nathan. *Two-Thirds of a Nation: A Housing Program.* New York: Alfred A. Knopf, 1952.

Strong, Josiah. *The Challenge of the City.* New York: The Young People's Missionary Movement, 1907.

Thrupp, Sylvia L. *The Merchant Class of Medieval London, 1300–1500.* Ann Arbor: The University of Michigan Press, 1962.

Tugwell, Rexford G. *The Battle for Democracy.* New York: Columbia University Press, 1935.

———. *The Democratic Roosevelt.* Garden City, New York: Doubleday and Company, Inc., 1957.

Tunnard, Christopher, and Boris Pushkarev. *Man-Made America: Chaos or Control.* New Haven: Yale University Press, 1963.

Tunnard, Christopher, and Reed, Henry Hope. *American Skyline: The Growth and Form of Our Cities and Towns.* New York: Mentor Books, 1956.

Walker, Mabel L. *Urban Blight and Slums.* Harvard Planning Studies. Vol. 12. Cambridge, Mass.: Harvard University Press, 1938.

Warner, George A. *Greenbelt: The Cooperative Community.* New York: Exposition Press, 1954.

Whitaker, Charles H., et al. *The Housing Problem in War and Peace*. Washington, D.C.: The American Institute of Architects, 1918.

Wright, Henry. *Rehousing Urban America*. New York: Columbia University Press, 1935.

Articles

Aikman, Duncan. "Tugwelltown: The Story of Greenbelt, the Government's New Socialized Community," *Current History* 44 (August, 1936): 96–101.

"Alphabet Soup in a Washington Mansion," *Literary Digest* 120 (August 31, 1935): 10–11.

"American Housing: A Failure, A Problem, A Potential Boon and Boom," *Life* 3 (November 15, 1937): 45–52.

"Architectural Contracts," *Architectural Record* 74 (July, 1933): 57.

Belair, Felix, Jr. "Greenbelt:: An Experimental Town," *New York Times Magazine*, October 10, 1937.

Bennett, Victor W. "Consumers and the Greenbelt Cooperative," *Journal of Marketing* 6 (July, 1941): 3–10.

Bishop, Warren. "A Yardstick for Housing," *Nation's Business* 24 (April, 1936): 29–31.

Bliss, W. D. P. "The Garden City Association of America," *The Garden City* 2 (February, 1907): 268–69.

Bliven, Bruce. "Suicide of a Dreamer," *The New Republic* 87 (July, 1936): 238–39.

Bolles, Blair. "The Sweetheart of the Regimenters: Dr. Tugwell Makes America Over," *American Mercury* 39 (September, 1936): 77–86.

Bone, Hugh. "Greenbelt Faces 1939," *The American City* 54 (February, 1939): 59–61.

Braden, Roy S. "A Plan for Community Living: Greenbelt, Maryland," *Public Management* 20 (January, 1938): 11–14.

Brown, Philip S. "What Has Happened at Greenbelt?" *The New Republic* 105 (August 11, 1941): 183–85.

"Businessmen Make a New Deal Idea Work," *Business Week*, March 10, 1962, pp. 92–94.

Cheney, Charles. "Urban Development: The Pattern and the Background," *The Planners' Journal* 1 (November-December, 1935): 34–35.

Churchill, Henry S. "America's Town Planning Begins," *The New Republic* 87 (January 3, 1936): 96–98.

"City, The," *The Planners' Journal* 5 (July-September, 1939): 70–71.

"City, The," *Time* 33 (June 5, 1939): 66–67.

"Comparative Architectural Details in the Greenbelt Housing," *American Architect and Architecture* 149 (October, 1936): 20–36.

"Constitutionality of Federal Relief Measures, The," *Harvard Law Review* 50 (March, 1937): 803–13.

"Co-Op: R.A.'s First Community Becomes a New Deal Guinea Pig," *Newsweek*, September 13, 1937, p. 12–13.

"Coop Stores Grow in Greenbelt," *Business Week*, May 14, 1938, pp. 17–18.

"Cooperative Corners: Greenbelt, Maryland," *Literary Digest* 124 (October 16, 1937): 16–17.

Crane, Jacob. "Safety Town," *Public Safety*, August, 1937, pp. 28–30.

Delano, Frederic. "To Meet the Housing Needs of the Lower Income Groups," *The American City* 52 (January, 1937): 45–48.

Drier, John. "Greenbelt Planning," *Pencil Points* 17 (August, 1936): 405–9.

Elkins, Stanley, and Eric McKitrick. "A Meaning for Turner's

Frontier," *Political Science Quarterly* 69 (September, 1954): 321-53.

Feiss, Carl. "New Towns for America," *Journal of the American Institute of Architects* 33 (January, 1960): 85–89.

Fernback, Richard. "Greendale," *The Planners' Journal* 3 (November-December, 1937): 161–62.

"Fever Chart of a Tugwell Town," *Nation's Business* 26 (November, 1938): 13.

Form, William H. "Status Stratification in a Planned Community," *American Sociological Review* 10 (October, 1945): 605–13.

Fulmer, O. Kline. "Superblock vs. Gridiron," *The American City* 55 (July, 1940): 72–73.

"Garden Cities in America," *Charities and the Commons* 18 (April 27, 1907): 114.

"Garden City Association in America," *The Garden City* 1 (December 1906): 252.

"Greenbelt," *Time*, September 13, 1937, p. 10.

"Greenbelt Towns," *Architectural Record* 80 (September, 1936): 215-34.

Gutheim, Frederick A. "Greenbelt Revisited," *Magazine of Art* 40 (January, 1947): 16–20.

Hartzog, Justin R. "Planning of Suburban Resettlement Towns," *The Planners' Journal* 4 (January-February, 1938): 29–33.

Kroening, Walter B., and Frank L. Dieter. "Utility Planning for Greendale, Wisconsin," *Civil Engineering*, February, 1938, pp. 94–98.

Johnston, Alva. "Tugwell, the President's Idea Man," *Saturday Evening Post*, 209 (August 1, 1936): 8–9 ff.

Lansill, John S., and Jacob Crane. "Metropolitan Land Reserves as Illustrated by Greendale, Wisconsin," *The American City* 52 (July, 1937): 55-58.

Larson, Cedric. "Greenbelt, Maryland: A Federally Planned

Community," *National Municipal Review* 27 (August, 1938): 413–20.

Lorwin, Lewis L. "Planning In a Democracy," *Plan Age* 1 (February, 1935): 4–5.

"Low Cost Furniture," *House Beautiful* 79 (April, 1937): 131–33.

"Low Cost Furniture," *Retailing*, July 26, 1937, p. 2.

Lubove, Roy. "Homes and 'A Few Well Placed Fruit Trees': An Object Lesson in Federal Housing," *Social Research* 17 (January, 1961): 469–86.

———. "New Cities for Old: The Urban Reconstruction Program of the 1930's," *Social Studies* 53 (November, 1952): 203–13.

McKernon, Edward. "Selling the Planning Idea," *The Planners' Journal* 3 (July–August, 1937): 85–87.

Mayer, Albert. "Greenbelt Towns for the Machine Age," *New York Times Magazine*, February 3, 1936.

———. "Greenbelt Towns Revisited," *Journal of Housing* 24, no. 2 (February-March, 1967): 80–85.

———. "Greenbelt Towns: What and Why?," *The American City* 51 (May, 1936): 59–61.

———. "Why Not Housing?," *The New Republic* 84 (September 4, 1935): 96–98.

Morris, George. "$16,000 Homes for $2,000 Incomes: Greenbelt, Maryland," *Nation's Business* 24 (January, 1938): 21–23.

"National Conference on Planning," *Planning and Civic Comment* 1 (April-June, 1935): 32.

"Notes from Abroad," *The Garden City* 2 (September, 1907): 411–414.

"Planned Community Appraised, A: Greenbelt, Maryland," *The Architectural Record* 22 (January, 1940).

"Planning Considerations in the Location of Housing Projects," *The Planners' Journal* 5 (March-June, 1939): 34–45.

"Realtors Want Drastic Change in Residential Development," *Business Week*, May 28, 1930, pp. 21–22.

Reiss, Richard L. "American Greenbelt Towns," *Town and Country Planning* 6 (January, 1938): 16–18.

Rishel, Virginia. "Greenbelt, A Modern Utopia for Moderate Income Earners," *The Democratic Digest* 14 (June, 1937): 21–22.

Roosevelt, Franklin D. "Growing Up By Plan," *The Survey* 67 (February, 1932): 483–85.

Sibley, Eldridge. "Fertility in a Greenbelt Community," *Social Forces* 20 (May, 1942): 476–77.

"Site Planning and Sunlight Developed by Henry Wright," *American Architect and Architecture* 149 (August, 1936): 19–22.

Stein, Clarence S. "New Towns for the Needs of a New Age," *New York Times Magazine*, October 8, 1933, pp. 6–7, 13.

Stephenson, Flora C. "Greenbelt Towns in the United States," *Town and Country Planning* 10 (Winter, 1942–43): 121–23.

Strong, Josiah. "The Industrial Revolution: Its Influence on Urban Development," *The Garden City* 1 (October, 1904): 2–4.

Thornhill, Fred, and Fred DeArmond. "Another Social Experiment Goes Sour," *Nation's Business* 28 (October, 1940): 23–25 ff.

Tugwell, Rexford G. "Changing Acres," *Current History* 44 (September, 1936): 57–63.

———. "Cooperation and Resettlement," *Current History* 45 (February, 1937): 71–76.

———. "Down to Earth," *Current History* 44 (July, 1936): 38–45.

———. "Magical Greenbelt Is Rising; Model Maryland Community," *Work: A Journal of Progress*, October, 1936.

———. "The Fourth Power," *Planning and Civic Comment* 5, pt. 2 (April-June, 1939): 14–18.

———. "The Meaning of the Greenbelt Towns," *The New Republic* 90 (February 17, 1937): 42–43.

Unwin, Raymond. "Land Values and Town Planning," *The Annals of the American Academy of Political and Social Science* 51 (January, 1914): 17–24.

Walker, Hale J. "Some Minor Technical Problems Encountered in the Planning of Greenbelt, Maryland," *The Planners' Journal* 4 (March-April, 1938): 34–37.

Walker, John O. "A Demonstration in Community Planning," *Shelter* 3 (February, 1939): 29–36.

———. "Greenbelt Towns," *Shelter* 3 (January, 1939): 20–25.

———. "Life in a Greenbelt Community," *Shelter* 3 (December, 1938): 16–23.

Walker, Robert A. "Is the City Planning Commission Meeting Today's Problems?", *The American City* 55 (December, 1940): 67–71.

Weaver, Robert C. "The Negro in a Program of Public Housing," *Opportunity* 16 (July, 1938): 198–203.

Wilson, Corwin. "Mr. Mumford's Castle," *Shelter* 3 (November, 1938): 23–25.

Wood, Edith Elmer. "Housing: United States," *Britannica Book of the Year: 1938*. Chicago: Encyclopedia Britannica, Inc., 1938. Pp. 223–28.

Other Published Sources

American Federation of Labor. *Report of the Proceedings of the Fifty-sixth Annual Convention of the American Federation of Labor*. Washington, D.C.: Judd and Detweiler, 1936.

Bettman, Alfred. "City and Regional Planning in Depression and Recovery," in *Planning and National Recovery: Planning Problems*. Presented at the Twenty-fifth National Conference on City Planning. Philadelphia: William F. Fell Company, 1933.

National Association of Housing Officials. *Housing Yearbook*. Chicago, 1935–38.

INDEX